Small Scale Industry
Concept, Status and Policy

Small Scale Industry
Concept, Status and Policy

Veena Bhatnagar

Foreword by
L. C. Jain

Kaveri Books
New Delhi - 110 002

Title: Small Scale Industry: Concept, Status and Policy
Author: Veena Bhatnagar

First Published in 1995
Edition 2026

ISBN-10: 81-7479-000-4
ISBN-13: 978-81-7479-000-2

Price Rs. 750.00

Published by
Kaveri Books
4832/24, Ansari Road
New Delhi-110002 (India)
Tel: 011- 47072321
E-mail : info@kaveribooks.com
kaveribooks@gmail.com
Website: www.kaveribooks.com

PRINTED IN INDIA

Aknowledgements

It is with a deep sense of gratitude that I acknowledge the appreciative review given to this book by Dr. L.C. Jain, former member Planning Commission. His view on role of small scale industries are held in great esteem by economist and policy makers alike. As such, I am grateful to him for his valuable comments.

I am highly indebted to my meutor and guide Dr. Govind Khanna, ex. Prof. Punjabi University, under whose supervision the thesis on which this book is based, was prepared.

My gratitude is also extended to Dr N. N. Srivastava, Prof. Lucknow University, for the encouragement given in the initial stages of my thesis.

Lastly and not the least, I extend my gratitude to my family members— my parents, husband and children for their suggest and encouragements.

VEENA BHATNAGAR

Foreword

India's interest in small scale industries is not derived so much from the fact that the scale is small — but because of India's over-riding need for creating large scale employment. In the past 40 years since planning was initiated the numbers of the unemployed kept rising. Nearly 80 per cent of our investible resources have gone to the large scale industry or infrastructure required to support the large scale industry. Yet the employment which the large scale industry has yielded is not only very small but minor.

In the manufacturing sector the contribution of the large scale to employment is below 20 per cent. 80 per cent of the employment is provided by the small scale sector. Therefore, the crucial importance of this sector to the Indian economy—indeed to the population of India, for giving it opportunities to gather its livelihood on their own initiative.

Recent trends in employment show that the large scale industry is shrinking employment even further while expanding its production and profits under the stimulus of new economic policy. These trends confirm that the small scale sector in India will become even more important in the years ahead.

One thing which the small scale sector suffers from is lack of insightful studies which bring out the internal and external constraints faced by small scale units. Studies of this nature have therefore a very important role to play. The present study on the small scale industries: concept, status and policy is, a valuable contribution and Dr. Veena Bhatnagar, its author deserves appreciation for the painstaking efforts and analysis. It should command attention of the policy makers, practitioners and the academics alike.

New Delhi
13th. July, 1994

L.C. Jain
Former Member
Planning Commission

Preface

Encouragement to small scale industry has been adopted as a policy goal in many countries including India. A key position has been accorded to this sector in Indian plans for achieving such objectives as removal of unemployment, decentralised growth, reduction of inequalities etc. Successive policy statements have repeatedly emphasised the growth of this sector and reiterated support to it wherever required.

The fact that significance is being attached to this sector in many countries, raises a variety of issues relating to policy formulation which in turn reveals differences in approaches and opinions concerning the industries in which small scale units should be encouraged, the extent of support to be provided, etc.

Viability can be judged by different parameters. Studies conducted in this field have revealed considerable ambiguity.

These differences can be attributed to a certain extent to:

(A) Generalisation of the results of research carried out in one area and/or industry, to small scale units in all areas and/or industries.

(B) Different ways of defining small scale units. Different criteria have been used this purpose.

(C) Differences in the methodology adopted.

In this book an attempt has been made to integrate certain theoretical and policy aspects of small scale industries, with special reference to India.

A chapter has been devoted to research done in this field. Basic thrust however, is on various implications of the way the concept has been defined from the point of view of policy formulation and for international comparisons.

The book has been divided into three sections—

The first section deals with the conceptual aspect—the various definitions adopted and their implications for efficiency analysis. The 'Study' specially discussed in this section pertains to my Ph.D research in the field.

No attempt has been made to study this aspect in a scientific manner, though opinions have been expressed by economists on the possible implications of differences in approach to the concept, (viz. the different criteria used to define the SSI), by different countries, institutions and researchers. The study in this book is an attempt to fill this lacuna.

The implications of these differences for small scale industry policy have also been discussed in this section, and subsequently in the third section.

The second section is on status of small industry. It briefly reviews the growth of the industry in developed and developing countries and then goes on to describe the present status of the small scale industry in India.

The third section is devoted to a critical analysis of the small scale industrial policy in India — its evolution and changes with the changing structure of the economy.

A debate has been going on for quite some time about the rationale for a policy of consistent support for the small scale sector. This section critically analyses the same and specially focuses on the new developments in the policy as a sequel to the rapid pace of liberalisation measures undertaken by the government during the 90's.

VEENA BHATNAGAR

Contents

A Survey of Research Done in the Field of Small Scale Industries

Considerable research has been done in the field of small scale industries. The literature on the subject can be broadly categorised into:

(a) literature of an analytical nature, which also provides policy prescriptions on issues relating to structure and performance of small scale industrial units;

(b) the second group of studies are a large number of publications in the form of model schemes, project plans and progress reports, published by government or other national and international organisations. These are mainly of descriptive and informative nature.

A survey of research work would mainly require a review of the former, even though the significance of the latter cannot be overlooked.

Analytical Studies

The analytical studies can be further divided into:

(i) studies dealing with the rationale, the viability, the employment generating capacity, capital saving potential etc. of small scale enterprises in general, in comparison with large scale industrial units;

(ii) studies, which, having accepted small scale industrial development as an avowed objective of government policy analyse the working of small scale industries under different organisational set ups, such as, industrial estates and areas, ancillary and independent units. These studies may be related to particular regions, or confined to one industry (in a region or in the whole economy). Thus, the objective may be to study the efficiency of various types of organisations, or to assess the effectiveness of government policy of encouragement of small scale industrial units in specific industries.

1. General Studies: The studies under this category, are based on the theoretical-mathematical models, such as those of P.C. Mahalanobis,[1] A.K. Sen,[2] Nurkse,[3] Joan Robinson,[4] Rosenstein Rodan,[5] etc. These studies were mainly concerned with the choice of technology in a developing economy, under different investment criteria. Various authors focussed attention on the relationship of capital, labour and output under alternative techniques and assessed the surplus generated under different methods/conditions of production. Some of the economists who joined the controversy were K.N. Raj, P.N. Dhar, H.F. Lydall, J.C. Sandesara, B.V. Mehta, A.K. Biswas, etc.

Technological Choice : If the problem is viewed as allocation of additional investment in an industry which has a spectrum of alternative technological choices, several aspects have to be considered. The resultant debate led to the formulation of interesting propositions, some in the nature of truisms, but most of them are empirically testable hypotheses.

A summary view is presented below. Regarding labour cost, it was pointed out that labour should be valued at the increase in consumption due to additional employment, even if opportunity cost of labour is not. As Sen[6] and Amlan Dutta[7] point out, "The more successful the state is in siphoning off the previous rural consumption of the new labourers, through taxation or other means, the less becomes the relevant labour cost and hence is the degree of capital intensity and the better is the economic growth; if a choice of technique exists. Sen points out that different propensities to consume may be associated with different techniques.

Regarding capital cost, as has been pointed out by Sen,[8] in a country facing balance of payments difficulties, it is important to study the import intensities of different techniques.

Sukhmoy Chakraborty[9] in his article "Time and Choice of Techniques", points out that life span of capital assets determines the ratio of new investment. Capital intensive methods make possible a larger total of new investment as compared to labour intensive methods.

Different techniques may have varying periods of gestation. Sen[10] points out that "the technique with shorter lag" will have the advantage of what M. Dobb calls "the compounding effect" as the pace of re-investment of surplus will be quicker. Sen[11] also points out that the relative position of labour intensive methods with respect to surplus per unit of capital would tend to deteriorate if account is taken of working capital also.

Regarding generation of surplus, it has been pointed out that although labour intensive techniques might result, in the short run, in maximizing employment and even aggregate output, their surplus generating capacity is limited, for the incomes generated are likely to be small and spent almost entirely on consumption. Dhar and Lydall[12] support this view. Besides, it has been pointed out that more of the surplus could be collected in the form of profits and invested in capital intensive techniques.

Tinbergen[13] and Bhagwati[14] and Chakraborty point out that at the empirical level, re-investable surplus may be higher in technique A (Labour intensive technique), than in technique B (Capital intensive technique), if only the first stages of production are considered, but the ranking may reverse if both direct and indirect investable surpluses were to be taken into account.

Besides, not only the final products obtained through varying techniques have to be considered, but also the industries and activities that are directly or indirectly related to each technique of production.

Spengler points out that "cottage industry produces goods and services only, it does not produce additional side effects that cause the marginal social benefits associated with cottage industry to exceed its marginal private benefits.[15]

Bhagwati and Chakraborty[16] point out that alternative techniques may have different impacts on quality and hence on export performance.

These were some of the broad considerations that were brought out by the discussion on choice of technique and hence of small scale as against large scale industrial units. Mahalanobies[17] approach appeared as a compromise of the two extreme views— one wanting protection and expansion of household sector for ideological reasons with Gandhian over-tones, and the other considering it as a "clog on progress a deliberate turning away from efficiency in favour of antiquated methods of production and dishonest concession to tradition."

Vakil[18] and Brahmananda[19] on the other hand, utilised Mahalanobie approach and argued for the use of surplus labour for the creation of capital assets, instead of production of consumer goods. The approach of subsidising traditional household industries was considered as a curious case of internal tariff protecting rural hand workers against low cost factory goods produced in the same country. Nurkse,[20] while supporting the approach of Vakil and Brahmananda mentioned, "If the hand workers drawn from disguised unemployment in agriculture are to enjoy tariff protection from the competition of Indian factory products, they will, through higher prices, still be receiving subsidy from the rest of the community, just as they were subsidised on the farm where their marginal productivity fell short of their consumption. This means that the locus of disguised unemployment is shifted. One make-work scheme replaces another."

Dr. K.N. Raj[21] provided the rationale for development of small scale industrial enterprises. He argues that "even if the surplus per unit of labour employed in less efficient variants is only a fraction of that possible on the basis of the more efficient ones, the total surplus available for capital accumulation in the former case could still be larger. Raj also highlighted the leakages in the form of doles to be paid to the unemployed as a part of the cost of using more mechanised techniques and cost of social overheads in setting up highly mechanised new units.

Biswanath Goldar[22] has compared for 37 industries, the relative efficiency of large and small scale industries in terms of labour, capital and total factor productivities. He concluded that the SSI sector is relatively inefficient in a large number of industries. He has also tried to relate relative efficiency to short term bank credit borrowings and finds that availability of bank credit has an adverse effect on SSI efficiency. This conclusion seems to fall in line with J.C. Sandesara's[23] conclusion that bank asisted units have not done as well as the non-assisted units.

I.M.D. Little, John Page & Mazumdar[24] examined the relationship between factor productivities and intensities and employment size of firms in Japan, India, Columbia, Taiwan and Korea.

On the other hand Dipak Mazumdar, V.S. Patvardhan and S.R. Hashim[24] have recently analysed factor and product markets and linkages. Mazumdar has taken up the issue of wage differentials. Patvardhan has focussed on access of SSI to institutional finance and Hashim has highlighted the role of SSI sector as an instrument of regional dispersal and check on concentration of economic power.

Whatever may have been the difference in policy prescriptions arising out of researches of such theoretical types, they brought out the usefulness of overall programming approach to the problem and laid the ground work for research studies of the more specific kind.

2. Specific Studies: As already mentioned, these are fact finding empirical studies, relating to traditional and modern small scale industries, the efficiency of different size group units in specific industries, and the relative merits of different types of organisational set ups of small scale industries.

Traditional Small Scale Industry: In the field of traditional small scale industries, which include village industries like khadi, handloom, edible oils, coir, tannery etc. that are mainly concerned with the processing of raw materials for local markets and also non-factory sector covering both artisans and household units, fact finding studies have been made both by official and non-official agencies. The official studies have been mainly concerned with studies of their performance and progress, e.g. the Karve Committee Report in 1956.

A large part of unofficial studies have also been in the nature of survey reports based on case studies of selected industries in different localities with a view to collecting information on existing structure and developmental potential. The studies differed in coverage and concept used. Significant among these unofficial studies are those conducted by Baljit Singh[25], T.K. Lakshman,[26] Lakdawala and Sandesara[27] etc. Most of these studies made a strong case for modernization.

The problem of marketing and finance and capacity utilization were also studied by Shetty,[28] McCrory[29], Baljit Singh[30] and Dhar and Lydall.[31]

Apart from the theoretical discussion on the choice of technology, economists explored this aspect through empirical studies in the field of traditional small scale industry. Debate in this field was centered around weaving and spinning techniques of Indian Cotton textile industry. Among these are those done by K.N. Raj,[32] A.K. Sen[33] and Naqvi.[34]

More recently, George Waardenburg,[35] H.H de Haan,[36] Nirmala, Bannerjee[37] and K.B. Suri,[38] conducted studies on leather shoe manufacturing units in Agra, sugar industry in Uttar Pradesh, electric fan industry in Calcutta, and laundry soap industry in Delhi, respectively.

These studies try to explain the co-existence of small and large units in the respective industries. Each study takes up a unique case and attempts to identify a specific set of factors in order to explain the phenomenon of co-existence in that particular industry.

Waardenburg's study of small leather shoe making units shows that with an increase in size, labour intensity decreases very sharply, without any significant increase in capital intensity. Among the factors aiding the co-existence of different types of units, variation in factor proportions, cost of production, quality, price of product and the caste factor might be playing an important role.

De Haan, while attempting an evaluation of the modern technology of the large scale mill sector and the intermediate technology of the sugar industry, comes to the conclusion that while the former has higher capital intensity and shows greater efficiency in terms of output and quality, the latter has higher employment generating capacity but has definite disadvantage with respect to quantity and quality of sugar recovery.

Nirmala Bannerjee, in her study of electric fan industry

in Calcutta, had focussed on the coexistence of small and large units, the former operating as ancillaries to the large firms for certain specified processes. The large firms in the face of uncertain demand from the domestic and foreign markets use the small unorganised units to meet the sporadic excess demand without investing to expand capacity.

K.B. Suri in his study on the co-existence of different level technologies in the soap industry, has attributed this phenomenon to quality differentials, differentiated factor markets as reflected in wage differentials, structured markets, govt. policy etc.

Modern Small Scale Industry: Coming to the research in modern small scale industry, which are mainly urban based, better integrated with large scale units, and turn out relatively more sophisticated products employing techniques for markets which often transcend purely local demand, the subject has been given extensive coverage, ranging from fact finding area studies to comprehensive treatment about their role in the overall economic framework. Literature in this field has been supplied by Indian as well as foreign economists.

The Indian literature has generally concerned itself with an examination of scale and efficiency correlates and problems and prospects of specific areas and industries in the light of various promotional measures adopted by the government, including development of industrial estates, ancillary units, etc.

Studies regarding relative efficiency or productivity of modern small scale enterprises vis-a-vis large scale units have been conducted by Dhar and Lydall,[39] S. Hajara,[40] D.T. Lakdawala and B.V. Mehta,[41] Prem Prakash[42] and J.C. Sandesara.[43]

These studies have compared relative efficiency through inter-relationships between capital and labour, output and surplus. The conclusions however, have been conflicting.

Dhar and Lydall[44] compared the output-capital ratio for a number of reasonably homogeneous industry groups each depicting size variation. They concluded that for factories which employ twenty or more persons, output-capital ratios increased with size of the units. Compared to unregistered small scale enterprises also, the relative position of modern small scale industries was noticed to be unfavourable. For enterprises employing less than 20 workers, the output-capital ratio was generally more favourable than those immediately above them, bot not necessarily more favourable than large enterprises.

Thus Dhar and Lydall found small scale units using modern machinery, and hiring up to 40 workers to be the most capital intensive. However since the size criteria is labour employed, it does not tally with the government's later classification of small industry on the basis of capital employed in which case the findings may not be valid, since less labour need not mean less capital also and so the frequency distribution of the units studied would change. Sandesara[45] extending the analysis, studied the scale and efficiency correlation over a period of time unlike Dhar and Lydall, whose study related to a point of time. Sandesara examined the relationship between size and capital intensity (i.e. capital labour ratio), and also between size and other economic characteristics like output, wages and surplus, each per worker, and output and surplus per unit of capital. Sandesara's study revealed lack of positive association between size and capital intensity, but size and output capital ratio, size and surplus-capital ratio and size and wage were seen to be positively associated, thus further supporting the conclusions of Dhar and Lydall.

Mehta,[46] however, doubted the efficacy of measuring size variation by employment units, for this was likely to include large scale units employing only a skeleton staff, or new units undergoing teething troubles, in the category of small scale units and thus affect the findings.

Thus Mehta employed the capital investment criteria for defining size and examined capital-labour, output-labour and output capital ratios for three size classes (small-fixed capital up to Rs. 5 lakhs, medium-fixed capital up to Rs. 25 lakhs, large-fixed capital over Rs.25 lakhs, covering 32 industries). He found that in almost all industries, capital-labour ratios increased with size, which further increases the likelihood that the size groups taken by Dhar and Sandesara on the basis of labour employed may change if they had taken capital investment as criteria, this would also change their conclusions. Labour productivity was also generally found to increase with size, but not in the same proportion as capital intensity, and as a natural corollary, output-capital ratio was noticed to decrease with size.

Watanabe and Susmme[47] in their article "Reflections on Current Policies for Promoting Small Enterprises and Sub-contracting", have pointed out that coefficients of some Japanese industries have revealed that small enterprises are less capital intensive in terms of capital-labour ratio, if production equipment alone is considered, but may not be true in the smallest size groups (below twenty labourers in his classification of units) if overhead capital such as building, land and other infrastructure is included. The same picture is revealed with regard to capital-output ratio. Productivity of labour rises steadily with the size of enterprises. On the basis of these findings he comes to the conclusion that small enterprises are a costly means of increasing employment, specially entrepreneurs with less than 20 workers, except where the enterprises are used as shed etc. This is the case in Japan, which makes the Japanese small units economically viable.

Subcontracting : Apart from the competitive aspect of the relative efficiency of small and large size groups in specific industries, studies have been undertaken in the field of complementarity of small and large groups, for small units near large ones may be more conducive to optimum rate of growth. Studies conducted by Berna[48] and George Rosen[49] in Bombay reveal a tendency towards self-sufficiency and very little subcontracting.

Several factors seem to have hampered the growth of ancillary units. Rosen mentions failure of small units to meet the orders in time and meet desired specifications.

Japanese economists Sakuna and Nakamura[50] and Watanabe and Susmme[51] have conducted some studies on the inter-dependence of small and large enterprises. Watanbe and Susmme point out that the success of small scale units, in spite of their relatively low efficiency coefficients, is very much due to the subcontracting relationship between large and small units, and the patronage given by large units to small units. Sakuna and Nakamura's study provides a useful framework for studying linkage patterns.

T.S. Papola and R.S. Mathur[52] in their study on "Inter-sectoral linkages in Manufacturing" in Kanpur, point out that as regards the types of linkages, they take one or more of the following forms: (i) transfer of equipments, (ii) sharing of technical knowledge; and (iii) transfer of skills. The extent and pattern of technical cooperation between large and small sector enterprises, generally follows the pattern of their market relations—independent, interdependent or competitive. As regards the motivation for sub-contracting, they point out, that this comes because it provides an opportunity to make fuller use of whatever little productive capacity they have, and a measure of protection against competition. As regards the large entrepreneur, it comes from either the non-availability of machinery to carry out the work which they contract out, or because they have machinery, but their capacity is not enough to meet the demand for their goods. It is also to avoid official constraints associated with large size e.g. higher taxes, employment rules etc. Motivation is also provided by shortage of space, seasonal demand, etc.

Industrial Estates : Research has been done on the functioning and relative efficacy of industrial estate and non-estate units.

Setting up of an industrial estate is essentially an attempt to provide basic overhead facilities like suitable accommodation on rental basis to a group of small entrepreneurs who are otherwise not able to get them at a reasonable price, so that a cluster of factories run by small entrepreneurs, comes up in a selected location, taking advantage of the economies of scale and external economies.

Work in this field has been done by William Bredo,[53] Alexander,[54] Kalyani Bandopadhyaya[55], Kashyap,[56] and R.L. Sanghvi[57] etc. Bandopadhyaya and Sanghvi have made a comparative study of efficiency of units in industrial estates and outside, in West Bengal and Gujarat respectively. These studies reveal that in majority of estates there is under-utilisation of the accommodation, with quite a large proportion of sheds remaining unoccupied. Sanghvi[58] has shed light on the problems of such estates and has come to the conclusion that estates situated near large industry and in semi-urban areas have been more efficient than the rural estates, thus bringing out the limitations of this tool for the policy of industrial dispersal and regional development. It has also been noticed that the performance of estates with linkages between units has been better than those where no such linkages existed. Bandopadhyaya[59] showed that at least in one estate of West Bengal, the benefits from inter-trading and inter-servicing accrued and there existed effective interdependence and complementarity relationship between units. Another aspect that has been studied by Dhar and Lydall[60] and Kashyap[61] is the one relating to the type of entrepreneurship that should be attracted in such estates.

The financial costs of development of industrial estates in India have been discussed. There is also discussion on the type of assistance and extent of assistance that should be given to industrial estates, that is, what should be the rent charged, whether it should recover the cost of construction of estates or whether they should be subsidised and to what extent to keep the rents low.

A UN Seminar on Industrial Estates in the ECAFE region[62] suggested a distinction between special inducements proposed for the establishment of industrial estates and those proposed for the units in the estates, and observed that while the industrial estates had a developmental objective, the intention was not to create a privileged section of entrepreneurs, who would enjoy special facilities and concessions denied to those outside the estates. The provision of readymade factory accommodation at subsidised rent should be regarded as sufficient inducement.

Some studies also point out the importance of anticipating the secondary growth effects of industrial estates and emphasized the need for coordination and integration of industrial projects with urbanisation of industrial plots, slum clearance and regional planning. Bredo, in the study of Rajkot Industrial Estate, showed that "a good deal of haphazard growth of industrial and commercial enterprises is taking place......(and) industrial estates might become completely surrounded by uncontrolled growth of business enterprises which could turn a well conceived project into a congested industrial slum."[63] Dhar and Lydall[64] also observed a similar pattern with reference to the Ludhiana Industrial Estate.

The studies on industrial estates, however, are hardly sufficient, and an examination of issues such as the manner in which units in industrial estates are to be clustered, the type of financial assistance provided, the type of emerging interdependence, and isolation of the area in which planning process is fattening, would bridge wide gaps in literature for policy prescription.

Growth Aspect : One of the other aspects of small scale industries that has been researched upon is the growth aspect, i.e. what is their potential to harness latent resources, and the rate of plough back of profits of these as compared to that of large ones. Mc Crory[65] conducted such a study in a North Indian town with regard to craftsman entrepreneurs. Berna[66] on the other hand, conducted a study of metal working firms. Both arrived at different conclusions. While the first gave a negative picture, Berna arrived at a relatively favourable picture regarding plough back of profits. Rao also arrived at the same conclusions as Berna. However, growth behaviour of small units has to be examined not only with reference to their plough back of profits, but also in relation to their technical progressiveness or otherwise, optimum size of the plant for a product line and other organisational and entrepreneurial factors.

Entrepreneurship Promotion: The role of small industries in the promotion of entrepreneurship has also been examined by some economists. They have studied the need for setting up a special climate for attracting entrepreneurship. UNESCO studies have also gone in this field. A useful comparative study has been done by SVS Sharma on 'Small Entrepreneurial Development in some Asian Countries.'[67] The study covers problems of small entrepreneurs the promotional measures undertaken in various countries and their effects. The various studies have come to the conclusion that factors like caste, tradition, etc. and some important economic forces like access to capital, possession of business experience, etc. played an important part in giving rise to entrepreneurship. SVS Sharma's study proves that though promotional measures have been taken in various countries to solve the problems of finance, availability of sight for plant, training facilities etc., they are not enough and the motivation for the activities is not conducive to efficient functioning of promotional activities.

Decentralization Aspect : On this aspect also various studies have been conducted. Staley and Morse[68] argue that the flexibility of small scale units with regard to location depends upon the product manufactured, the type and level of technology etc. Generally, there is a tendency that initially small scale units flourish best in large cities, and efforts to 'grow' small industry where nothing else grows, are not likely to succeed. Instead of a global strategy of regional dispersal of industries, some studies have argued for a phased programme. The elements of this programme consist in (a) selecting intermediate urban growth points, (b) promoting comprehensive development of the growth points and (c) developing urban rural linkages. It has also been argued that large scale units and not small scale ones are more suited for opening an underdeveloped area. Florence,[69] however, argued that a "bunched dispersal" of small scale units can offer similar economics as found in a single large plant i.e., setting up of industrial estates, but as already mentioned, a lot depends upon the location of industrial estates and the types of linkages established within the estates.

Equity Aspect : Regarding equity or social aspect of small scale industry, some like Dhar and Lydall[70] have argued that the price of greater equality now may be a small income in the future, or the price of more jobs now may be fewer jobs later. This presumes the small scale units to be inefficient, hindering output, real income etc. However, Staley amd Morse argue that this need not be so and efficiency can be ensured through "properly selected types of small factories functioning as independent enterprises, but stimulated and aided by a well concieved government programme, which encourages modernisation and development.[71]

Governmental Programme : On government programme for development of small scale industry, various studies have argued that instead of favouring small firms, the attitude should be to remove their disabilities and encourage them to grow into least-cost size units.

J.C. Sandesare in a paper has evaluated govt.[72] programmes of support to SSI sector and has compared the performance of reserved with non-reserved sector.

Arun Ghosh,[73] in his paper "Govt. policies concerning small scale industries—An Appraisal", has raised a number of policy related issues.

Dipak Mazumdar[74] in yet another paper, has examined govt. policy towards the textile industry.

J.C. Sandesara[75] has analysed implications and prospects of New Small Enterprise Policy of the Indian Government.

After a brief survey of the above mentioned research studies on small scale industry, we notice that often conclusions on the same aspects of study have been conflicting.

The differences in conclusions, however, can be attributed to complications about definitions, inadequacy of treatment given, inherent limitations of statistical analysis, assumptions of product homogeneity (involving different techniques), different valuations of capital (because of different depreciation practices, or different age span of capital, and because a large part of capital of small factories may consist of working capital.

Thus the differences in conclusions point to the inadequacy of research and the need for more accurate studies.

References

1. P.C. Mahalanobis, "The Approach of Operational Research to Planning in India", *Sankhya*, Dec. 1955-56, pp.3-130.
2. (a) A.K. Sen, "On Choosing Technique", *The Economic Weekly*, July 1956, 8, 857-858.

   (b) A.K. Sen, *Choice of Techniques: An Aspect of Theory of Planned Development*, 1962, Oxford, Blackwell Publishers.
3. Ragnar Nurkse, "Reflections on India's Development Plan" *Quarterly Journal of Economics*, 1957, 71, pp. 188-204.
4. Joan Robinson, "The Choice of Techniques", *The Economic Weekly*, June 1956.
5. Rosenstein Rodan, "How to Industrialize an Underdeveloped Area", in W. Isard (Ed.) *Regional Economic Planning Techniques*, 1961, Paris.
6. A.K. Sen, "Labour Cost and Economic Growth", *The Economic Weekly*, Sept. 1956, 8, pp. 1159-1169.
7. Amlan Dutta, "Welfare versus Growth Economics", *Indian Economic Journal*, October 1956.

8. A.K. Sen, *op. cit.*

9. Sukhamoy Chakraborty, "Time and Choice of Technique", *The Economic Weekly*, Sept. 15, 1956, pp. 1097-1098.

10. A.K. Sen, *op. cit.*

11. *Ibid.*

12. P.N. Dhar and H.F. Lydall, *The Role of Small Enterprises in Indian Economic Development*, 1961, Delhi, Asia Publishing House.

13. J. Tinbergen, "Mill versus Cottage Industries", *The Economic Weekly*, Jan. 1957, 9, pp. 81-83.

14. Jagdish N. Bhagwati and Sukhamoy Chakraborty, *Contribution in Indian Economic Analysis; A Survey"*, 1971, Bombay.

15. J.J. Spengler, "Cottage Industries: A Comment", *Economic Development and Cultural Change*, 1956-57, pp. 371-373.

16. J. Bhagwati and Chakraborty, *op. cit.*

17. Mahalanobis, *op. cit.*

18. Off the Record, "Will the Cottage Sector Deliver the Goods—is it intended to ?", *The Economic Weekly*, Aug. 1955, pp. 993-994.

19. C.N. Vakil and P.R. Brahmananda, "Planning for an Expanding Economy", 1956, Bombay.

20. Nurkse, *op. cit.*, p. 194.

21. K.N. Raj, "Small Scale Industries—Problems of Technological Change: Part I," April 1956, 8, pp. 435-438; and *Ibid*, Part II, *The Economic Weekly*.

22. Biswanath Goldar, "Relative Efficiency of Modern Small Scale Industries in India", A paper in "Small Scale Enterprises in Industrial Development"—Edited by K.B. Suri, 1988, Sage Publications.

23. J.C. Sandesara, Small Industry Development Programmes in India—Efficacy, Explanations and Lessons: "Some field studies", A paper in "Small Scale Enterprises in Industrial Development" Edited by K.B. Suri, 1988, Sage Publications.

24. I.M.D. Little, John Page, Mazumdar, "Small Manufacturing Enterprises": A comparative study of India and other countries, A World Bank Publication. Dipak Mazumdar, V.S. Patvardhan and S.R Hashim, "Small Scale Enterprises in Industrial Development". A compilation of papers edited by K.B. Suri, Sage Publications.

25. Baljit Singh, "The Economics of Small Industries—A Case Study of Small Scale Industrial Establishments of Moradabad", 1961, Delhi.

26. T.K. Lakshman, "Cottage and Small Scale Industries in Mysore", 1966, Mysore.

27. D.T. Lakdawala and Sandesara, J.C., *"Small Industry in a Big City; A Survey in Bombay,"* 1960, Bombay University.

28. M.C. Shetty, *Small Scale and Household Industries in a Developing Economy*, 1963, Bombay.

29. J.T. McCrory, *"Small Industry in a North Indian Town"*, 1956, Delhi.

30. Baljit Singh, *op. cit.*
31. Dhar, B.N., "*Small Scale Industries in Delhi,*" *1958*. Bombay; Asia Publishing House.
32. K.N. Raj, *op. cit.*
33. A.K. Sen, *op. cit.*
34. K.A. Naqvi, "*The Economics of Ambar Charka*", *The Economic Weekly*, July 1956, pp. 833-34.
35. J. George Waardenburg, "Small Scale Leather Shoe Manufacturing in Agra": A case study in Small Scale Industry in India's Development, "Small Scale Enterprises in Industrial Development," Edited by K.B. Suri.
36. H.H. de Hann, "Sugar Processing in India: The Scope for Intermediate Technology"—K.B.Suri.
37. Nirmala Bannerjee, "Small and Large Units: Symbiosis or Malsyanya", K.B. Suri.
38. K.B. Suri, "Technology, Firm Size and Product Quality."
39. Dhar and Lydall, *op. cit.*
40. S. Hajra, "Firm Size and Efficiency in Manufacturing", *The Economic Weekly*, August 1965.
41. D.T. Lakdawala and B.V. Mehta, "Small Scale Units in Engineering Industry", *The Times of India Supplement*, 28 February 1958.
42. Prem Prakash, "Relationship between size and productivity in selected Indian Industries", *Asian Economic Review*, May 1961, 11, pp. 237-248.
43. J.C. Sandesara, "Scale and Technology in Indian Industry" *Bulletin of the Oxford University Institute of Economics and Statistics*, 1956, 28, pp. 181-186; and "*Size and Capital Intensity in Indian Industry*", 1969, University of Bombay.
44. Dhar and Lydall, *op. cit.*
45. Sandesara, *op. cit.*
46. B.V. Mehta, "Size and Capital Intensity in Indian Industry", *Bulletin of Oxford University, Institute of Economic Statistics*, 1969, 31, pp. 189-204.
47. Watanabe and Susumme, "Reflections on Current Policies for Promoting Small Enterprises and Sub-contracting', *International Labour Review*, 1974, Vol. 110, No. 5.
48. James Berna, 'Industrial Entrepreneurship in Madras State", International Industrial Development Centre, Stanford Research Institute, 1960, Bombay.
49. George Rosen, *Industrial Change in India; Industrial Growth, Capital Requirements and Technological Change*, Centre for International Studies, HIT, 1958, Greece.
50. Itasu Sakuna and N. Nakamura, "Size of Business in Japanese Inter Industry Relations 1951-55", *Bulletin of the Oxford University, Institute of Economics and Statistics*, August 1969, 26, pp. 217-228.
51. Watanabe and Susmme, *op. cit.*
52. T.S. Papola and R.S. Mathur, "*Intersectoral Linkage in Manufacturing—A*

Study of Metal Engineering Industry in Kanpur", Giri Institute of Development Studies, Lucknow, 1978.

53. William Brede, *Industrial Estates*, 1962, Bombay. Callier Macmillan Limited.
54. P.C. Alexander, *Industrial Estates in India*, 1963, Bombay.
55. Kalyani Bandopadhyaya, *"Industrialization Through Industrial Estates*, Bookland Pvt. Ltd., 1969, Calcutta.
56. S.P. Kashyap, "Government sponsored Industrial Growth: The Jaipur Estates", *The Economic Weekly*, June 1964, 16, pp. 1021-1027.
57. R.L. Sanghvi, *Role of Industrial Estates in a Developing Economy*, 1979, Multi-Technical Publishing Co., Bombay.
58. R.L. Sanghvi, *ibid.*, pp. 161-163.
59. K. Bandopadhyaya, *op. cit.*
60. Dhar and Lydall, *op. cit.*
61. S.P. Kashyap, *op. cit.*
62. United Nations, Department of Economics and Social Affairs, *Industrial Estates in Asia and the Far East*, 1962, New York.
63. W. Bredo, *op. cit.*, pp. 52-53.
64. Dhar and Lydall, *op. cit.*
65. McCrory, *op. cit.*
66. James J. Berna, *Industrial Entrepreneurship in Madras State*, 1960, Bombay. International Industrial Development Centre.
67. SVS Sharma, *Small Entrepreneurial Development in some Asian Countries*, 1979. New Delhi, Light and Life Publishers.
68. E. Staley and Richard Morse, *Modern Small Industry for Developing Countries*, Mc Graw Hill Book Company, 1969, New York.
69. P.S. Florence, "Investment, Location and Size of Plants", Cambridge University Press, 1948.
70. Dhar and Lydall, *op. cit.*
71. Staley and Mores, *op. cit.*
72. J.C. Sandesara,"New Small Enterprise Policy", *Economic and Political Weekly*, Oct. 19, 1991.
73. Arun Ghosh, "Government Policies Concerning Small Scale Industries", K.B. Suri.
74. Dipak Mazumdar, "Indian Textile Policy", K.B. Suri.
75. J.C. Sandesara, *op. cit.*

Section A

Concept

1

Definition

There is considerable ambiguity surrounding the concept of small scale industry, because it does not lend itself to scientific definition. The phrase "small scale industry" itself is considered a misnomer. Dhar and Lydall[1] argue that only when all the units in an industry are operating on small scale, one might legitimately call it small industry. Otherwise the more appropriate phrase would be small scale enterprise or unit. For, while the term small scale refers to the scale of operation in any enterprise, the term "industry" has a particular "commodity" connotation.

Another problem is that "small" is relative and what is small in one economic setting may not be so in another. Although attention is often focussed on the manufacturing sector, discussion of small scale enterprise can extend into virtually all non-agricultural sectors of production, each with different relative standards of what is "small".

Delimitation by size differs according to the purpose one has in mind, and hence is based on different criteria such as employment, capital, technology etc.

The use of the word is different in different regions. Japan calls them "small enterprises", India "small industry", others "small business", and some others, "rural or cottage industries". These different expressions are more than merely semantic variations. Japan for instance, includes service or commercial activities such as retail marketing, beauty saloons and laundry, in small enterprises programme, while India till recently excluded all but manufacturing enterprises. The range of products turned out by the small industry sector, is very wide, depending on the stage of development and resource endowment of a country—from precision electronic and optical instruments produced in Japan, to basket making or net weaving in some other less developed regions—a highly incomparable variety for a generalised and comparative study.

The current definitions are both functional and statistical in nature. Functional definitions broadly tend to view the production methods and/or the nature of market served as the demarcating factors, taking into account characteristics such as (a) little specialisation in management, (b) close personal contact, (c) handicaps in obtaining capital and credit, and (d) no dominant position in the market.

The statistical definitions use some index of size to define and demarcate small industry. The employment figure has been considered as the most convenient and least objectionable. But the quantum of employment used has been varying. ECAFE's working party on industry and trade in 1951, defined small industry as one operating mainly with hired labour and not exceeding twenty if using power, or up to 50 if not using power. The Standard Research Institute[2] for international comparisons, classified units employing up to 100 workers, in the category of small enterprises.

Apart from employment, capital has been used singly or along with employment, as a determinant of size. The index differs as between countries also and within the same country it changes periodically, which is symptomatic of growth. Many countries have linked their definition to investment alone. Pakistan, Thailand and a few others merely judge the industry by its investment in fixed assets. But in Africa, many countries relate it to the number of workers employed. A number of countries, however, employ both criteria. In Japan, the Basic Law of 1963 defined small enterprises as—(i) enterprises in the manufacturing sector with capital less than 50 million Yen or having less than 300 workers, (ii) enterprises in the commercial and professional service sector with capital less than 10 million Yen and with workers less than 50.

Thus if either the capital or the employment criteria is satisfied, the unit comes under the category of small enterprises.

In practice it is found that it is the number of employees that operates as a ceiling, with the industrial units becoming more capital intensive. Any enterprise which employs 300 persons, needs capital far in excess of 50 million, in fact sometimes as much as ten times the investment ceiling specified in the definition. Thus many units categorised as "small scale" in Japan would be regarded in other developing countries as medium or even large scale, which correspondingly modifies the results of the studies.

In USA, the Small Business Act 1953 defines small business as one which is independently owned and operated and which is not dominant in its field of operation. It allows other criteria, however, such as number of employees and dollar volume of business. The criteria vary from industry to industry and reflect different characteristics of the industry.

In UK, small enterprises located in rural or depressed areas alone are entitled to special benefits. The criteria employed is, villages or country towns with less than 10,000 inhabitants and firms employing less than 20 skilled workers.

All this further brings out the difficulty in making any meaningful comparisons between countries.

The Indian Concept

The concept, as it has developed in India also shows confusion and lack of clarity. Before independence, the term small scale 'industry' was meant to denote the village based and/or urban cottage industry, manufacturing handicrafts.

In the Industrial Policy Resolution of 1948 and the document of the First Five Year Plan, the only criteria to define small scale enterprises was their non-registration under the Factory Act. Thus small scale enterprise meant all units which (a) used power and employed less than 10 workers (including family labour, or (b) did not use power and employed up to 20 workers.

Later on, during the First Five Year Plan, the distinction between "small scale industry" and village industries was made. Small scale enterprises were described as those small units which did not form an integral part of the village economy and were defined as (i) those units which employed less than 50 workers, if using power; or (ii) less than 100 workers if not using power; or (iii) having capital assets not exceeding Rs. 5 lakhs. Thus three criteria—capital, employment and use of power—were adopted.

Later, in1960, employment and power were given up and only capital investment was retained as the determinant of size, capital investment being taken as investment in plant and machinery and excluding land and buildings. As per 1966 definition, all industrial units with a capital investment of not more than Rs. 7.5 lakhs (irrespective of the number of persons employed) were treated as small scale units. For ancillary units, the limit was kept higher at Rs. 10 lakhs.

In view of inflationary pressures, the limit of capital investment was again raised in 1974 to Rs. 10 lakhs in the case of small units and 15 lakhs for ancillary units, which was subsequently again raised to Rs. 20 lakhs and Rs. 25 lakhs respectively on 23 July, 1980.

In 1982 it was decided to include even service oriented units within the small scale sector, provided they are set up in rural areas and towns with a population of 5 lakhs or less, and subject to a ceiling of investment in plant and machinery of Rs. 2 lakhs. In addition, a new sector, the "TINY" sector, was also defined which included units with less than Rs. 2 lakh investment. In 1985 the limit for small scale industry was further raised to 35 and 40 lakhs.

In the New Small Enterprise Policy announced in Aug. 1991, the investment limits in plant and machinery of small scale industries have been raised to Rs. 60 lakhs and those of ancillary and export oriented units has been raised to 75 lakhs. Thus extra incentive has been given to exports from small scale industry. For the "TINY" enterprises, the limit has been raised from the present Rs. 2 lakhs to Rs. 5 lakhs respectively, irrespective of location.

In recognition of the fact that the service sector is a fast growing area and needs support, and also in view of its vast potential to provide employment specially to the educated small entrepreneurs, all industry related services and enterprises, irrespective of their location, would be recognised as small scale industries, and their investment ceilings would correspond to those of Tiny enterprises.

Year	1966	1976	1980	1985	1991 (a)
Description	Investment Ceiling for Plant & Machinery (Rs. in Lakhs)				
Small Scale Industries	7.5	10	20	35	60
Ancillary Industries	10	15	25	45	75
Small Service Establishments	-	-	2*	2*	5
Expert Oriented Small Scale Industries	-	-	-	-	75
Small Scale Service & Business (Industry related) Enterprises (SSSBE)	-	-	-	-	5

* Located in rural areas and towns with population of 5 lakhs.

(a) In the case of Small Scale industrial undertaking referred to in (a) above, the limit by investment in fixed assets in plant and machinery shall be Rs. 75 lakhs provided the unit undertakes to export at least 30% of the annual production by the end of the year from the date of its commencing production.

Source : Report on the Second All India Census of Small Scale Industrial Units.

Thus the Small Scale Units included in the category of "small scale and village industries", are of a type ranging from the age-old household industries to modern mechanical small-scale units. Broadly they can be divided into (i) traditional industries based on traditional techniques and skills, and (ii) modern small scale industries using modern techniques as well as artisan workshops engaged in activities such as repair of implements, machinery, vehicles etc. The traditional industries can further be divided into (i) handicrafts producing goods of high skill workmanship (wood and ivory covering, carpet making etc.) and (ii) village and household industries providing common consumer goods of low skill variety (pottery, leather products, hand woven textiles etc.) and are highly labour intensive.

As can be noticed, constant changes have been incorporated in the concept of the small scale industries. These are indicative of the economy's coming of age. The inclusion of the service sector in the New Small Enterprise Policy '91, is no more than the acceptance of the fact, that this sector has now come to play a very important role in the economy and is likely to become more and more significant in the coming years. Similarly, the significance accorded to the small scale industries export sector, is a recognition of the fact that the nation, in the new economic scenario, cannot ignore the growing importance of trade, as also the role that the small scale export sector can play in earning valuable foreign exchange. Thus the concept of SSI has been undergoing a change to accommodate all these policy changes in conformity with changing requirements.

References

1. P.N. Dhar and H.F. Lydall, *The Role of Small Enterprises in Indian Economic Development*, 1961, Delhi, Asia Publishing House.
2. S. Nanjundan, H.E. Robinson and E. Staley, *Economic Research for Small Industry Development*, 1962, Bombay.

2

Investment Criteria and Role of Small Scale Industry

The concept of SSI was developed basically with the presumption that a small scale unit inherently possesses certain economic advantages which justify its existence, and if initially given "baby" protection from the grabbing and bullying attitude of the "big brother", i.e. the large scale sector, it may be able to prove more efficient and economically viable than its large competitor. It may also develop and provide certain other advantages to the economy which the large scale sector is unable to do.

The Investment Criteria

The role that small scale enterprises can play in an economy depends upon the criteria that guides the investment pattern in an economy. It is thus pertinent to start an analysis of the rationale for small scale industries by first studying the criteria that may be chosen in undertaking investment activity and then go on to see how far small scale industries fit into the pattern in the light of such criteria.

The fundamental economic problem facing any decision making unit, be it a firm, an individual or a nation, is the allocation of scarce resources. There exist a wide variety of opportunities for the productive employment of funds.

Broadly speaking, the opportunities may be put into two categories—consumption and investment. The basic difference between consumption and investment is one of time preference.

Thus, investment may be defined as an act involving the sacrifice of an immediate and certain satisfaction in exchange for a future expectation.

This decision having been made, the question arises about the choice of the criteria for investment, which in turn depends upon the object of investment. For a private enterprise, there is no dispute about the object and hence about the choice of criteria. The object being profit maximization, investment decisions are made in the light of a set of figures which express some form of relationship between the cost of the project and the incremental profit expected to accrue to the firm from the project. The central problem therefore, is one of evaluating the uncertain future cash flows and relating them to outlay in the immediate present.

However, from larger social point of view, i.e. for the nation as a whole, the investment decision assumes a more complex character because of the multiplicity of objectives which throw up a number of investment criteria, often conflicting with each other.

Choice has to be made between the different sectors and the different techniques of production. As regards the first, in an underdeveloped country, the problem is of raising the standard of living of the people and of providing productive full time employment. So major significance is accorded to the development of industries.

Within the industrial field also there may be a wide range of possibilities—whether the country should have basic or intermediate industries, processing industries or consumer goods industries.

The choice of technique of production involves basically a choice between labour intensive and capital intensive methods of production. Various combinations of labour and capital may be considered as representing different techniques of production which produce different results with regard to the cost of production, productivity of capital and labour, etc. In this connection also it may be pointed out that while a technical variation may generally be possible in the production of a majority of commodities, there may be some industries where only capital intensive or labour intensive technique is possible.

On the other hand, there may be some industries which, though allowing for alternative techniques, eliminate the question of choice, because the study of their efficiency may allow for either of the techniques being equally justified. Prof. Sandesara[1] conducted a study of eleven industries for technique and their economic characteristics and found that in two of these industries there was no scope for change in technique, in the case of four industries, there is a clear benefit in adopting either labour or capital intensive technique; while five industries exhibit no difference, so that either technique could be adopted.

The emphasis that should be accorded to different sectors, to the different industries within the industrial sector, as well as to the technique of production that should be adopted, depends upon the objectives of national economic policy and the major constraints that exist in a developing economy.

The broad objective of any central authority is to maximize social welfare. This may require increase in output and income, generation of more employment as well as more equitable distribution of income. Related to the equality or distributive objective is the problem of reducing the widening gulf between the more prosperous and backward regions. If this aspect is neglected, the comparatively prosperous regions tend to become more affluent, while the backward areas grow at a slower pace. In such a situation it is necessary to evolve a new strategy of industrialization that is suited to the needs of the newly developing nations. It is not advisable to follow a policy of concentrating on a few more developed regions, and wait for the diffusion effect to operate and bring about development in other regions. Competition is becoming increasingly imperfect, so that the automatic working of the economic system is unlikely to generate the beneficial effects it was expected to, by earlier economists. Thus, a balanced development of the regions also becomes an important objective of economic policy.

A developing economy normally faces certain constraints which hamper the pace of economic development. The major constraints in the economy are:

(a) ability to invest, because of scarcity of capital;

(b) ability to import because of shortage of foreign capital,

(c) availability of skilled labour; and

(d) availability of entrepreneurial talent.

In this connection, i.e. with regard to the existence of economic constraints, it has been pointed out[2] that it is necessary to free ourselves from the assumption of stable functions for the supply of savings and skill, as also the demand for skill. The supply of capital as well as skill can be changed within a generation to a great extent, as has been shown by both Japan and the USA. Thus a complete transformation of the 'mutable factors' as A.J. Brown[3] puts it, is possible within two generations. Capital imports have reduced the dependence on domestic savings only. The tendency towards increased automation and mechanization is reducing the problem of skill formation and technical know-how is being freely imported by developing countries from the developed ones. Thus, some of the significance of these constraints is being reduced. In the initial stages, however, one does have to take into account such constraints for the choice of a criteria for a programme of industrialization.

On the basis of the goals and constraints mentioned above, different criteria have been proposed. Every criteria however, does not take into account all the objects and constraints. A choice may therefore have to be made at the cost of one or the other objective. The different criteria reflect differences of opinion as to what less developed countries ought to attempt to maximize.

Some of the main criterias[4] are:—

(a) The Minimum Capital-Output Criteria: It is also known as the highest rate of turnover criteria. It emphasizes capital's strategic role in the growth process. The object is to minimize $\frac{1}{0}$ and maximize $\frac{0}{1}$, where $\frac{1}{0}$ is the incremental capital-output ratio.

(b) The Social Product Criteria: The aim according to this criteria should shift from minimum use of capital to maximum social product. Social marginal productivity (SMP) is taken as the difference between the annual value of output (V) and social costs (C), expressed as a ratio of the capital invested (K), i.e. $SMP = \frac{V - C}{K}$. The social marginal product will exceed private product where the opportunity cost of a factor is less than what private investors must pay for it. In less developed countries this may happen in the case of a wide range of products, and if such projects are not to be neglected, this criteria of investment should be applied.

(c) The Marginal Re-investment Criteria: This criteria given by Galenson and Leibenstein, lays emphasis on maximization of output and consumption in the future, as against the present. Resources should be so allocated that the marginal re-investment quotient between projects is equalised. Thus, emphasis is upon generation of maximum surplus per head.

(d) Labour Absorption Criteria: The criteria suggests that if an economy has a surplus of labour for employment, together with scarcity of capital, investment should be made with a view to absorb maximum labour per unit of capital as opposed to product maximization.

(e) Balance of Payments Criteria: Growing recognition is being paid to foreign exchange as a scarce resource in developing economies, because of the significance of imports in the development process. If foreign exchange is the dominant scarce factor which may be the case in the take off stage, there may be a strong case for diversion of investment to export oriented or import substitution investments.

Thus the choice of a criteria would depend upon the objects and constraints, which themselves may change at different stages of development.

Role of Small Scale Industry

Having discussed the concept of small scale industry, the ambiguity that surrounds it, the goal and constraints of an underdeveloped economy, as well as the criteria of investment, we are now in a position to see how far small scale industry can serve these goals. If the goal is maximization of output and the constraint is scarcity of capital with an "unlimited supply" of labour at a given wage rate, a case for small scale units can be built if it can be proved that they have a higher output-capital ratio than large scale units. In fact, economists do build up a case for small scale industry on the ground that small scale units are less capital intensive than large scale enterprises, though the productivity of labour may be lower.

Biswanath Goldar[5] in his paper "Relative Efficiency of Modern Small Scale Industries in India", has also come to the conclusion that SSI generally have low capital intensity, high capital productivity and low labour productivity.

I.M.D. Little, Page & Mazumdar, in a World Bank Study[6] of LDCs have concluded that by and large this conclusion holds for manufacturing industry in general but this hypothesized relationship of direct relationship between capital intensity and size breaks down at the disaggregated level. The smallest size is quite often not the most labour intensive.

If we take maximization of output in "future" as the object, "maximum per capital re-investment" would be the appropriate criteria for investment. Small Scale enterprises would then be preferred if they generate more surplus per unit of capital invested, than the large scale units. It has been pointed out that the share of wages in the output is higher in small scale units than in large ones, which leaves a lower surplus for re-investment. This is again borne out by Sandesara's[7] study, according to which small scale units have a lower surplus per unit of capital as well as per unit of labour.

In a country where there is an abundance of labour, the major problem can be one of generating more employment. In such a situation a case for small scale enterprise can be made on the ground that it was more labour intensive than a large scale unit. It thus fits in the "labour absorption" criteria. However, some studies do not show a clear relationship between size and capital intensity as is borne out by many studies as mentioned earlier.

In so far as small scale units can be located in the villages, they can solve the problem of unemployment and under employment. The capital-labour ratio will be lower, the higher the capacity of the government to mop up their previous consumption by taxation. This is more so in the case of industries based on traditional technology.

Developing countries often suffer from scarcity of foreign exchange. As such, the balance of payments criteria may be adopted for determining the direction of investment and the technology to be employed. It is presumed that a small scale unit based on simple techniques of production, requires less foreign capital and hence saves a scarce resource. A strong case for small scale enterprise has recently been made on the ground that new technological advances in the field of automation, synthetic alloys, die casting and precision instrumentation, have removed some of the technical constraints of small scale production. But these very technical advancements also reduce the viability of the main argument in their favour, that they are less capital intensive and import light. However, another aspect of this development has been the entry of these very industrial units as exporters in the international market, thus developing foreign exchange earning capacity. e.g. electronics and software exports.

It is also pointed out that small scale industry encourages growth of entrepreneurship and forms the basis of training of entrepreneurs for modern large scale production. A World Bank study of African industries says, "In general, the owners of small scale enterprises in Africa originate from within the small enterprise sector. Data from enterprise surveys indicates that more than 60 per cent of entrepreneurs of small firms received training as apprentices in other small scale enterprises. Where general surveys of small scale enterprises have been undertaken, less than 10 per cent of the respondents among small entrepreneurs indicated that their prior experience had been in modern, large scale industry."[8] The report further states that the levels of formal educational attainment among small business proprietors were quite modest. Same is the case as far as requirement of skill from labour is concerned. It is contended that small scale enterprises by and large required less of skilled labour.

A case for small scale industry is often built on ground of social justice. It is pointed out that being labour intensive, workers get a large proportion of value generated by small enterprises. Also, small enterprises maintained competition, thus preventing growth of monopoly or concentration of economic power. As against this argument, some have pointed out that the productivity of labour in small scale units being low, the wages of workers employed in these are generally lower than in larger units. Further, lower incomes mean lower savings with reduced capital investment and lower rate of growth of national income. Thus, in the long run, their potential for generating more jobs is doubtful.

An argument for small scale industry is also advanced on grounds of bringing about decentralization. It is pointed out that because these require small initial investment and do not require on elaborate infrastructure, these are ideally suited for bringing about balanced regional development and avoid the evils of concentration of industry in urban areas. However, the identification of small industry with rural development is wrong. All industries are not suited for a rural location, even if a small size is technologically or otherwise advantageous. This applies specially to those industries which are not economically linked with agriculture.

The development of technologically efficient but light small industries and the dispersal of suitable ones into rural location, will also call for intensive planning, in fact more intensive than a development plan based on large industries. These industries will not grow unless a definite bias towards them is created. This will require a complete control of location of investments, arrangements for finance and final responsibility for the maintenance of prices. But planning by its very nature operates better with a smaller number of large industries than with a large number of small ones.

It is also argued that a small size may not be technically viable. This argument may be countered by the fact that so long as unemployed/under employed labour is there, the wastes of small size may be smaller than the wastes due unemployed/underemployed labour. Still more important is the possibility that a dispersed system of rural industries may create investment incentives by its very existence.

Lastly, it is seen that a developing economy is faced with a high inflationary pressure and a need for a rapid rise in the standard of living. So the industries chosen should be such that the gestation lag is small. The anti-inflationary requirements and the requirements for development are often in conflict, and a compromise can be found in the industries which have, as J.R. Hioks[9] called, a high "fruit coefficient" (or a high ratio between planned output and investment), and also a short "fruition lag".

It can thus be concluded from the above discussion that prima facie, no generalised case can be built for small scale units in all the industries. Each industry has to be viewed on its own merit on the basis of different criteria, before a programme of encouragement to small scale units can be decided upon.

To quote a World Bank paper on small enterprise development, "A dynamic and growing small scale enterprise sector can contribute to a wide range of development objectives held in common by governments, donors and international agencies: efficient use of resources; employment creation; mobilization of domestic savings and investment; expansion of the role of domestic entrepreneurs; training of managers and semi-skilled workers; use of local resources; more equitable income distribution; and growth of production oriented towards basic consumer needs. Whether small scale enterprise promotion represents an efficient mechanism for job creation, entrepreneurial and management development, or other policy goals, however, depends crucially on the current size structure of industry, on the costs and benefits of promotional efforts and ultimately, on the economic efficiency of small enterprises themselves.[10]

In each case, two questions need to be answered— (a) what is the factual basis on which to believe that small scale enterprises differ in their behaviour from industrial enterprises in general? (b) If they do in fact differ, what is the argument for intervention in the economy on their behalf?

Role of Small Scale Industry in the Indian Economy

A discussion on the Role that the SSI has been assigned and has played in the Indian economy involves a discussion of its definition. The role and the definition, which has been changing over time, are closely linked.

In the earlier stage of the development of the country (i.e. the late 19th Century and early 20th Century) the association of the idea was essentially with the indigenous industry engaged in the production of articles of "indigenous arts and manufactures", based on traditional technology. Since this was about the only industry in existence in the country at the time, giving employment to skilled labour and having an edge in the international economy also, the "self rule" movement had it on its agenda protection of this industry as an item of importance.

Thus in the initial stages, indigenous industry and small scale industry were synonymous and no distinction was made between the two. These industries gained immense significance in the Swadeshi movement.

Gopal Krishna Gokhale emphasized modernisation of these industries, and this laid the foundation for the distinction to be later made between cottage and small scale industries.

The role assigned to traditional small scale industry got another shot with Mahatma Gandhi's propagation of decentralized economic system and emphasis on rural self sufficiency.

The same period also saw the growth of some large scale sector based on high technology and hence a debate on the relative desirability of small versus large scale industry. It also gave rise to the possibility of co-operative rather than competitive growth of the two segments of the industrial sector.

Soon Cottage and "Small Scale" industries came to be clubbed together from the point of view of policy and the difference between "Small & 'Large' came to be associated with scale rather than technique. The Industrial Policy Resolution of 1956 specially emphasized the need for modernisation of the small scale sector, to become ultimately self sustaining. However, the need to support this sector in its infancy stage, and the role that it could play in generating diffusion effects of economic development, continued to be recognised and emphasized.

Prof. Mahalanobis made the potential of the small scale industry to meet increasing consumer demand, the basis of Second Five Year Plan model, because of their high output capital ratio and low fruition lag. The assumption of higher labour output ratio and hence the higher employment multiplier effect, in the face of an exploding population, added another dimension to the role assigned to the SSI.

Later however, another debate got generated—that of relative efficiency of the two segments of the economy as sources of employment and output generation, and possibility of SSI being attracted to the rural sector without creating adequate supporting system in the form of infrastructure and industrial demand. This in turn gave rise to the need for setting up industrial estates and ancillary centres.

Thus, as Prof. Hashim[11] puts it, three clear lines of thought have emerged about the role of Small Scale Industries — (a) the Protectionist ideology, particularly for rural traditional handicrafts, to sustain employment in them in the absence of other employment avenues; (b) the view that they have an edge in terms of production function efficiency; and (c) the diffusion effect of SSI.

The scope for future growth of the SSI sector depends upon their technical and organizational structure. The traditional skill based industries, depending on government support and middle men for marketing of their products, will continue to exist, but do not have much scope for expansion with development.

On the other hand, the other nonskill based traditional industries like gur and khandsari which compete now with the mill sector, have not much scope for survival even, unless they modernise or get absorbed under the brand name of the organised sector.[12]

Another aspect to be looked into from the point of view of the place that SSI will occupy in future, is connected with the changing nature of the SSI sector. New Technological advances have opened up rare vistas in this sector, specially in the field of electronics. The earlier technological developments fell more in the field of heavy engineering and electrical operations involving vertical disintegration of processes, thus accounting for the growth of ancillary and subsidiary units. The later advances are in the field of electronics where the scale advantage disappears and in some cases the advantage lies only in the availability of high skilled labour. In these fields India has an advantage and hence has immense possibilities of competitive growth even in the international field. These newer industries also require entrepreneurial skills which can help in solving the problem of educated unemployed, towards which focus has been shifted.

As Prof. S.R. Hashim has pointed out, at a stage where production technology is neutral to scale, small scale units have two distinct advantages—diffusion of ownership and dispersion in space.

Role of SSI in other Developing Countries

With the exception of India, other developing countries showed no interest in SSI till the 70's. The policy of trade regulations, interest rate manipulations and credit controls, and expanding large sector investment, discriminated against the SSEs by giving them an edge in obtaining information and concessions.

This limited concern for SSEs is understandable because of the concern of these countries to step up their rates of industrialization, which, in the absence of a local entrepreneurial class, could be achieved only through the growth of public sector or foreign enterprise. In any case most of the small locally owned enterprises that did exist in Asia and Africa were of the craft style. World Bank studies have proved that entrepreneurial class for medium and large enterprises cannot be generated from craftsman class. So the role of SSEs as a training ground for potential large scale entrepreneurial class was recognised, but remained insignificant in the under-developed economies of Asia and Africa.

Small Scale enterprises have played an innovative role in the industrial countries, but one cannot expect the same in developing countries where innovation involves learning, choosing, imparting, absorbing, and modifying foreign technology. Larger firms have an advantage in this respect.

The strongest argument that could be raised in developing countries in favour of SSEs was their employment generating potential.

It was only in 60's when the international organisations like the ILO recognised the menace of growing unemployment in underdeveloped countries, that the role of SSE's came to be recognised. The ILO's Kenya mission took up and popularised the concept of the "informal" sector, which is labour intensive and hence should form an integral part of the development strategy.

Later on the role of SSEs in reducing poverty and inequality in underdeveloped economies came to be debated in international forums, which strengthened the case for SSI in some countries like Philippines and India, and brought about a change in the policies of governments of UDCs towards the SSEs.

References

1. J.C. Sandesara, *Size and Capital Intensity in Indian Industry,* University of Bombay, 1969, p. 6.
2. Amlan Dutta, *Economics of Industrialization,* World Press Pvt. Ltd., 1952.
3. A.J. Brown, *Industrialization and Trade,* 1943, pp. 25-27, Oxford, Royal Institute

of International Affairs.

4. A.P. Thirlwall, *Growth and Development*, London, MacMillan Publishers Ltd., 1972.

5. Bishwanath Goldar, "Relative Efficiency of Modern Small Scale Industries in India" In "Small Scale Enterprises in Industrial Development", Edited by K.B. Suri.

6. IMD Little, J.S Page & D. Mazumdar, "Small Manufacturing Enterprises: A Comparative Study of India and other Countries," A World Bank study.

7. J.C. Sandesara, *op. cit.*

8. John Page and William Steel, *Small Enterprise Development— Economic Issues from African Experience, World Bank Technical Paper, No. 26, 1984.*

9. J.R. Hioks, "World Recovery after War—A Theoretical Analysis", *E.J. June* 1947, p. 160.

10. John Page and William Steel, *op. cit.*

11. Prof. S.R. Hashim, "Nature of Small Scale Industry and its Developmental Role", In "Small Scale Enterprises in Industrial Dev". Edited by K.B. Suri, Sage Publications, 1988.

12. Prof. S.R. Hashim, *op. cit.*

3

An Empirical Study of Efficiency Ratios on the Basis of Conceptual Differences

Introduction

It is clear from the foregoing discussion that perception of the role that the small scale industries can play in the development process of an economy as well as in the development of an egalitarian society, depends on the perception of the nature of small scale industries i.e. the definition adopted.

Many researchers have come up with conflicting conclusions with respect to efficiency of SSI, possibly because of conceptual differences.

This section is devoted to an empirical analysis of efficiency ratios on the basis of conceptual differences i.e. different criterias for measurement of size.

Three criteria have been taken, viz. employment, capital investment and capital intensity, and relative efficiency of different size groups analysed on the basis of each classification.

Hypothesis and Concepts

Following hypothesis have been tested:

(1) Large units are relatively more productive than small units irrespective of the criteria adopted for determining size.

(2) Smaller units require less capital per unit of labour than larger units.

(3) Smaller units generate lower output per worker than larger ones.

(4) Smaller units have a lower wage per worker than larger ones.

(5) Smaller units generate lower surplus per worker.

(6) Smaller units generate higher output per unit of capital.

(7) Small units generate less surplus per unit of capital.

(8) Larger units have a higher output-input ratio than smaller units.

Thus, corresponding to the above, seven efficiency ratios have been used—

(i) C/L i.e. capital-labour ratio—indicator of employment generating potential of capital. It has relevance where the objective is maximization of employment.

(ii) O/L i.e. output-labour ratio—indicating productivity of labour. It has relevance where labour is the scarce factor and output has to be maximized with the given labour force.

(iii) WG/WRK indicates wage per worker. Together with productivity of labour, it can be used to study wage productivity relationship.

(iv) S/WRK i.e. surplus per worker.

(v) S/C i.e. surplus-capital ratio. Together with S/WRK, this indicates capacity to generate reserves, again depending on whether capital or labour is the limiting factor. It thus has future growth implications, rather than the maximization of present output.

(vi) O/C. i.e. output-capital ratio—indicates productivity of capital. It has significance where capital is the scarce factor.

(vii) O/I i.e. output-input ratio—indicates total productivity.

Concepts

All values taken are book values and refer to the period between 1st of April and 31st of March. Wherever stock values are taken, they refer to closing values and not opening values.

In this study, since the data refers to 1979 and 1980, the period taken is between 1st April 1979 to 31st March 1980 and that between 1st April 1980 to 31st March 1981.

Size is denoted by employment and capital, and technique by capital intensity.

Employment: Employment refers to all employees number. It relates to all persons engaged by the factory in work connected directly or indirectly with the manufacturing process. It includes all the administrative staff as also labour engaged in the production process. The number of employees is an average number per working day (days on which the manufacturing process is carried on).

Capital: The term here has two connotations depending upon its usage. Where capital intensity of technique is being measured, the term refers to gross value of plant and machinery. In all other cases the term refers to overall productive capital, i.e. total of fixed and working capital closing.*

Worker: A worker is defined as a person employed whether for wages or not, in any manufacturing process. Persons holding managerial or supervisory positions are excluded. The number of workers is also an average number per working day.

Labour: Labour refers to mandays of workers, i.e. the number of mandays worked by the factory during the accounting year. This is obtained by summing up the number of persons of all categories attending in each shift over all the shifts worked on all days.

Wages: Include all payments made to workers in cash as compensation for work done during the year. It includes apart from basic pay, allowances, bonus, overtime etc.

Input: Comprises all manufacturing costs of the factory. It includes costs of fuel and materials consumed, office supplies, stationery, technical magazines, periodicals etc., purchase value of goods sold in the same condition as purchased, purchase value of products reported for sale in the previous year but consumed during the survey year for further manufacture and the costs of services purchased.

Output: Refers to value added by manufacture and provides

---

* Here it is relevant to mention that where C/L is taken to measure capital intensity i.e. technique, only investment in machinery is taken. Where C/L is taken as efficiency ratio, it refers to economy in the over use of capital for employment generation.

a measure of the contribution made by labour and capital in producing the output of an activity. It is obtained by deducting the inputs and depreciation from the total value of output.

Surplus: is the excess of the value added or output over emoluments.

Working Capital: comprises stock of material, stores, fuels, semi-finished goods and finished goods, cash in hand and at the bank, net balance of amounts receivable over amounts payable, as at the end of the accounting year. It excludes fixed deposits, long term loans and investments.

Coverage

Industry: Only the engineering industry has been taken up for study. The products included are those which fall under the National Industrial Trade Classification Code Numbers: 330-339; 340-349; 350-359; 360-369; 370-379; 380; 381; 382; 386.

Area: With regard to the area of coverage, since each area has its own problems and resource availability, the study has been confined to the Chandigarh area, which seems to offer a wide potential for the growth of this industry. Most of the units in the area are concentrated in industrial estates or industrial areas. It has a dynamic, enterprising and educated population, as well as availability of skilled labour. A wider coverage was not possible because of the obvious restrictions of an individual study. However, the affiliation of the ancillary units outside Chandigarh, but in its close vicinity, has also been taken into account.

Data could be obtained for two years only, viz. 1979-80 and 1980-81. This naturally limits time series analysis, but this limitation again is inescapable in a one person study as well as in a regional study where published material for separate units is conspicuous by its absence.

The units covered are only those which are registered under the Indian Factories Act i.e. those which employ not less than 10 labourers using power, and not less than 20 working without power.

Nature of the Sample

The total number of units covered are 81 in 1979-80 and

76 in 1980-81. The number of units falling under various industrial codes is given in Table 3.1.

Table 3.1

National Industrial Classification Code Number	Number of units in 1979	Number of units in 1980
330-339	5	8
340-349	41	30
350-359	23	23
360-369	5	9
370-379	6	4
380	1	2
Total	81	76

As can be seen there is a concentration of units in the NIC 340-349 and 350-359 i.e. in the manufacture of metal products and machinery, machine tools and parts. This can be attributed to the fact that there is a larger demand for agricultural machinery as well as cycles, scooters, etc. in Punjab and Haryana. There are three large scale units—the Hindustan Machine Tools, Punjab Tractors and Eicher Tractors—producing tractors and agricultural machinery in the neighbourhood of Chandigarh.

Size Group-wise Classification of the Sample Units

The units in each year have been classified into various size groups on the basis of

(a) Investment in plant and machinery.

(b) Employment.

(c) Capital intensity.

(a) Investment: On the basis of investment in plant and machinery, the units have been classified into seven size groups. The investment-wise classification and the number of units in each group is given in Table 3.2.

Table 3.2

Size Group	Investment (Rs. Lakhs)	Number of Units 1979	1980
I	Under 1	19	16
II	1 to under 2.5	31	32
III	2.5 to under 5	11	10
IV	5 to under 7.5	8	5
V	7.5 to under 10	4	7
VI	10 to under 20	3	2
VII	20 and above	5	4

Thus, on the basis of the definition of small scale units at the time the study was conducted (i.e. units below Rs. 20 lakhs investment), the first six groups fall in the small scale sector. Only the large size group belongs to the medium or large scale sector according to the definition then adopted. Thus 76 units in 1979 sample and 72 in 1980, belong to the small scale sector. Even in the largest size group some of the units may be ancillary units.

(b) Employment: On the basis of employment the units have been classified into five size groups. The level of employment and the number in each size groups is given in Table 3.3.

Table 3.3

Size Group	Employment	Number of Units 1979	1980
I	Upto 19	47	47
II	20-49	20	19
III	50-99	7	7
IV	100-199	3	None
V	200 and above	4	3

There are no units falling in the fourth size group in the 1980 data.

(c) Capital Intensity: On the basis of capital intensity, the units have been classified into six size groups. The capital intensity of each size group and the number of units in each group is given in Table 3.4.

Table 3.4

Size Group	Capital Intensity (Investment in plant and machinery in Rupees per unit of labour	Number of Units	
		1979	1980
I	Under 20	14	15
II	21-40	21	12
III	41-60	18	17
IV	61-80	11	9
V	81-100	8	9
VI	101 and above	9	14

It may be mentioned here that the number of units in certain groups are too small to warrant definite conclusions regarding them.

As can be seen, there is a concentration of units in the first three size groups of the first two criteria of classification and more than 65 per cent of the units belong to the 'tiny' sector. Fixed capital investment in the tiny sector* was Rs. 95.2 lakhs in 1979, which was 12.5 per cent of the total fixed capital investment in the surveyed units. Employment in this sector was 1129, accounting for 28.6 per cent of total employment in the surveyed units. The share in value added was 16.5 per cent with a total of Rs. 90.3 lakhs.

In 1980, the fixed capital investment was Rs. 93.8 lakhs in the tiny sector accounting for 13.6 per cent of the total investment in the surveyed units. Employment was 1078, with its share in the total employment in the surveyed units rising to 30.2 per cent. The share in value added of the surveyed units also rose to 23.8 per cent with a total of Rs. 115 lakhs.

The increase in the value added in 1980, while the level of investment and employment declined, may be due to better performance of the existing units, though some may have closed down. The number of ancillary units is also smaller.

Classification on the Basis of Organisation

The number of units falling under various organizational

set up in each year, is given in Table 3.5.

Table 3.5

Organisation	1979	1980
Proprietorship	10	5
Joint Family Enterprises	2	3
Partnership others	53	51
Public Limited Companies	2	2
Private Limited Companies	13	14
Co-operative Society	1	1

As can be seen, more than 60 per cent of the units in both the years are partnerships. Both partnership and proprietorships together account for more than 75 per cent of the total.

Most of the units have been started in the seventies. Hardly any dateback beyond the sixties. Thus the age of the units generally ranges between 10-20 years.

Classification on the Basis of Amount of Capital Investment

Investment in fixed capital has been one of the most common criteria adopted for measuring the size of a unit. As already mentioned, it has been adopted as the criteria of size in our country for quite some time. Many of the industry studies are also based on this criteria.

As already stated, the sample has been divided into seven size groups on this basis and seven structural ratios have been used for gauging their economic efficiency. The relationships between specific variables have been analysed for each size group as given by the following formula;

$$\sum \frac{X_i / Y_i}{n}$$

where X and Y are the economic variables, i the unit and n refers to the number of units in each size group.
For clarity, a graphical presentation of the result has also been given. Thereafter, the Rank Correlation method has been used to reinforce the results of the size group analysis.*

* Details of this method have been discussed in the Appendix of this section.

Capital-Labour, Output-Capital and Surplus-Capital Ratios

Capital-labour ratio is indicative of the degree of capital intensity, a study of which is relevant for an assessment of employment generated by enterprises of different size groups. Output per unit of capital and surplus per unit of capital pertain to efficient utilization of capital.

Table 3.6 shows these ratios in each size group. Broadly speaking, capital per unit of labour (C/L, Column 2) seems to increase both in 1979 and 1980, up to a point, i.e. till the Rs. 10 lakhs limit, after which it shows a decline. The capital size range between Rs. 2.5 lakhs and Rs.10 lakhs seems to represent the enterprise where capital intensity is maximum. The tiny sector definitely represents the less capital intensive group. The very low value of capital-labour ratio in the sixth size group in 1979 data is attributable to the very low value of working capital of one of the units. This may be due to under-utilization of capacity of the unit due to some reason.

The output-capital ratio (column 3), though not indicating a definite trend, is maximum in the largest size groups, i.e. in the above Rs. 10 lakhs investment groups. Thus capital productivity does not seem to coincide with higher capital intensity. In fact, even the tiny sector, comprising investment below Rs. 2.5 lakhs has higher productivity of capital than the most capital intensive groups in the 1979 data. However, the same is not supported by the 1980 data.

The surplus per unit of capital (column 4), once again does not show a clear trend. But by and large, the surplus generating potential of the enterprise is higher in the above Rs. 20 lakhs investment group.

Thus while the productivity of capital as indicated by its output and surplus generating potential are higher in the largest size groups, capital intensity seems to be highest in the middle range of the small scale sector.

Output-Labour Ratio, Wager Per Worker, Surplus Per Worker and Output-Input Ratio

Output per unit of labour, wager per worker and surplus per worker, are ratios which relate to efficiency of labour. These are given in Table 3.7.

Productivity of labour (O/L, Column 2), shows maximization

Table 3.6: Technical Coefficients of Different Size Groups (Capital Investment Criteria)

	Size Group	Capital Invesment (in Rs.)	C/L		O/C		S/C	
			1979	1980	1979	1980	1979	1980
		1	2		3		4	
1.	Under one lakh		66.8	86.1	.74	.55	.42	34
2.	One lakh to under 2.5 lakhs		75.3	83.1	.69	.58	.44	.32
3.	2.5 lakhs to under 5 lakhs		200.7	123.0	.44	.68	.28	.54
4.	5 lakhs to under 7.5 lakhs		380.8	151.2	.48	.63	.33	.45
5.	7.5 lakhs to under 10 lakhs		199.3	225.4	.62	.41	.51	.28
6.	10 lakhs to under 20 lakhs		36.0	124.1	.99	.74	.45	.58
7.	20 lakhs and above		149.1	153.6	.85	.74	.68	1.14
	Overall average		129.7	111	.66	.59	.42	.41

C/L is capital-labour ratio.
S/C is surplus per unit of capital.
O/L is output per unit of labour.

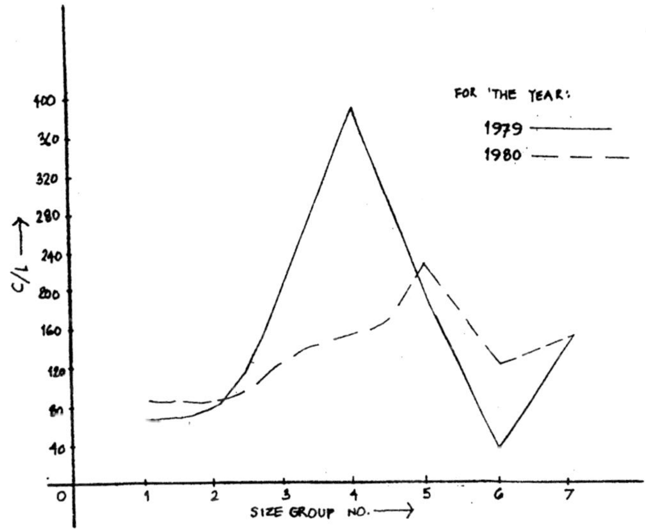
FOR THE YEAR:
1979
1980
C/L →
400
360
320
280
240
200
160
120
80
40
0
1
2
3
4
5
6
7
SIZE GROUP NO. →

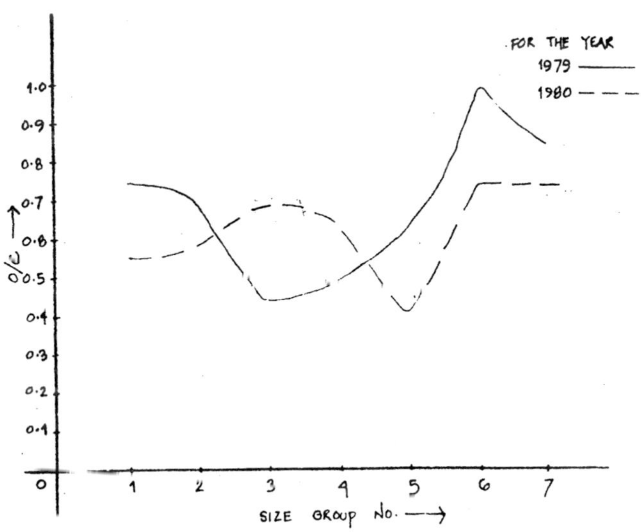
FOR THE YEAR
1979
1980
O/C →
1.0
0.9
0.8
0.7
0.6
0.5
0.4
0.3
0.2
0.1
0
1
2
3
4
5
6
7
SIZE GROUP No. →

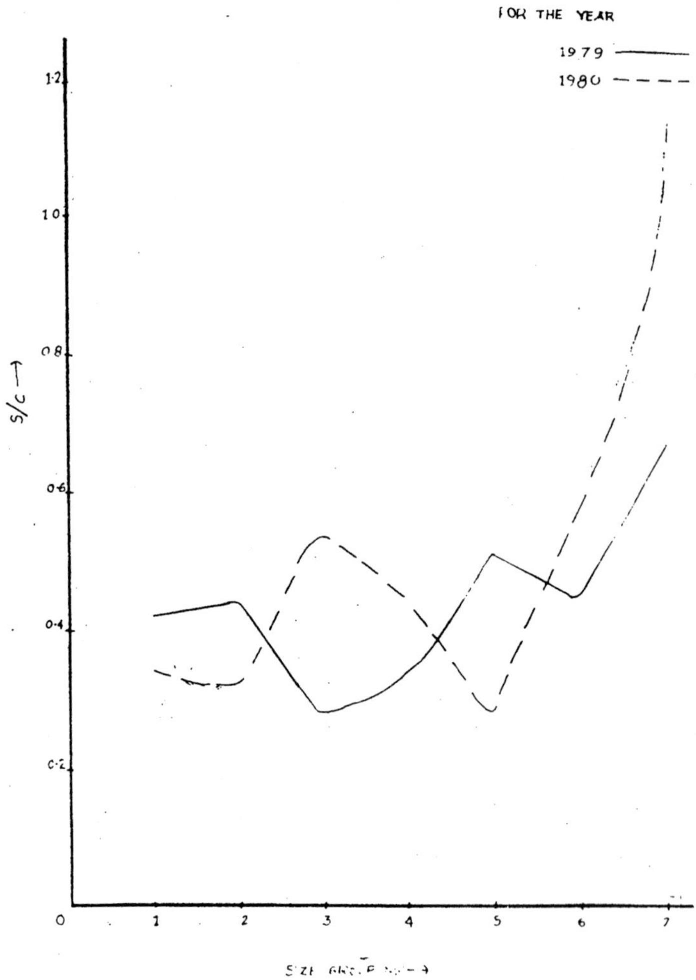
FOR THE YEAR
1979
1980
S/C
1·2
1·0
0·8
0·6
0·4
0·2
0
1
2
3
4
5
6
7

Table 3.7: Technical Coefficients of Different Size Groups (Capital Investment Criteria)

1	2		3		4		5	
Size Group Capital Invested (in Rs.)	O/L		WG/WRK		S/WRK		O/I	
	1979	1980	1979	1980	1979	1980	1979	1980
1. Under one lakh	34.1	35.4	3674.3	4095.9	6187.0	7195.0	4.9	5.3
2. 1 lakh to under Rs. 2.5 lakhs	40.5	39.4	4130.4	4758.4	7781.4	7574.2	3.5	4.0
3. 2.5 lakhs to under 5 lakhs	56.1	64.7	4162.5	4604.3	1572.9	15114.9	5.0	4.2
4. 5 lakhs to under Rs. 27.5 lakhs	133.5	58.7	4916.9	4718.2	33877.4	13178.3	16.0	6.6
5. 7.5 lakhs to under 10 lakhs	145.5	63.8	4281.3	4894.7	39784.1	14433.3	4.2	.84
6. 10 lakhs to under 20 lakhs	27.5	94.6	3991.6	4684.2	4355.6	24459.9	9.4	3.2
7. 20 lakhs and above	100.0	47.8	4158.6	4639.3	13676.5	13254.6	5.5	4.2

O/L is output per unit of labour.
S/C is surplus per unit of capital.
WG/WRK is wage per worker.
O/I is output input ratio.

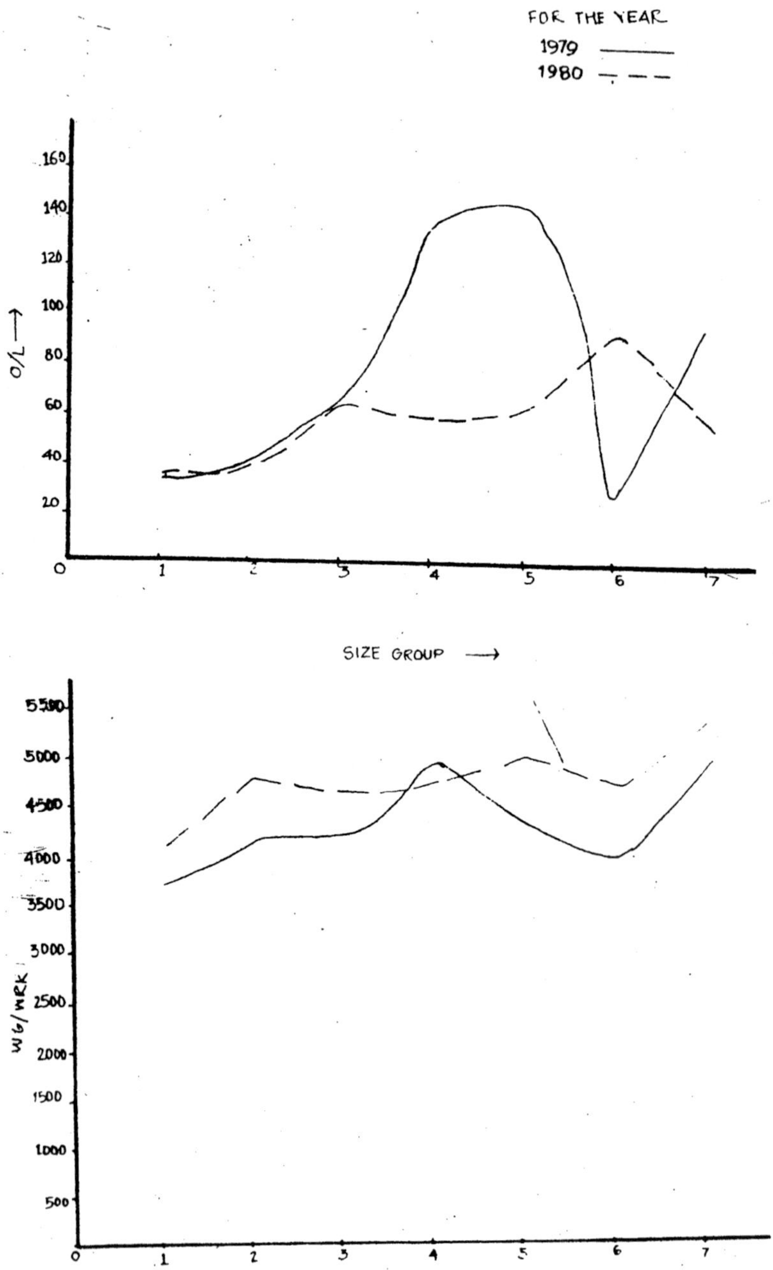
FOR THE YEAR
1979
1980
O/L →
160
140
120
100
80
60
40
20
0
1
2
3
4
5
6
7
SIZE GROUP →
WG/WRK
5500
5000
4500
4000
3500
3000
2500
2000
1500
1000
500
0
1
2
3
4
5
6
7

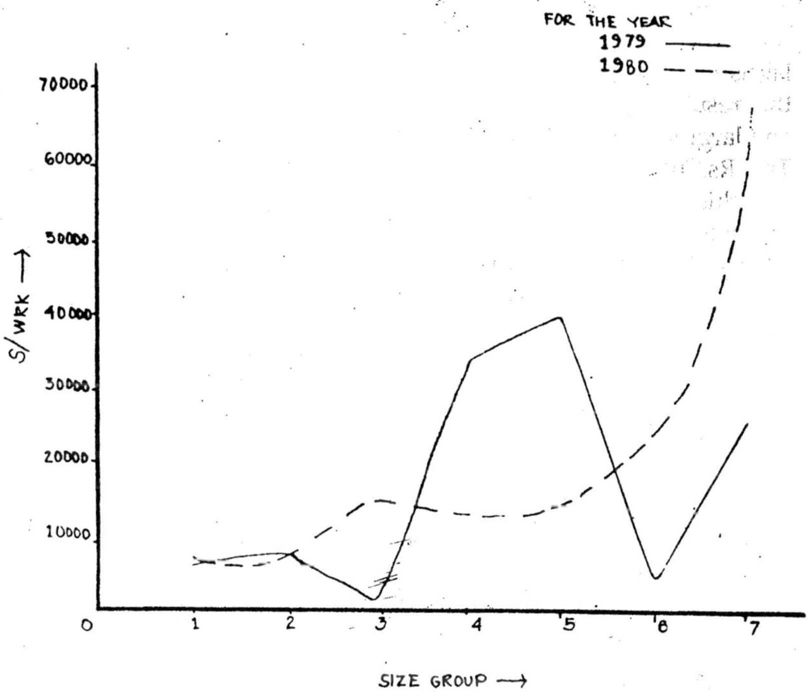
FOR THE YEAR
1979
1980
70000
60000
50000
40000
30000
20000
10000
S/WRK →
0
1
2
3
4
5
6
7
SIZE GROUP →

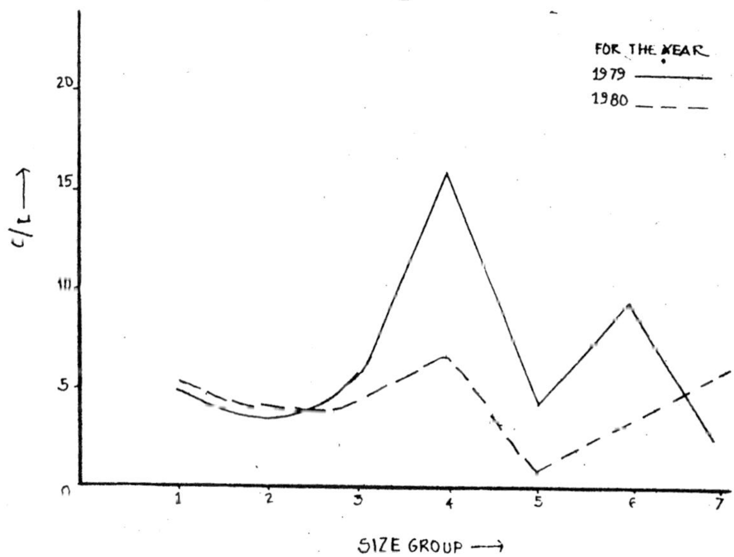
FOR THE YEAR
1979
1980
20
15
10
5
0
C/L →
1
2
3
4
5
6
7
SIZE GROUP →

in the middle size range, i.e. between Rs. 2.5 lakhs and under Rs. 10 lakhs investment group in 1979, and between Rs. 2.5 lakhs to Rs. 20 lakhs group in 1980. It thus partly corroborates the result of capital intensity analysis. Wage per worker by and large shows a rising trend with increase in capital investment. The Rs. 10 lakhs to Rs. 20 lakhs group is the only exception. But this may be treated as of no significance as the number of units in this group are too small, viz 2 in the sample of 1979 and 3 in that of 1980, to warrant any significant conclusion.

Surplus per worker also by and large shows an increasing trend with size.

Thus the larger size units provide better remuneration than the smaller units and also generate more surplus.

Finally, the aggregate productivity ratio (O/I, column 5) shows no definite results. The variations between the different size groups are too erratic and wide. This suggests the influence of exogenous variables, not accommodated for in the calculation of the ratio. The result is not conclusive, though in a very weak way they seem to support the results of capital productivity i.e. optimization in the middle size range.

Generally speaking, the units falling in the capital investment groups above Rs. 7.5 lakhs, show higher efficiency. Thus on the whole, capital does seem to be a significant determinant of productivity. This will be further tested in a later section with the help of regression analysis.

Rank Correlation Coefficients

The data was also subjected to Rank Correlation analysis to establish some clear relation between size on the basis of investment in fixed capital, and the ratios. The results of the correlation analysis are given in Table 3.8.

Table 3.8

Rank Correlation Coefficients (For Capital Investment Criteria)

Ratios	Correlation Coefficients	
	1979	1980
C/L	0.37	0.30
O/L	0.33	0.47
WG/WRK	0.25	0.27
S/WRK	0.28	0.46
O/C	-0.10	0.01
S/C	0.04	0.15
O/I	-0.03	0.00

Capital-Labour Ratio: Judging the relation between investment in fixed capital and capital labour ratio on the basis of rank correlation, though correlation is positive in both the years, the values do not indicate a strong correlation. Thus though by and large they are directly correlated, the relationship is not very definite. Mehta's study[1] also shows a positive relationship between size and capital labour ratio.

Output-Labour Ratio: The same positive but not strong correlation is revealed by the rank correlation values for the output Labour ratio. This shows that productivity of labour by and large increases with fixed capital investment. The same result was also borne out by the size group analysis. Professor Mehta's[2] analysis also shows similar relation between the two variables.

Wage Per Worker: The correlation between fixed capital investment and wage per worker reveals a positive correlation as was generally brought out by the size group analysis. The rank correlation value, however, is low.

Surplus Per Worker: The correlation value for this again is positive, showing that surplus per worker increases with fixed capital investment. The correlation is much higher in 1980 than in 1979.

Output-Capital Ratio: The Correlation value for this ratio is negative in 1979 and positive in 1980, though both values are very low. The values show almost no correlation between productivity of capital and fixed capital investment. The size group analysis did not reveal a negative correlation or negligible relation. This could be because the grouping of units may be partially reducing the negative effect. Mehta's[3] analysis on the other hand brings out a definite negative correlation between the two variables.

Surplus Capital Ratio: Correlation between capital investment and surplus per unit of capital is positive in both years, but again very low.

Output Input Ratio: The coefficient of correlation between fixed capital investment and output per unit of input has a very low negative value in 1979 and zero correlation in 1980. Both show that there is no correlation between the two variables.

In general we can say that Rank Correlation analysis by and large shows low correlation between fixed capital investment and the efficiency ratios. Fixed capital investment does seem to exert comparatively more influence on capital intensity (C/L), labour productivity (O/L), surplus per worker (S/WRK) and wage per worker (WG/WRK), as revealed by slightly higher value of rank correlation.

It exerts hardly any influence on productivity of capital and surplus per unit of capital.

Thus labour efficiency seems to be affected more by fixed capital investment, than capital productivity.

Classification on the Basis of Volume of Employment

Employment is another criteria of classification that has been frequently adopted for measuring size - both in government classification and for research purpose. Most of the surveys are also conducted on this basis.

The merit of this method of classification lies in the fact, that while 'capital is subject to conceptual, theoretical and practical difficulties of definition and calculation, the employment criteria faces no such problems'.

The employment criteria was used by the Indian government also before the adoption of the capital investment criteria.

This chapter will be devoted to an analysis of the data on the basis of this classification.

The sample has been classified into five groups, as already mentioned. There is no unit in the fourth size group, in 1980.

Each ratio will be analysed for both years on the basis of the methods used for analysis in this study.

Capital-Labour, Output-Capital and Surplus-Capital Ratios

Three ratios, viz capital per unit of labour, output per unit of capital and surplus per unit of capital are given in Table 3.9.

Table 3.9 : Technical Coefficients of Different Size Groups (Employment Criteria)

Group Number	Employment (Number of workers	C/L		O/C		S/C	
		1979	1980	1979	1980	1979	1980
1	1 to 19	106.0	107.1	.59	.51	.35	.31
2	20 to 49	199.4	105.6	.64	.73	.44	.48
3	50 to 99	106.2	126.7	.91	.63	.67	.45
4	100 to 199	93.3	None	.88	None	.65	None
5	200 and above	129.2	177.2	.98	.76	.59	1.39
	Overall Average	126.7	11.3	.66	.59	.42	.41

C/L is capital unit of labour.
O/C is output per unit of capital.
S/C is surplus per unit of capital.

A glance at the capital-labour ratio (column 2) indicates that there is no clear tendency towards an increase or decrease with increase in number of people employed in the 1979 data. Capital intensity however, does seem to increase with employment in the 1980 data. But while highest capital intensity is in the 20 to 49 workers group in 1979, it is highest in the largest employment group in the 1980 data. Thus no conclusive evidence is revealed about the relation between employment and capital intensity.

Regarding productivity of capital (column 3), the behaviour is erratic. It, however, seems to be higher in the larger size groups where employment is more than 50 workers.

Surplus per unit of capital (column 4) shows broadly an increase with employment in both the years. Thus efficiency

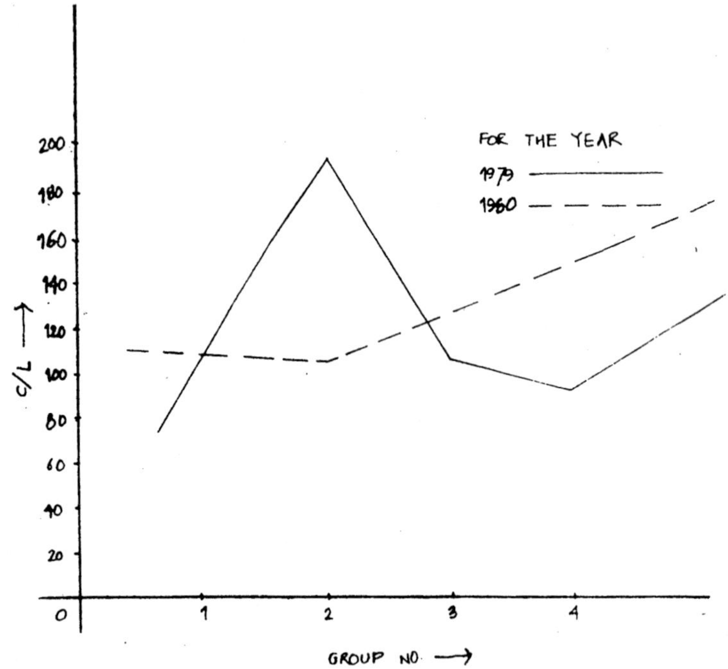
FOR THE YEAR
1979
1980
c/L →
200
180
160
140
120
100
80
60
40
20
0
1
2
3
4
GROUP NO →

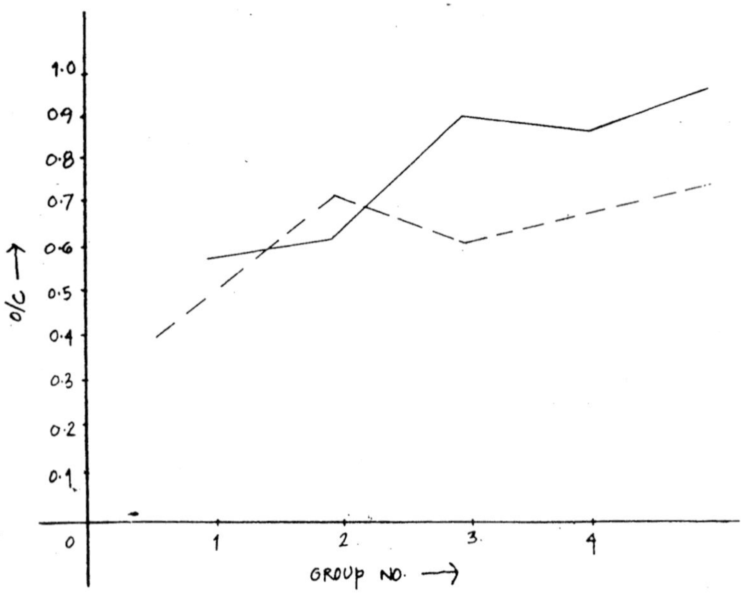
O/C →
1.0
0.9
0.8
0.7
0.6
0.5
0.4
0.3
0.2
0.1
0
1
2
3
4
GROUP NO. →

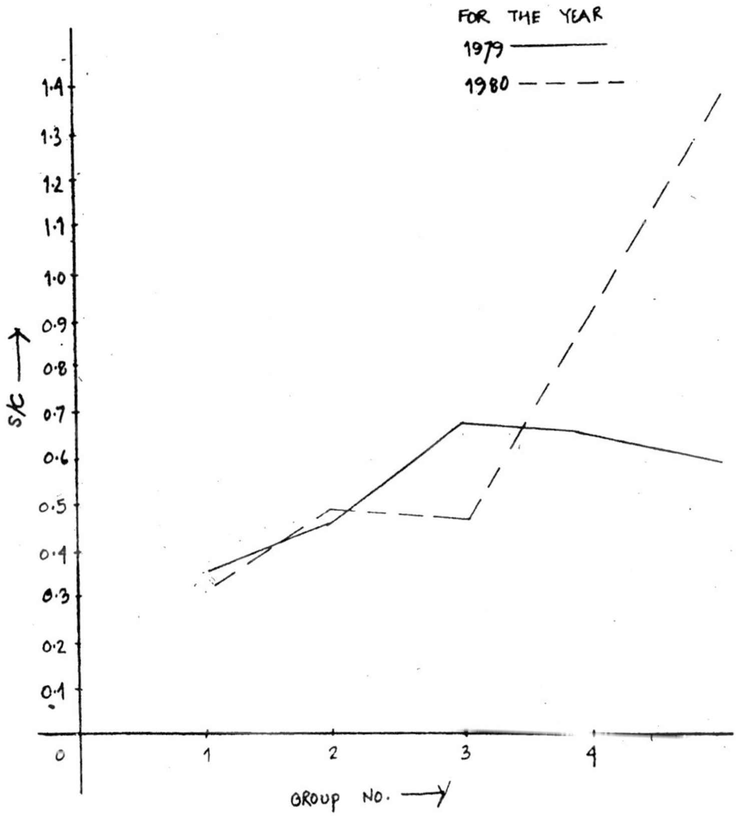
FOR THE YEAR
1979
1980
1.4
1.3
1.2
1.1
1.0
0.9
0.8
0.7
0.6
0.5
0.4
0.3
0.2
0.1
0
1
2
3
4
S/C
GROUP NO.

Table 3.10: Technical Coefficients of Different Size Groups (Employment Criteria)

Size Group No.	Employment (No. of Workers)	O/L		WG/WRK		S/WRK		O/I	
		1979	1980	1979	1980	1979	1980	1979	1980
1	1 to 19	45.1	44.9	4128.8	4853.7	8911.6	9160.3	4.5	3.7
2	20 to 49	81.9	48.8	4242.7	4162.5	19995.5	10809.3	8.4	5.4
3	50 to 99	85.8	60.3	3535.2	4316.6	21585.4	14090.6	6.7	3.8
4	100 to 199	85.3	None	4977.1	None	21023.5	None	2.7	None
5	200 and above	72.4	58.0	4565.5	5053.9	18718.1	90934.3	2.2	5.5
Overall Average		60.5	47.8	4158.6	4639.3	13676.5	13254.6	5.5	5.5

O/L is output labour ratio.
WG/WRK is wage per worker.
S/WRK is surplus per worker.
O/I is output input ratio.

of capital seems to get maximized in the large size groups if employment is taken as criteria of size.

Output-labour Ratio, Wage Per Worker, Surplus Per Worker and Input-Output Ratio

Labour efficiency ratios are given in Table 3.10. Productivity of labour, as indicated by output-labour ratio (column 2) shows a continuous rise till the group where up to 200 workers are employed and seems to optimize in the middle range of employment, viz enterprises having between 50 to 200 workers.

Wage per worker (column 3) does not show any clear indication of an increase or decrease with increase in employment. But remuneration is highest in the units having more than 100 workers. However, the number of units in these two groups being too small and the 1 to 20 workers group also showing higher remuneration than the other larger employment groups, in 1980 data, definite conclusion cannot be drawn.

Surplus per worker (column 4), by and large, shows an increase with increase in number employed. However, while it seems to reach a maximum in the 50 to 100 employment group in 1979 data, its peak is in the above 200 employment group in 1980 data. Thus no definite conclusion can be inferred.

The output-input ratio (column 5) reveals an erratic behaviour showing wide variations in both the years, with the result nothing can be said about optimization of overall efficiency at any employment level.

By and large, efficiency, both of labour and capital is higher in the units having employment above 50 workers. However, none of the ratios analysed on the basis of the size group analysis project any definite results. Hence once again we will take a glance at the Rank Correlation coefficients of the various ratios, to find out what is the degree of correlation that exists between the level of employment in a unit and its labour or capital efficiency.

Rank Correlation Coefficients

The correlation coefficients for different ratios with respect to the employment level are given in Table 3.11

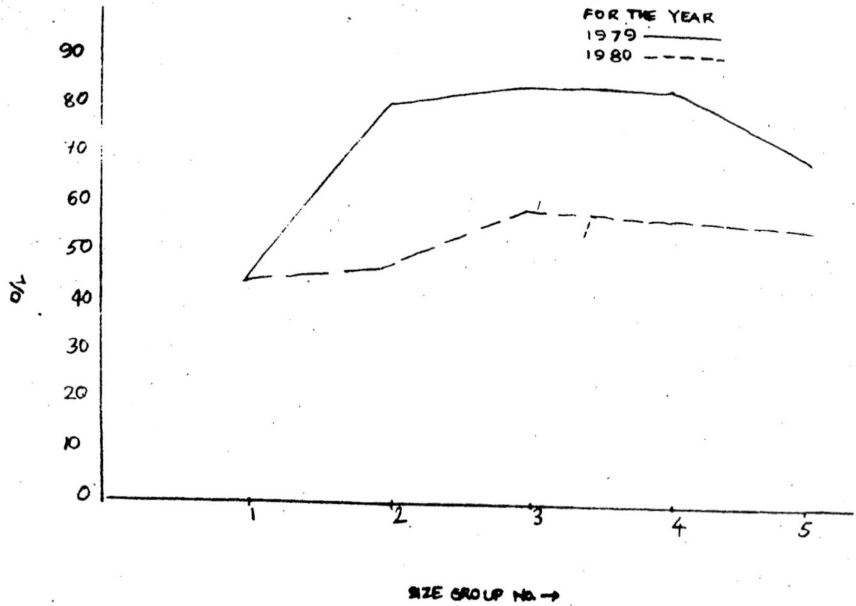
FOR THE YEAR
1979
1980
90
80
70
60
50
40
30
20
10
0
O/L
1
2
3
4
5
SIZE GROUP NO. →

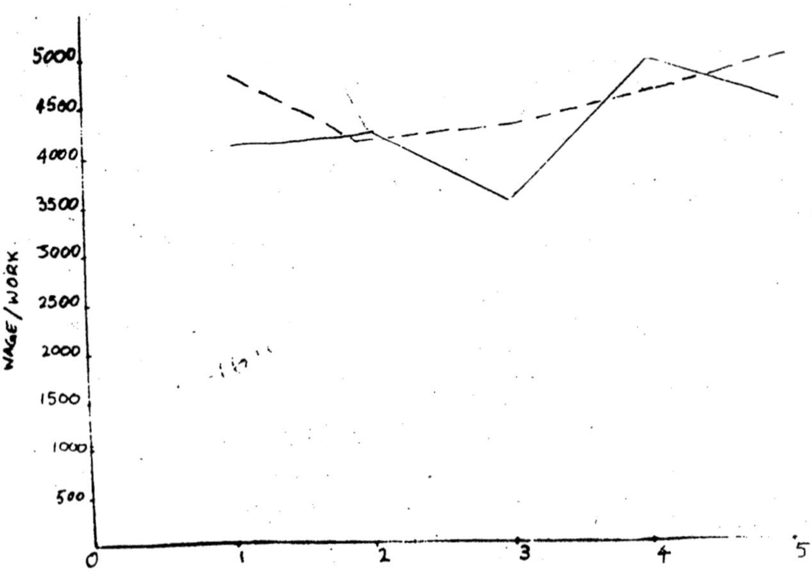
5000
4500
4000
3500
3000
2500
2000
1500
1000
500
0
WAGE/WORK
1
2
3
4
5
SIZE GROUP NO. →

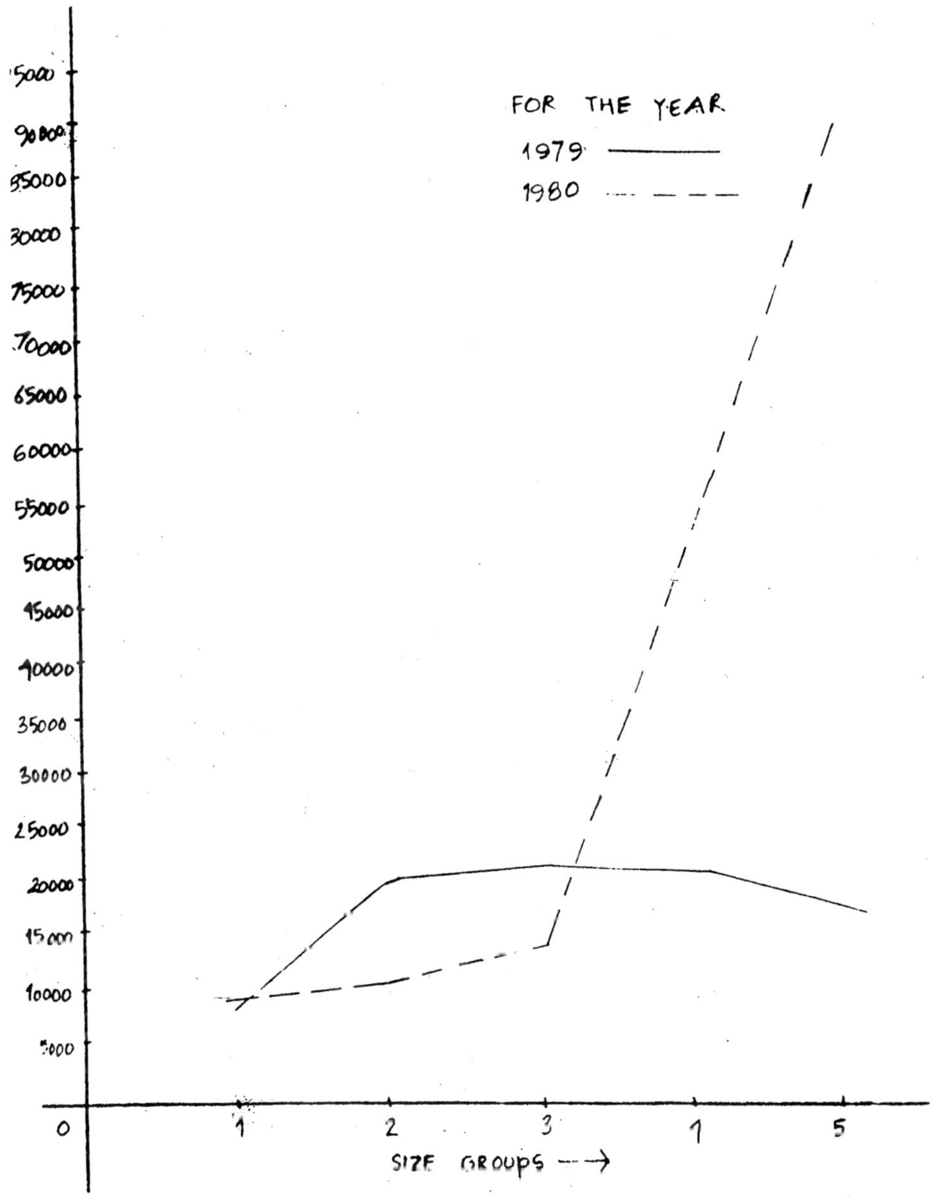
FOR THE YEAR
1979
1980
60000
55000
50000
35000
30000
25000
20000
10000
0
1
2
3
5
SIZE GROUPS

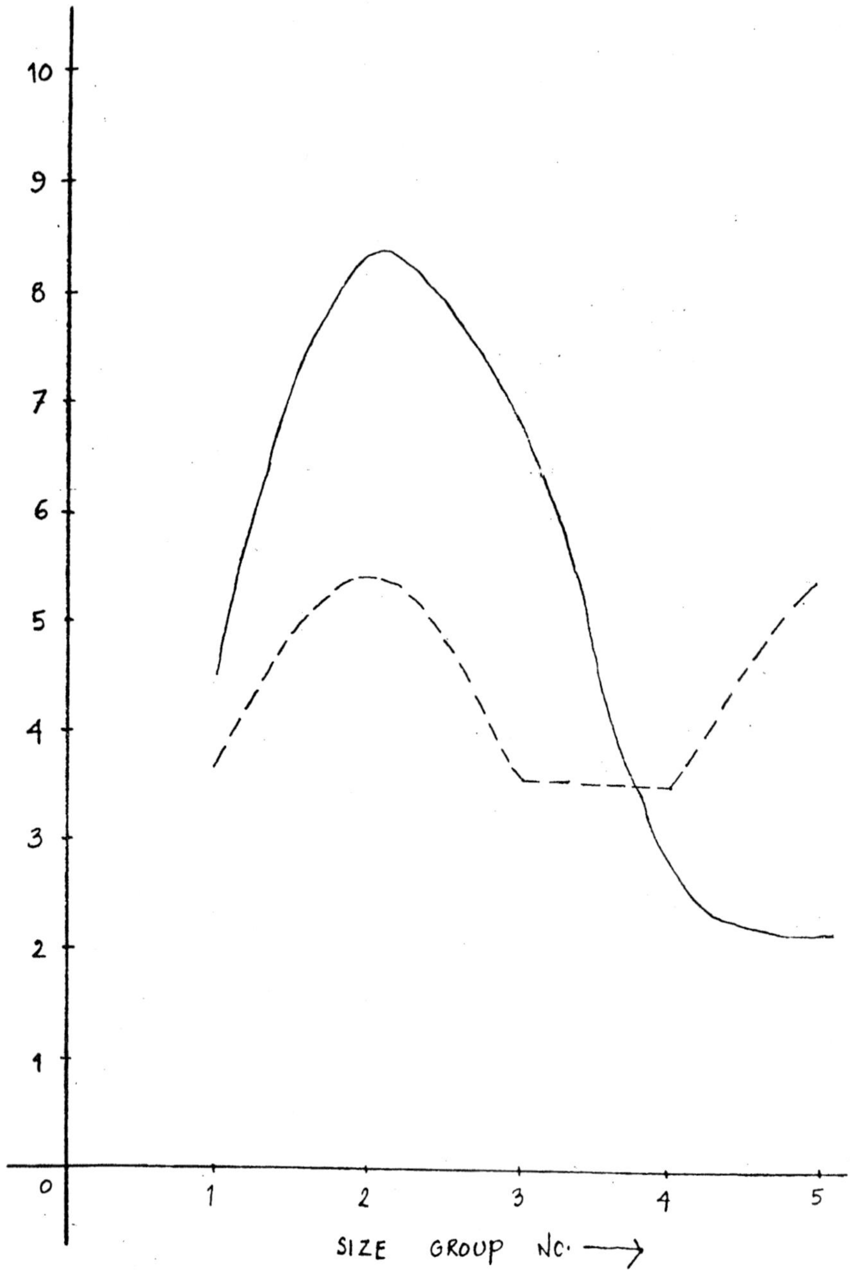
10
9
8
7
6
5
4
3
2
1
0
1
2
3
4
5
SIZE GROUP NO. →

Table 3.11 Rank Correlation Coefficients (Employment Criteria)

Ratio	Correlation Coefficients	
	1979	1980
C/L	-0.05	-0.03
O/L	0.15	0.21
WG/WRK	-0.05	-0.18
S/WRK	0.17	0.28
O/C	0.26	0.22
S/C	0.32	0.34
O/I	-0.13	0.01

Capital Labour Ratio: The correlation between size on the basis of employment criteria and C/L is negative both in 1979 and 1980. It is also extremely low, the values being -0.05 and 0.03 respectively. This shows absolutely no association between size and capital per unit of labour, a result which is also corroborated by the size group analysis. The same conclusion is borne out by Sandesara's study also.[4]

Output-Labour Ratio: The value of rank correlation between the level of employment and labour productivity, in 1979 and 1980, are positive but again very low, showing that labour productivity does not have any strong association with level of employment.

Wage Per Worker: The correlation values for wage per worker are negative and very low in both the years. This brings out that not only does the level of employment have very little effect on remuneration of workers but an increase in employment in a unit may even lower it.

Surplus Per Worker: The relation between size and surplus per worker is positive in both years, but both values are very low and thus do not reveal any strong effect of employment on surplus per worker.

Output-Capital Ratio: Productivity of capital does seem to be positively related to level of employment, as revealed by the positive values of rank correlation for both the years. However, the values are not high and hence do not show a strong correlation between the two.

Sandesara's study[5] also brings out a positive correlation

between size and productivity of capital on the basis of rank correlation, with employment as the criteria of size.

Surplus-Capital Ratio: Surplus per unit of capital is positively related with employment. But the relation is not strong and employment does not seem to exert much influence on surplus generated per unit of capital. The same result is borne out of Sandesara's correlation analysis.

Output-Input Ratio: The correlation coefficient for this ratio is negative in one year and positive in another. The values in both years, however, are very low, showing almost nil effect of employment on output per unit of input.

Generally speaking, the values of rank correlation with regard to capital productivity (O/C and S/C) are higher than those for labour productivity. So where capital is the limiting factor, and output maximization is the goal, a larger size may be advisable. At the same time, since C/L also shows a negative correlation in both years, though very low, there is more justification for encouraging a larger size for employment generation, than a smaller size.

Classification on the Basis of Capital Intensity

In this section, the criteria adopted is capital intensity. The term "capital intensity" has different connotations. Dhar and Lydall[6] have used the term to refer to productivity of capital taking output-capital ratio as an indicator of capital intensity. However, here we are concerned more with the technical aspect of the term. Hence it is with reference to technique of production that the term will be used. Most economists e.g. J.C. Sandesara[7] and Mehta[8] use this term in the latter sense.

Technical connotation would mean taking C/L as the indicator of capital intensity. Though most economists take total capital labour ratio as the measure of capital intensity of technique, it is felt that since technique is related to machinery, it is meaningless to include working capital.

The units in this section will be classified on the basis of fixed capital-labour ratio, to signify the labour intensity or capital intensity of technique.

Since there is no clear demarcating line between the two, an increase or decrease in the ratio is presumed to represent more or less capital intensive technique. Thus the concept is relative and not absolute.

This classification has not been used by any of the government bodies in any country. However, the policy of encouragement to small or big units has been adopted in various countries often on the presumption that a larger size means more capital-intensive technique, and smaller size, less capital intensive technique. The conclusions with regard to other ratios with changes in size are also often based on the same presumption.

Hardly any studies have been done to study the relationship based on C/L ratio (taking only fixed capital) and other ratios. So this section is devoted to such a study and to find out how far the hypothesis presumed in this study holds good with regard to technique also.

The units are classified into six groups in increasing order of C/L ratio (fixed capital-labour ratio).

In this section also, as in the previous two sections, the relationship of each ratio with technique will be taken up.

Capital-Labour, Output-Capital and Surplus-Capital Ratios

The C/L, O/C and S/C ratios have been taken up in Table 3.12.

Table 3.12 : Technical Coefficients of Different Groups (Capital Intensity Criteria)

Group Number	Fixed Capital Per Unit of Labour (in Rs.)	C/L		O/C		S/C	
		1979	1980	1979	1980	1979	1980
1.	Up to 20	41.0	82.6	.86	.62	.44	
2.	21 to 40	62.9	77.9	.82	.88	.54	
3.	41 to 60	82.4	81.4	.62	.68	.40	
4.	61 to 80	135.3	83.7	.49	.60	.33	
5.	81 to 100	96.2	114.2	.36	.49	.20	
6.	101 and above	541.2	223.1	.55	.24	.47	
Overall Average		129.7	111.3	.66	.59	.48	

C/L is total capital labour ratio.
O/C is output per unit of capital.
S/C is surplus per unit of capital.

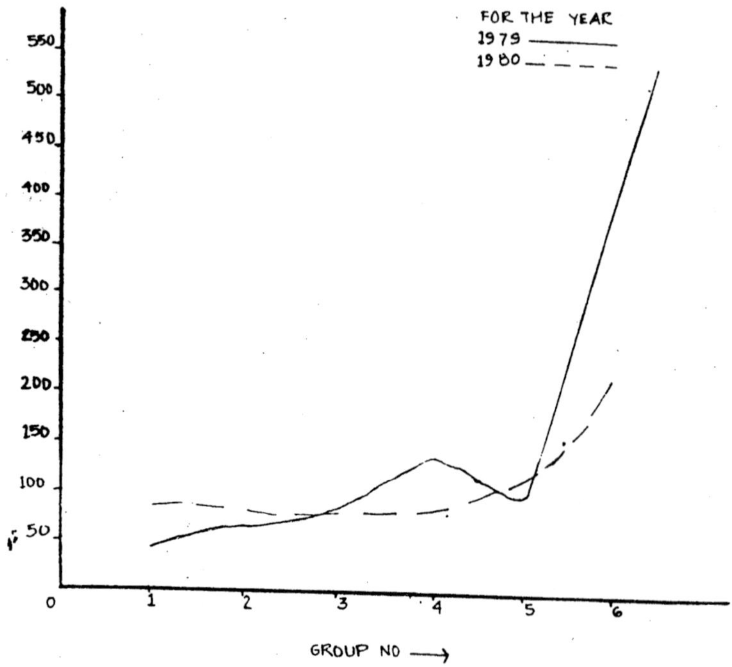
FOR THE YEAR
1979
1980
550
500
450
400
350
300
250
200
150
100
50
0
1
2
3
4
5
6
GROUP NO →

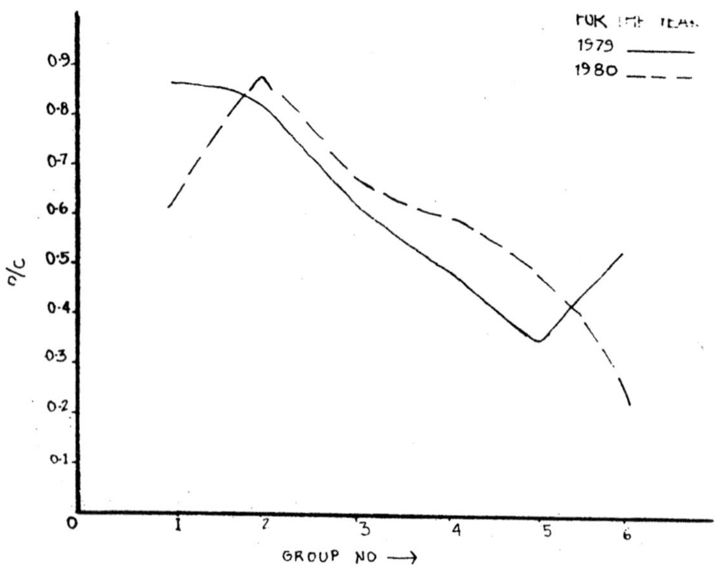
1979
1980
0·9
0·8
0·7
0·6
0·5
0·4
0·3
0·2
0·1
O/C
0
I
2
3
4
5
6
GROUP NO →

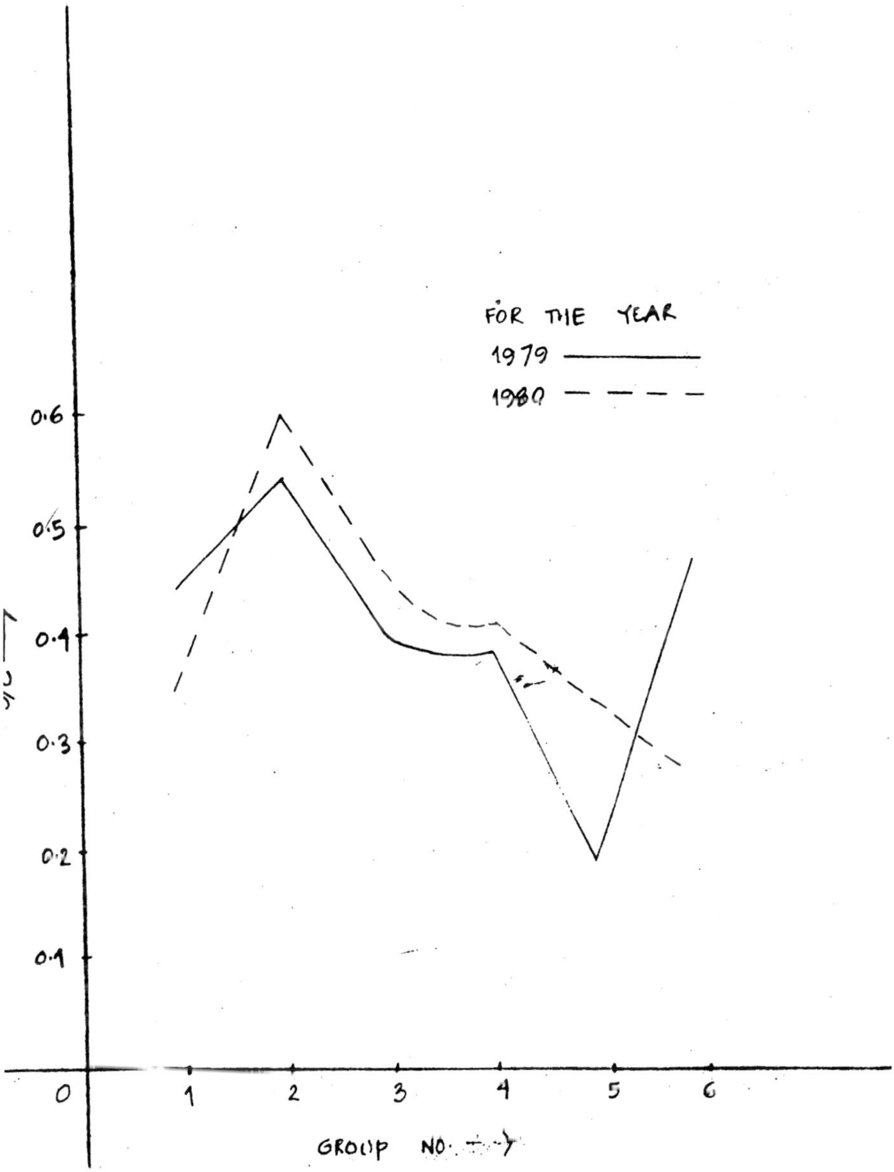
FOR THE YEAR
1979
1980
0.6
0.5
0.4
0.3
0.2
0.1
0
1
2
3
4
5
6
GROUP NO.

The ratio of total capital per unit of labour (column 2) shows a definite trend towards an increase with increase in capital intensity of technique, in both the years. The fifth group (i.e. Rs. 81 to Rs. 100 of fixed capital investment per unit of labour) is the only exception and that too only in the 1979 data. This could be taken as a freak case, or may be due to the existence of certain other forces. Otherwise maximum capital investment per unit of labour is shown by the most capital intensive group.

Productivity of capital (column 3) shows a declining trend with increase in capital intensity of technique, though it increases in the second group and is also the highest in both the years in this group.

Surplus per unit of capital (column 4) also shows the same result. It is also maximum in the same group.

Thus, by and large the less capital intensive groups are showing higher productivity of capital.

Output-Labour, Wage Per Worker, Surplus Per Worker and Output-Input Ratios (Table 3.13)

Productivity of labour (column 2) seems to change in a manner which does not show any clear result, though the most capital intensive group in the 1979 data shows a markedly higher productivity than the other groups.

Wage per worker by and large does seem to be more in the more capital intensive groups. Same is the case with surplus per worker. The fifth group in 1979 is the only exception, which also has a low total capital labour ratio and labour productivity in the same year. This could be due to certain other factors not accounted for in the study.

The results regarding the ideal technique to be used are very clear in 1979 data. The sixth group, representing the most capital intensive technique, is ideal from the point of ideal labour utilization as revealed by its having the highest O/L, WG/WRK and S/WRK. It also has the highest output-input ratio showing higher overall efficiency of production.

From the point of view of capital utilization, however, the

Table 3.13: Technical Coefficients of Different Groups (Capital Intensity Criteria)

Group Number	Fixed Capital per unit of labour (in Rs.)	O/L		WG/WRK		S/WRK		O/I	
		1979	1980	1979	1980	1979	1980	1979	1980
1	Up to 20	24.2	30.5	3559.8	4133.0	4253.9	5820.8	3.7	5.5
2	21 to 40	42.5	63.1	3888.8	4220.4	8504.3	14620.3	4.5	4.7
3	41 to 60	43.9	43.5	4244.7	4556.0	8580.7	8706.6	4.9	2.2
4	61 to 80	65.0	49.8	4233.9	4708.5	15142.3	10496.6	6.8	3.3
5	81 to 100	35.7	50.6	4404.0	5491.1	5103.2	10812.1	4.9	4.0
6	101 and above	209.1	55.5	5237.6	5050.1	56423.3	28914.5	11.0	5.6
	Overall Average	605.8	47.8	4158.6	4639.3	13676.5	13254.6	5.5	4.2

O/L is output per unit of labour.
WG/WRK is wage per worker.
S/WRK is surplus per worker.
O/I is output input ratio.

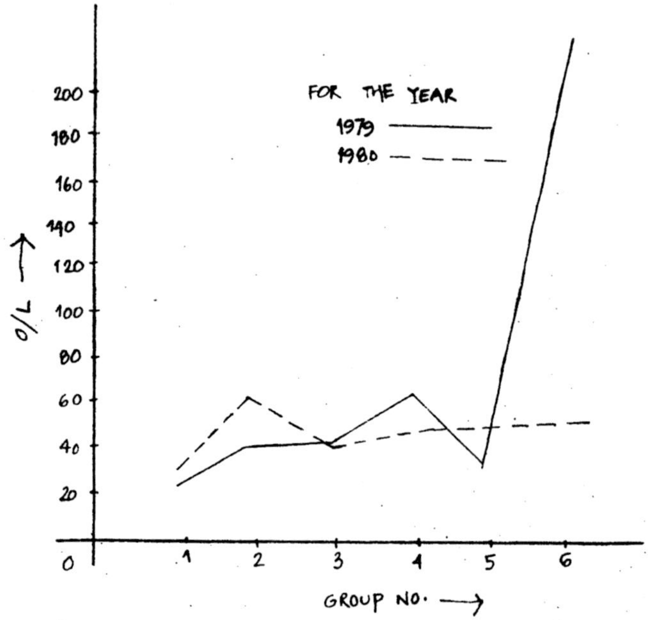
FOR THE YEAR
1979
1980
O/L →
200
180
160
140
120
100
80
60
40
20
0
1
2
3
4
5
6
GROUP NO. →

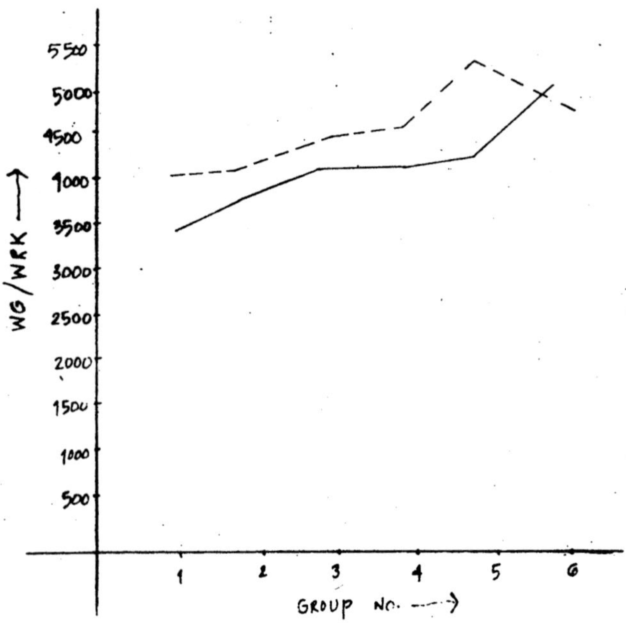
WG/WRK →
5500
5000
4500
4000
3500
3000
2500
2000
1500
1000
500
1
2
3
4
5
6
GROUP NO. →

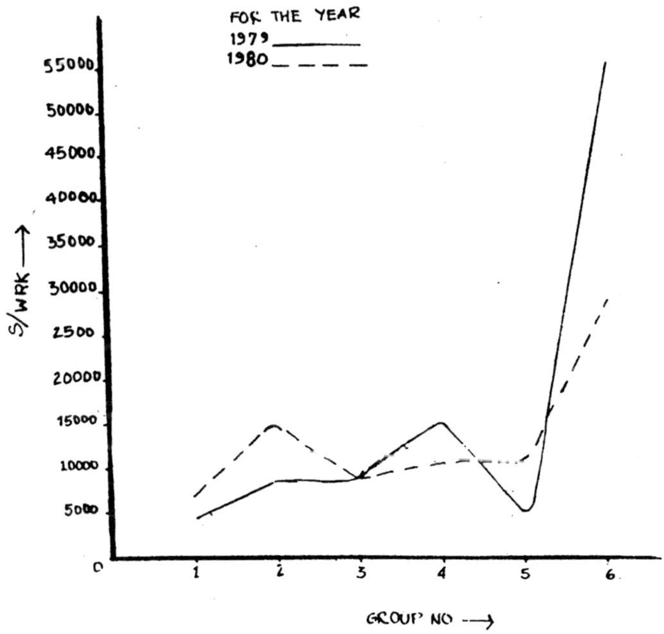
FOR THE YEAR
1979
1980
S/WRK
55000
50000
45000
40000
35000
30000
2500
20000
15000
10000
5000
0
1
2
3
4
5
6
GROUP NO

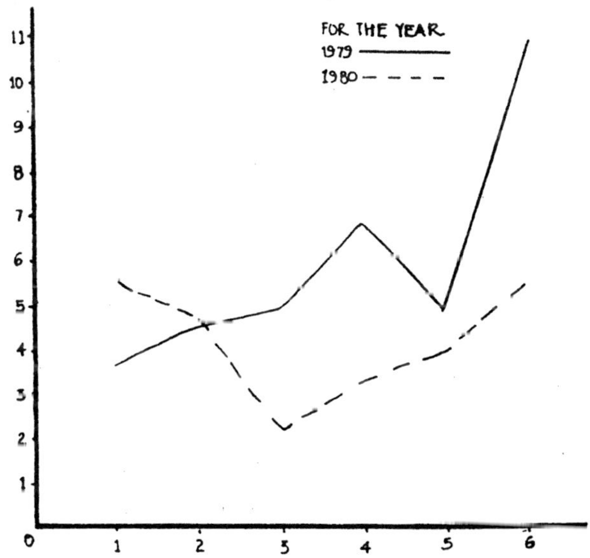
FOR THE YEAR
1979
1980
11
10
9
8
7
6
5
4
3
2
1
0
1
2
3
4
5
6

first two groups representing the least capital intensive groups, are most efficient as revealed by the highest output-capital and surplus-capital ratios.

The 1980 data does not give a clear indication of best technique from the point of view of either labour or capital productivity. By and large one can say that while labour productivity seems to get maximized in the more capital intensive groups, capital productivity seems to be higher in the more labour intensive groups.

Rank Correlation

The rank correlation for different ratios in both the years with respect to the technique are given in Table 3.14.

Table 3.14 : Rank Correlation Coefficient (For Capital Intensity Criteria)

Ratios	Correlation Coefficients	
	1979	1980
C/L	0.69	.0.52
O/L	0.48	0.33
WG/WRK	0.29	0.36
S/WRK	0.39	0.27
O/C	-0.40	-0.28
S/C	-0.18	-0.14
O/I	0.17	0.10

Capital-Labour Ratio: The level of total capital utilization per unit of labour shows high correlation with the amount of fixed capital investment per unit of labour. In other words it shows an increase with capital intensity of technique.

Output-Labour Ratio: More capital intensive techniques generate higher productivity of labour. This is proved by the relatively high positive correlation value of this ratio.

Wage Per Worker and Surplus Per Worker : These also show a positive correlation with capital intensity of technique and the correlation values are also not too low, so as not to warrant a more or less definite relationship.

Output Capital Ratio: Unlike productivity of labour, productivity of capital shows almost a definite negative correlation with capital intensity of technique. Thus the more labour intensive the technique, the higher would be the capital productivity.

Surplus Capital Ratio: The negative rank correlation coefficients of this ratio for both the years, bring out the fact that surplus per unit of capital more or less decreases with increase in capital intensity.

Output-Input Ratio: Shows a positive correlation with capital intensity of technique, but the values are too low to give any definite conclusion.

Thus the rank correlation analysis re-inforces the conclusions of the size group analysis that labour productivity increases with capital intensity of technique, while capital productivity decreases. The same conclusion were brought out in the capital investment criteria analysis. But by and large the values of rank correlation for many ratios are higher in the capital intensity classification than the capital investment and employment classifications.

Broadly speaking, it can be said that while capital intensive techniques tend to increase labour efficiency as revealed by the higher values of efficiency ratios, there is a decline in productivity of capital with increase in capital intensity of technique. So if more has to be achieved by way of output per unit of capital, less capital intensive technique should be adopted. On the other hand if output per unit of labour is to be maximized, then capital intensive technique should be used. The former would thus be suited for countries having scarcity of capital and the latter for countries having scarcity of labour. If employment generation is the objective, then again a labour intensive technique is more suitable as shown by a high value of rank correlation for C/L.

Thus the employment objective and the output maximization objective seem to synchronise with regard to adoption of technique. If there is scarcity of capital, then both objectives point to the adoption of labour intensive technique of production.

Regression Analysis

The data was subjected to stepwise regression analysis, to study the influence of various variables in the determination of different parameters.

The following functions were used for the stepwise regression analysis and 't' values determined:

(1) O = f (O/L, O/C/, I/C, S/C, FC/L)

(2) E = f (O/L, O/C, C/L, I/O, S/C, S/L, WG, WRK, FC/L)

(3) S = f (O/L, O/C, C/L, I/O, WG/WRK, FC/L)

(4) O/L = f (FC, C, L, S)

(5) C/L = f (FC/L, WG/L, S/L)

(6) O = f (FC, C, L, S)

(7) O/C = f (L/C, S/C)

(8) S = f (C/L, O/L, O/C, FC/L)

where,

O = Output

E = Employment

S = Surplus

L = Labour

C = Total Capital

FC = Fixed Capital

I = Input

WG = Wages

WRK = Worker

Output and surplus have been used twice as independent variables, but the second equation of output has different independent variables. The variables are ratios in the first equation, while as in the second equation they are total values.

In the two equations where surplus has been used as a dependent variable, however, some of the variables are repeated. But in the second equation the number of variables is less.

The 't' values of the regression coefficients are high enough to warrant reliable conclusions being drawn on the basis of results obtained (Tables 3.15 and 3.16). An analysis of the results of each equation is given below:

Table 3.15 : Regression Coefficients 1979 Data

Equation	Variable	Intercept	Regression Coefficients	't' Value	R^2
(1)	S/C	369604.02	1582285.75	2.58	.11
	FC/L		5331.96	2.22	
			DF=75		
(2)	S/C	18.47	60.52	1.79	.03
			DF=72		
(3)	O/L	606934.6	20938.56	3.93	.23
	O/C		-820687.40	1.91	
	C/L		-8861.58	4.04	
	FC/L		9445.80	2.76	
			DF=74		
(4)	S	57.46	0.0004	3.22	.38
	L		-0.0009	1.19	
	FC		-0.00001	-1.17	
			DF=76		
(5)	WG/L	-30.12	2.0389	13.46	.95
	FC/L		1.04405	5.85	
			DF=77		
(6)	S/C	0.03	1.0318	46.49	.99
	L/C		10.6348	22.58	
			DF=78		

Table 3.16 : Regression Coefficients 1980 Data

Equation	Variable	Intercept	Regression Coefficients	't' Value	R^2
(1)	C/L	419489.7	4571.68	1.80	.14
	S/C		1766639.2	3.21	
			DF=75		
(2)	S/C	19.31	67.52	2.03	.05
			DF=72		
(3)	O/C	410458.01	1383070.38	3.18	.13
	C/L		5306.75		
			DF=74		
(4)	S	48.79	0.00002	4.28	.45
	L		-0.00108	-3.60	
			DF=76		
(5)	FC/L	64.41	0.3620	3.323	.43
	WG/L		0.5394	1.936	
			DF=77		
(6)	S	37099.2	1.19311	242.2	.99
			DF=76		
(7)	S/C	0.03128	0.9692	56.94	.99
	L/C		12.8641	21.27	
			DF=78		
(8)	O/L	-101104.16	12504.38	2.27	.25
			DF=76		

Equation (1): In equation (1) the two variables which affect output a little significantly are S/C and FC/L in the 1979 data and S/C and C/L in 1980 data, the values of R^2 being 11 per cent and 13.9 per cent respectively.

Equation (2): In employment generation also S/C is the only significant variable, though even this is not a highly significant variable. The values of R^2 are only 3 per cent and 5 per cent in 1979 and 1980 respectively.

Equation (3): The variables which affect total surplus generation significantly are O/L, O/C, C/L, FC/L in 1979 data and O/C and C/L in 1980 data. Together they account for 23 per cent change in surplus generation in 1979, and 13 per cent in 1980 data. However, while the Regression Coefficient values for O/C and C/L are negative in 1979 showing a fall in 'S' with a rise in these variables, it is positive in 1980. The positive correlation is logically better explained, but the conclusions remain uncertain on account of the different behaviour patterns in the two years.

Equation (4): In the 4th equation, 'S', 'L' and 'FC' come out as significant variables as the determinant of O/L or labour productivity in1979 data. However, only 'S' has a positive value of Regression Coefficient. Both 'L' and 'FC' have negative Regression Coefficient values. In 1980 data too 'S' and 'L' are significant variables, having R^2 value of 45 per cent. But once again 'L' has a negative Regression Coefficient value. The negative relationship of total labour with labour productivity proves the hypothesis, but that between total fixed capital and labour productivity, does not. The hypothesis is that labour productivity, i.e. O/L increases with capital intensity and vice-versa.

Equation (5): In the determination of C/L ratio i.e. total capital per unit of labour, WG/L and FC/L seem to exert a large influence as shown by the value of R^2 equal to 95 per cent in 1979 and 43 per cent in 1980. This is understandable, for the cost of labour would definitely play a very important part in determining the capital intensity of technique and extensive use of capital. The higher the wage rate, the higher will be the capital intensity of technique.

Equation (6): Just as in equation (1) S/C was significant in output determination, in equation (6) 'S' is the only significant variable, accounting for 99 per cent change in 'O' in 1979 and 99 per cent in 1980. Thus total profit as well as profit per unit of capital come out significant as determinants of output.

Equation 7: Productivity of capital (O/C), seems to be significantly affected by changes in S/C and L/C. The significance of the relationship between L/C and O/C was brought out in the size group analysis in the previous chapters also where O/C is seen to be directly related with L/C.

Equation 8: In equation (8) as in equation (3), 'S' is significantly affected by the four variables O/L, O/C, C/L and FC/L in 1979. O/C and C/L have negative regression coefficients. In 1980 data however, the only variable of significance is O/L.

Size Group Regression Analysis

The data of 1980 was subjected subsequently to Regression Analysis for two ratios for size groups classified on the basis of capital investment criteria (Table 3.17 and 3.18). For each size group the following equations were used:

(1) O/C= f(L/C S/C)

(2) S= f(C/L)

Table 3.17 : Size Group Regression Analysis Equation (1)

Size Group		Variable	Intercept	Regression Coefficients	't' Value	R^2
I.	Upto one lakh	Number of firms are too few for analysis.				
II.	1-2.5 lakhs	S/C L/C	0.6108 DF=29	0.91343 12.35908	14.140 9.199	.97
III.	2.5-5 lakhs	S/C L/C	0.0405 DF=7	0.9723 12.7131	23.513 4.619	0.98
IV.	5-7.5 lakhs	S/C L/C	0.0122 DF=2	0.9710 14.7684	53.686 7.803	.99
V.	7.5-10 lakhs	Number of firms too few for analysis.				
VI.	10-20 lakhs	Number of firms too few for analysis.				
VII.	Above 20 lakhs	S/C	0.0118 DF=1	1.1959	40.725	.99

Note: Size groups are classified on the basis of capital investment criteria.

Table 3.18 : Equation (2)

Size Group	Variable	Intercept	Regression Coefficients	't' Value	R^2
I. Upto 1 lakh	C/L	105751.34	-1862.200 DF=14	-1.673	.69
II. 1-2.5 lakhs	C/L	86872.87	-407.067 DF=30	-1.211	.24
III. 2.5-5 lakhs	C/L	159787.38	-421.254 DF=8	-1.084	.24
IV. 5-7.5 lakhs	C/L	669539.09	-1641.35 DF-3	-0.859	.33
V. 7.5-10 lakhs		Observations too few for analysis.			
VI. 10-20 lakhs	C/L	594706.13	-1038.124 DF-0	-1.318	.60
VII. Above 20 lakhs	C/L	6373932.10	-10651.426 DF=2	-0.899	.37

In equation (1) both independent variables L/C and S/C are highly significant with R^2 values of more than 90 per cent in almost all size groups. Thus profitability of capital and capital intensity seem to be most significant determinants of capital productivity. Higher the profitability, greater the productivity of capital. On the other hand, the lower the capital intensity or higher the labour intensity, higher the productivity of capital.

There is not much difference in Regression Coefficient values of S/C and L/C in different size groups, showing very little difference in results with changes in size. In other words, the influence of the variables on productivity of capital, is not affected much by size of the firm.

The second equation shows that while C/L i.e. capital intensity exerts significant influence on surplus generation in all size groups and as in the case of equations (3) and (8) relating to surplus, in the overall data analysis, the Regression Coefficient values are negative in all size groups, showing surplus to be negatively correlated to capital intensity.

By and large, as the size increases, greater changes in capital intensity are required to bring about any change in surplus as revealed by higher Regression Coefficient values for sizes 4th, 6th and 7th, though the first size group has a high value of Regression Coefficient. The seventh group comprising large scale units, has by far the highest value of Regression Coefficient. The same result is seen in the rank correlation analysis, when the value of rank correlation of S/C with capital intensity has a negative sign. This indicates the existence of diminishing returns to capital, when returns are measured in terms of profitability.

A Comparative Analysis of Ratios on the Basis of the Three Criteria

The chapters on sample analysis and regression analysis were devoted to a study of the structural ratios for different groups on the basis of three different criteria of classification viz:

(a) Level of investment in fixed capital

(b) Level of employment

(c) Capital intensity of the technique of operation.

An attempt was made to study the behaviour of each ratio in each size group. An attempt was also made to find the ideal size group or groups for each ratio as well as on the whole.

It will be endeavoured in this chapter to find common ground if any, regarding the 'trend' of ratios with change in size and technique, as well as the 'deal size' or 'technique'. Any discrepancy in the results of the three criteria will also be studied.

This chapter may involve repetition of certain conclusions of the previous chapters, but a comparative analysis becomes necessary to test the first hypothesis, that the behaviour of the structural ratios will be the same irrespective of the criteria of size adopted, implying similar conclusions. Besides, a comparative study becomes very significant in view of the fact that a policy of encouragement to small scale industries is being adopted in many countries on the basis of research done on the viability of such units, though the criteria adopted for classification of small units by researchers and in different countries, are different. This points to the acceptance of the absence of any discrepancy with regard to results on the basis of different criteria, which, as will be seen in this chapter, is not true. The limit up to which encouragement is to be provided on the basis of different criteria, may also turn out to be different depending on which criteria is adopted.

Thus, first a comparative study of 'trends' of all ratios on the basis of the three criteria will be undertaken, and then a comparative study of the ideal size depending on different objectives, will be done.

Trends

In a comparative study of trends of ratios, since the 'size group' analysis does not show any clear trends, the values of rank correlation, emphasizing the relation between size and efficiency are studied. Each ratio is taken up separately.

(1) Capital-Labour Ratio

As regards the capital-labour ratio, no clear trend in relation to size is revealed for groups classification on the basis of employment or capital investment.

The analysis on the basis of capital intensity on the other hand, does indicate a rise in the use of capital per worker, with increase in capital intensity.

The rank correlation analysis (Table 3.19) shows a positive correlation between size on one side and capital intensity and capital investment on the other. Though the values of correlation are very low for capital investment criteria, they are fairly high for technique.

The correlation for employment on the other hand, is negative and very low. Thus, there is a certain amount of discrepancy in the results of capital and employment criteria with respect to the relation between capital-labour ratio and size.

(2) Output Labour Ratio

No clear trend is revealed for the labour productivity ratio too on the basis of 'size group' analysis for all three criteria.

Only for the most capital intensive technique, for both years does the result show a rise.

As regards the relation on the basis of "rank correlation", it shows a positive correlation between size/technique and labour productivity, on the basis of all the criteria. However, while the correlation is very low for the employment criteria, it is not so low for the capital investment criteria and technique. The degree of correlation for capital investment and technique criteria is almost the same.

Table 3.19 : Rank Correlation Coefficients

Ratios	Correlation Coefficients	
	1979	1980
For Capital Investment		
C/L	0.37	0.30
O/L	0.33	0.47
WG/WRK	0.25	0.27
S/WRK	0.28	0.46
O/C	-0.10	0.01
S/C	0.04	0.15
O/I	-0.03	0.00
For Employment		
C/L	-0.05	-0.03
O/L	0.15	0.21
WG/WRK	-0.05	-0.18
S/WRK	0.17	0.28
O/C	0.26	0.22
S/C	0.32	0.34
O/I	-0.13	0.01
For Capital Intensity		
C/L	0.69	0.52
O/L	0.48	0.33
WG/WRK	0.29	0.36
S/WRK	0.39	0.27
O/C	-0.40	-0.28
S/C	-0.18	-0.14
O/I	0.17	0.10

(3) Wage Per Worker

With regard to wage per worker, the size group analysis on the basis of capital investment and employment, does not reveal any trend. The trend is not clear for capital intensity either, but it generally shows an increase in wage per worker with increase in capital intensity.

The 'rank correlation' value for capital investment criteria and capital intensity are positive but in both cases low. For the employment criteria the value is negative but again very low.

Thus, while for the capital intensity and capital investment criteria, there seems to be not much correlation between size/ technique and wager per worker, for the employment criteria, there is a negative relationship, if any.

(4) Surplus Per Worker

The surplus generating potential per worker, does not show any clear trend with respect to 'size groups' on the basis of employment. On the basis of capital investment also, the trend is not clear, though generally it can be said to be upward. With regard to technique, the ratio is definitely higher in the most capital intensive technique and is more or less the same in the first four groups.

As regards 'rank correlation', it is low for all the three criteria, but it is lower for employment criteria than for capital investment/technique.

(5) Output-Capital Ratio

The trend of productivity per unit of capital with regard to size on the basis of both capital investment and employment, is not clear. With respect to technique, the trend, though not clear, is more towards a decline in the ratio with increase in capital intensity.

The rank correlation for the ratio on the basis of employment is positive but fairly low. On the basis of capital investment, it is positive in one year and negative in another, but in both cases extremely low, showing almost no correlation. On the basis of technique however, the value of rank correlation is negative and not low, showing that generally there is a tendency for productivity of capital to fall with increase in capital intensity of technique.

(6) Surplus Capital Ratio

The trend of this ratio with regard to 'size group' is not clear on the basis of employment as well as capital investment, though it shows generally a rise with increase in size in the latter case. With regard to technique also, the trend is not clear.

The 'correlation' between size and capital investment as well as employment, and surplus per unit of capital is positive. But while in the case of employment criteria the value of rank correlation is not very low, it is very low in case of capital investment criteria. The correlation for technique is negative and very low. Thus, while the positive trend is more clear for employment criteria, the relation is very weak with regard to capital investment and technique.

(7) Output-Input Ratio

In the case of output-input ratio, the trend in the 'size group' analysis, is not clear, though in the case of groups based on employment and investment, there is generally a tendency towards a decline in the ratio with increase in size.

The 'rank correlation' for employment and investment classification is negative in one year, and positive in the other. However, in both cases it is extremely low. For technique, it is positive but very low. Thus, in all three cases, there seems to be no relation between output-input ratio and size/technique.

General Conclusions

On the basis of the above analysis of the different ratios, certain general conclusions can be drawn with regard to the relationship between size of the enterprise and the objective to be achieved.

(1) Employment Generation[9]: Taking maximum employment generation to be the objective, while a smaller size may be economical if capital investment is taken as the criteria of size, a larger size of the unit may be desirable if employment is taken as the criteria of size. As regards the technique of production the rank correlation value of C/L shows that a less capital intensive technique is more employment generating per unit of capital.

Thus, the conclusions are different if different criteria of size are adopted.

(2) Labour productivity Maximization: Where maximization of labour productivity is the objective, a bigger size based on capital investment criteria, may be more desirable.

Similarly, a capital intensive technique may give higher productivity per unit of labour.

On the basis of employment criteria of size, however, the relationship is not so clear and the value of 'r' not so strong as to give a clear indication.

(3) Capital Productivity Maximization: If capital productivity maximization is the goal, as is the case in most underdeveloped countries, because of scarcity of capital, a small size on the basis of capital investment criteria, and a bigger size on the basis of employment criteria may be more advisable, thus again giving contradictory conclusions.

With regard to technique, a less capital intensive technique would give a higher productivity of capital.

(4) Maximization of Surplus Per Unit of Labour: Where the objective becomes maximization of surplus per unit of labour, to achieve maximum growth in the future with an economy of labour, there is no contradiction in the analysis for the two criteria. A bigger size may be justified on the basis of both criteria, i.e. employment and capital. Similarly, a more capital intensive technique may be more desirable too from this angle.

(5) Surplus Maximization Per Unit of Capital: When the objective is maximization of growth in future with economy of capital, i.e. surplus maximization per unit of capital, no such uniformity prevails. While no conclusion can be drawn for capital investment criteria, preferably a bigger size on employment basis and a less capital intensive technique, may be more desirable. Since a less capital intensive technique has been seen to imply less total capital investment according to results of our correlation analysis, the employment and capital investment criteria give contradictory results.

(6) Welfare Maximization[10]: Taking welfare maximization as the objective, a bigger size on the basis of capital investment criteria and a more capital intensive technique are desirable as indicated by the relation between WG/WRK and size-technique. While as on the basis of the employment criteria, a smaller size may be more desirable. Here again the conclusions are contradictory.

Thus, the analysis proves that policy implications regarding the efficacy of a smaller or bigger size differ, depending on the criteria of size adopted and the type of technique referred as well as the goal desired to be achieved. *Generally speaking, one notices a somewhat similarity of results regarding trends of the ratios and correlation results on the basis of capital investment criteria and technique. On the other hand there seems to be more discrepancy on the basis of employment as a criteria as compared to capital investment and technique.*

This is an important finding, in so far as it has contradictory policy implications for the different criteria.

Generally, the correlation coefficients are opposite for labour and capital. They show higher labour productivity and lower capital productivity in larger size group on the basis of capital investment criteria and just the reverse is the case in larger size group on the basis of employment criteria. It is also noticed that the correlation values are higher in the case of capital investment criteria and technique, than for employment criteria. This shows that the former exert a greater influence on efficiency than the level of employment.

It is also seen that units falling in the various size groups of the three criteria may not follow the same pattern. For example, it is not necessary that the units falling in the smaller size groups on the basis of capital investment and employment criteria, will necessarily fall into the less capital intensive group and vice versa. This is revealed by the fact that while the units falling in the last three size groups on the basis of capital investment are only 12 in 1979, and on the basis of employment criteria only 14, on the basis of capital intensity there are 28 in the last three groups in the same year.

Similarly in 1980 also, while there are 13 units in the last three groups of capital investment criteria and 10 on the basis of employment criteria (4th group non-existent), there are 32 on the basis of capital intensity i.e. technique in the last three groups.

This clearly indicates that many of the small size units classified on the basis of employment or capital investment are capital intensive in technique.

The employment and capital investment criteria groupings may also not coincide. For example, a unit having investment of less than 1= 1/2 lakhs has employment equal to a unit having investment of Rs. 8 lakhs (32 employees). Former is only a family partnership while the latter is a private limited company. Thus, while the two fall into the second group by the employment classification, the former comes under the second group by the investment classification and the latter in the fifth group.

Similarly another unit having an investment of more than Rs. 8=1/2 lakhs has employment of only 23, thus barely managing to cross the smaller size group on the basis of the employment criteria. Yet another unit, having an employment of only 17, has investment in gross fixed capital of nearly Rs. 9 lakhs.

On the whole, the hypothesis with regard to the behaviour of structural ratios is borne out to be correct more with the capital investment criteria, than with the employment criteria. Moreover, the results of regression analysis also show that productivity of labour and capital, total employment and output, as well as surplus generation for future growth, are influenced most by capital intensity (C/L) or by profitability of capital (S/C), i.e. directly or indirectly by capital.

Hence it may be concluded that it may be more meaningful and fruitful if units are classified into small and large scale on the basis of fixed capital investment for the purpose of a policy of encouragement to small scale units and not on the basis of employment, as was being done in India earlier and is even now being done in some countries.

Limitations of the Study

Any research study is subject to certain limitations. There are some which are inherent in all studies of the type undertaken. There are yet others, which are specific to the study arising from the circumstances pertinent to the particular case.

General Limitations: In any study which pertains to efficiency and viability of industrial units, certain productivity and profitability ratios are used. Output-capital and output-labour ratios indicate technical efficiency. On the other hand surplus capital or surplus labour ratios indicate economic viability. They also indicate the ability of industrial enterprises to grow. However, there are certain limitations of arriving at these ratios.

(i) The data would normally be for one or two years. In the case of this study also it is only two years. This limits the possibility of a cross sectional-cum-time series analysis.

(ii) The existence of unutilized capacity would lead to under estimation of output-capital relationship. What is required is capacity output and what is available is only actual output to compute output-capital ratios.

Capital utilization would also affect the profitability of industrial enterprises.

Output-labour, surplus per worker and wage per worker, however, may not be affected by capacity utilization, since employment is a function of actual output. However, fluctuations in output do not necessarily lead to reduction in labour force.

(iii) Thirdly, productivity and profitability are influenced by many factors—size, age, level of capacity utilization, technique of production, organisation, government policy and so on. Even two industrial enterprises of equal size would exhibit vast differences in efficiency on account of the above factors. It is, however, impossible to take account of all of them in one study.

This particular study is also subject to the following specific limitations:

Firstly, the coverage of the area is small to draw definite general conclusions with regard to the behaviour of efficiency ratios, though confining the study to a smaller area has its advantage in so far as the problematic study becomes more meaningful.

Secondly, the limitation of the study to one industry only, while helping in making the sample uniform, may not lend such generality to the conclusions that they may be applicable to all units every where, because there would be regional and other variations.

Thirdly, above two limitations become significant also for the conclusions that the behaviour of ratios will differ depending upon the criteria of size adopted. It thus suggests further research in the field, in other industries also.

Lastly, but not the least, though an attempt was made to collect as much authentic information as possible, data collection in regard to industrial units is beset with problems which raise questions about its reliability.

References

1. B.V. Mehta, "Size and Capital Intensity in Indian Industry", *Bulletin of Oxford University,* Institute of Economics and Statistics.
2. *Ibid.*
3. *Ibid.*
4. J.C. Sandesara, *"Size and Capital Intensity in Indian Industry"*, 1969, University of Bombay.
5. *Ibid.*
6. Dhar and Lydall, *"The Role of Small Enterprises in Indian Economic Development,* 1961, Asia Publishing House, Delhi.
7. J.C. Sandesara, *op. cit.*
8. B.V. Mehta, *op. cit.*
9. For this purpose C/L is taken as an indicator.
10. Wage per worker is taken as a measure of welfare.

4

Ancillary Concept and Role

The development of the concept of ancillary units may be traced to the development of specialization among firms. Its applicability however, has increased in modern times with the development of new products which require high technology and large capital investment.

Initially, our industrial policy was directed at assisting and rejuvinating the entire small scale sector. Ancillary development as a means of promoting the development of small scale sector had not emerged as a policy goal. At best, policy pronouncements such as Industrial Policy Resolution of 1956, indicated that the development of the decentralized sector should be integrated with that of large scale industries. The working group of the Third Five Year Plan introduced the concept of ancillary industries. It recommended that in the interest of "developing viable ancillary units, a relaxation of Rs. 5 lakhs limit in fixed capital may be made in respect of such small scale units which are supplying parts and components to certain large scale industries".[1] The group felt that a limit of Rs.10 lakhs should be adopted for this purpose. A new category of small scale industries was thus born. The main emphasis, however, continued to be on introducing schemes to enable the small scale entrepreneurs to compete on level with large scale units.

Recent industrial policy, however, lays greater emphasis on the role of ancillaries. The Industrial Policy Statement 1980 visualizes a strategy where a few large nucleus plants will be set up which would generate ripple effects by which ancillaries will spring up, mushroom, and set the pace of industrialization.

The policy statement reads, "It will be government's endeavour to reverse the trends of the last three years towards creating artificial divisions between small and large industries, under the misconception that their interests are essentially conflicting. While making all efforts towards integrated industrial development, it is proposed to promote the concept of economic federation, by setting up a few nucleus plants in each district, identified as industrially backward, to generate as many ancillaries and small and cottage units as possible."

In pursuance of the policy announcement of 1980, a programme for the establishment of nucleus plants in selected backward areas was taken up by the ministry, assisted by organizations such as the Small Industries Development Organization.

The Concept

Ancillarisation involves essentially a process of subcontracting part of a business by a bigger firm to a smaller firm with the parent firm generally providing technical financial or other help to the subsidiary firm.

The Government of India Gazette dated 31 July 1980 defines ancillary units as having investment in fixed assets in plant and machinery, whether held on ownership terms or by lease or by hire-purchase, not exceeding Rs. 25 lakhs, and engaged in (a) manufacture of parts, components, subassemblies, toolings or intermediaries (b) the rendering services and supply, or rendering or proposing to supply or render 50 per cent of their production or total services, as the case may be, to other units, for production of other articles: providing that no such undertakings shall be subsidiary of, or owned or controlled by, any other undertaking.

Certain other clarifications regarding ancillaries have also been issued:

(i) The concept of 'parent' unit shall include small scale units also. Thus one small scale unit can function as ancillary to another.

(ii) A unit to be recognised as an ancillary, should supply or propose to supply at least 50 per cent of its production to one or more parent units.

Subcontracting, by which the small business contracts to supply parts or even completed equipment to a parent firm, has become a prominent feature of the Japanese industrial scene. The contract could be an exclusive one with a single contractor, or it could be a contract with several contractors such as the supply of the part to a number of assemblers. There could also be independent sale apart from supply to a prime contractor.

It is also found that the amount of subcontracting also varies from industry to industry. Between 25 per cent to 50 per cent of the products is delivered by subcontractors in machinery production, textiles, automobiles and sewing machines, etc.

It is estimated by the Ministry of International Trade and Industry in Japan, that almost 60 per cent of the small business acts as a subcontractor to a parent firm.[2] The practice is so extensive that at times one is inclined to wonder whether there is any independent industry in Japan at all.

Linkages

The assistance received by the subcontractor from the parent firm covers a wide range of activities, viz supply of basic raw materials, technical guidance, supervision on the job, financial assistance and an assured market. Sometimes important and expensive machinery is leased out to the subcontractors for the manufacture of the contracted parts.

Technical linkages between the parents firm and the smaller firm can take one or more of the following forms:[3]

(i) Transfer of equipments

(ii) Sharing of technical know-how

(iii) Transfer of skill

These technical linkages may be through—

(a) Subcontracting arrangements

(b) Sale or hire of machinery

(c) Organization of training programmes by large firms for smaller ones

(d) Deputization of skilled employees from large to small entrepreneurs.

Technical transfer may also be autonomous due to movement of skilled workers from large to small firms, or when an employee formerly engaged in a large firm sets up an independent small unit.

The type of linkages adopted would differ from firm to firm, depending upon the type of market relationships—independent, interdependent or competitive.

In the case of independent markets for products of both large and small sectors, any technical linkage would be restricted to input linkage. In case of a competitive market situation, small enterprises would be obliged to use a technique comparable to that used by the large enterprises. However, more often than not, this technology may be independently acquired and not on transfer from the large enterprises.

In a situation of interdependence, e.g. where ancillaries produce intermediate goods for large enterprises, technical cooperation is likely to be much more because technologically the two have got to be linked.[4]

Motivation

The motivations for subcontracting may be many—

(i) The small enterprises may have limited production capacity which they would need to utilize fully for maintaining a minimum production and income level. They normally lack an organised marketing organization and hence are faced with greater competition from larger enterprises. Linkage arrangements for these provide an opportunity to make full utilization of capacity. It also provides a measure of protection against competition.

(ii) Subcontracting by larger enterprises to small ones may be (a) by those which do not have the machinery to carry out the work which they contract out, or (b) by those which have machinery but their existing capacity is not adequate to meet the demand for their products.

It is also found that many large scale enterprises have resorted to subcontracting not for any specific advantages from subcontracting, but to escape some of the problems associated with expansion, e.g. the application of certain legal enactments such as Employees State Insurance Act etc., which become applicable when employment goes beyond a certain level. This raises the average cost of production. There are other inconveniences associated with larger sizes in the form of government interference, higher excise duties and other taxes etc. Higher minimum wages may also be required if the level of employment crosses a certain limit.

Other reasons for subcontracting by larger firms are lack of space and minimisation of fixed overhead costs and seasonal character of demand for the product.

Besides all these economical and technical factors, there may be a reluctance on the part of the family entrepreneurship to share managerial responsibility with outsiders in case of expansion.

The foregoing discussion proves that there are advantages gained by both large and small units from subcontracting. This raises the question as to whether subcontracting in any way raises economic and technical efficiency of small scale ancillary units vis-a-vis the non-ancillary ones, for, while advantages flowing to the ancillary firms are recognised, what is not taken cognizance of, are the various conflicting factors that operate in the parent ancillary syndrome. The next section is devoted to such a study.

A Study of the Ancillary Set Up in Chandigarh

The engineering industry has been chosen for study of ancillaries. This is for two reasons:

(i) It represents 'modern' industries in which there is a high degree of specialization and division of labour. The separability of manufacturing operations, the large number of parts and components that go into making a single product, offer enormous scope for ancillarisation. (ii) The precision and close supervision necessary for the manufacture of certain parts also make them eminently suitable for small firms where the entrepreneur is in a position to personally supervise operations. The region chosen is Chandigarh.

In 1984, (The year in which the study was done) the only large industry which had an ancillary set up in and around Chandigarh was the Hindustan Machine Tools Limited at Pinjore. The other two large scale units in the near vicinity of Chandigarh which provided major share of the market to most of the Chandigarh based small scale units were Punjab Tractors Limited in Haryana and Eicher Tractors in Parwanoo, Himachal Pradesh. However, the tie up of the small scale units with the latter is more in the nature of suppliers. They have no registered ancillaries. The Punjab Tractors Limited has 39 units in Chandigarh which supply components to it regularly.

The difference between units which act as suppliers and those which are registered ancillaries, is essentially in the nature of contract with regard to the demand by the large concerns. While demand was guaranteed from year to year in the case of the ancillaries, the contract was renewed every year with a supplier.

The Hindustan Machine Tools Limited which was the only parent concern in the whole of the Chandigarh ancillary set up, produced mainly Tractors, combine harvestors and machine tools.

The ancillaries of the Hindustan Machine Tools Limited are established in the industrial areas of Chandigarh. It, however, has an ancillary industrial estate in Panchkula (Haryana) also.

All the ancillaries of Hindustan Machine Tools were captive units, i.e. their total supply was to the Hindustan Machine Tools. There was no difference in the linkage of the units set up in the industrial areas of Chandigarh and those in the ancillary estate at Panchkula.

In the technical sphere, the Hindustan Machine Tools provides guidance to the maximum extent possible. This has been recognised by the ancillary units interviewed. However, it does not supply jigs, tools and fixtures etc. In this respect, the ancillaries do not seem to have much of advantage as compared to other suppliers to Hindustan Machine Tools as well as Punjab Tractors Limited. Punjab Tractors also provide technical guidance to small scale suppliers during manufacture of components. Besides, facilities like jig boring, heat treatment, inspection etc. are also provided. Help from Punjab Tractors Limited's standard room and Guage room is also available for validation and inspection of their gauges.

As compared to the units who are neither suppliers nor ancillaries, these units do seem to have an advantage in the technical sphere.

As regards raw material supply, though the parent concern does not arrange for supply of all raw materials, assistance is provided in arranging for supply of imported and scarce raw material. The units interviewed, however, did not express full satisfaction with respect to this facility offered by the Hindustan Machine Tools. Besides, Punjab Tractors Limited also offers this facility, i.e. arranging for supply of raw materials, depending upon complexity of input material to its suppliers.

In the sphere of offering training facilities to the ancillary units' staff and labour, the Hindustan Machine Tools does not make any arrangements.

The ancillary units do not receive any financial assistance either from the Hindustan Machine Tools.

With regard to the facilities available to the ancillary estate units as compared to those situated in Chandigarh Industrial Area, the ancillary estate units have a slight edge over the latter in so far as, while built in sheds along with water and power supply are provided in the ancillary estate, only land was provided along with power and water supply facility to the industrial area units. These units had to either construct their own sheds, or in some cases these are taken on rent from the owners of the plots and sheds by those who want to set up an industry. The rent was often higher than that of the ancillary estate sheds.

The biggest gain from linkage was in the form of an assured market for the product, which reduced risk. Though the other suppliers of the big units had also an yearly contract, the same had to be renewed every year. The ancillary units also had an edge over the non-ancillary suppliers in respect of payment received from the larger unit for their supplies. While the payment time limit fixed for ancillary units was 30 days, and they often received payments much ahead of the time limit, the period often is above this maximum limit, in the case of unattached suppliers.

Component development cost is also low for ancillaries, as technical guidance is available from parent unit and sometimes raw materials may be available on more economical terms.

Lastly, it is also easy for ancillary units to get loan from commercial banks and other government agencies, as these agencies become confident of getting back their loans, these units being captive units, assured of a market.

Status and Contribution of Hindustan Machine Tools Ancillaries for the half year ending 1.4.84 to 30.9.84

I.	**Details of Ancillary Units in Operation**		
		In the Industrial Estate	*Outside the Industrial Estate*
(a)	Number of Ancillary Units	29	10
(b)	Investment on plant and machinery	133 lakhs	22 lakhs
(c)	Installed capacity in terms of value	498 lakhs	110 lakhs
(d)	Number of persons employed	730	104
II.	**Purchase from Ancillary Units**		
		Current half year	*Previous half year*
(a)	Located in the ancillary estate	252 lakhs	224 lakhs
(b)	Outside the Ancillary estate	50 lakhs	37 lakhs
III.	Number of small scale units other than those covered in serial number I	450	450
IV.	Purchases from small scale units under serial number III	653 lakhs	616 lakhs
V.	Total purchases from ancillaries and other small scale units (II+IV)	956 lakhs	817 lakhs
VI.	Total value of purchases made by the undertaking	2556 lakhs	
VII.	Percentage of ancillary supplies to total purchases	37 per cent	

Source: Hindustan Machine Tools Administrative Office.

Efficiency Study

In this section an attempt has been made to study the efficiency of ancillary units vis-a-vis non-ancillary units, on the basis of the sample covered in the study. Since the sample covers only the units situated in Chandigarh, the ancillary units situated in the ancillary estate (Panchkula) are excluded. However, since the linkage in Chandigarh units and ancillary estate unit is the same, as also the assistance offered (except for the availability of sheds in ancillary estate), the conclusions may hold good for the ancillary estate units also.

The efficiency ratios used are the same as those used in the previous portion of the study. Only output working capital ratio (O/WC), has also been added.

The number of ancillary and non-ancillary units, as well as the values of the ratios for the two types of units for the two years 1979 and 1980, are given in Table 4.1. The ratios have been calculated by the following method:

$$\frac{(Xi)^*}{Yi}$$

The sample has been divided into two groups (i) ancillary (ii) non-ancillary. The number of units in the ancillary group are 13 while as those in the non-ancillary group are 68 in 1979. In 1980, the numbers are 9 and 67 respectively. Though the number in the first group is much smaller than that in the second group, it is not small enough not to warrant a comparative study. Each efficiency ratio will be taken up separately for comparative study.

(1) Capital-Labour Ratio: Both in 1979 and 1980, the capital labour ratio is lower in the ancillary group than in the non-ancillary group, showing greater overall capital intensity in the non-ancillary group.

(2) Output-Labour Ratio: The output labour ratio is higher in the non-ancillary group, showing lower labour productivity in the ancillary group. The productivity of labour thus seems to be directly linked with capital intensity.

(3) Wage Per Worker: This ratio is also higher in the non-ancillary group as compared to the ancillary group in both the years.

(4) Surplus Per Worker: As regards this ratio, the conclusion is not clear. While in 1979, the ancillary group shows a higher ratio, in 1980 the non-ancillary group shows a much higher ratio. This is probably because 1979 was a bad period for industrial

* Details of this method have been discussed in the Appendix of this section.

Table 4.1: Efficiency Ratio of Ancillary and Non-Ancillary Units

	No. of Units	C/L	O/L	WG/WRK	S/WRK	O/C	O/WC	S/C	O/I
1979									
Ancillary	13	92.3	59.0	4074.4	13902.6	.69	18.2	.51	5.3
Non-ancillary	68	136.9	60.8	4174.7	13633.3	.66	5.1	.41	5.5
1980									
Ancillary	9	63.9	40.1	4166.9	7950.6	.62	2.4	.36	6.3
Non-ancillary	67	117.7	48.9	4702.8	13867.1	.58	4.5	.41	3.9

production on the whole, while 1980 showed recovery. While the ancillary units did not suffer much in 1979 because of linkage, the non-ancillary group may have been hit badly.

(5) Output Capital Ratio: Capital productivity, as revealed by output capital ratio, is higher in the ancillary group as compared to the non-ancillary group. This once again proves that productivity of capital is inversely related to capital intensity.

(6) Output-Working Capital Ratio: The result with regard to this ratio is inconclusive. While it is much higher in the ancillary group in 1979, it is much lower for the ancillary group in 1980. The reason could again be probably sought in the adverse economic climate in 1979. There may have been an accumulation of inventories in 1979 in the case of the non-ancillary group. It may thus bring out the risk bearing capability of the ancillary groups. Labour productivity was also only marginally lower in 1979.

(7) Surplus Capital Ratio: This ratio is higher in the ancillary group in 1979, but lower in 1980. This is in conformity with the performance of the ancillary group with regard to O/C.

(8) Output Input Ratio: This ratio is marginally lower for the ancillary group in 1979, but markedly higher in 1980. Thus the picture is not clear at all with regard to the overall efficiency ratio.

On the whole, for 1979 as well as 1980 the C/L is higher for the non-ancillary group. As regards other ratios, in 1979, the ancillary group has higher O/C, O/WC and S/C, showing higher productivity of capital. In 1980 it has higher O/C and O/I.

The non-ancillary group has higher O/L, WG/WRK and O/I in 1979. In 1980 it has higher O/L, WG/WRK, S/WRK, O/WC and S/C. This shows higher labour productivity in the non-ancillary groups.

Lower capital intensity may be due to the nature of products supplied which are mainly components and parts. These may not require very capital intensive technique as compared to the other small scale units in the non-ancillary groups, some of which may be producing complete products requiring more advanced techniques.

From the foregoing analysis, it is clear that the ancillaries do not seem to gain any substantial advantage out of the linkage with the parent concern. This may be attributed to the fact that there is not much assistance offered by the parent concern to these units. The only advantage is the guarantee of demand, which may account for their better performance in1979. Thus full impact of linkage benefit is not felt by them.

An interesting study of ancillary relationship has been done by Nirmala Banerjee, in her paper "Small and large units—Symbiosis or Matsyanyaye".[5] She investigates the economic rationale of the ancillary relationships which has been continuing inspite of the apparent losses of SSUs in the fan industry in Calcutta. She finds that the large firms use the small unorganised units to meet the sporadic excess demand in an uncertain market situation, instead of themselves investing in additional capacity. In this way the demand uncertainties are transmitted to the small scale segment as well. The payments made to the SSUs are meagre and often do not cover their cost of production. To cover up such a production condition, the small scale units on their part pay the bare minimum subsistence wages and give them irratic employment. By using obsolete techniques and inferior quality inputs, they compromise on quality. While the smaller units sacrifice higher profits because of this compromise, the larger units loose out further on demand by consciously ignoring quality. The ancillary set up thus, instead of being complementary and mutually beneficial, has turned into a low level trap for all concerned. Even the minimum advantage of a guaranteed regular demand is not available to the SSUs in this case.

References

1. Govt. of India, Ministry of Commerce and Industry. Report of the Working Group: Small Scale Industries— *Programme of Work for the Third Five Year Plan,* New Delhi, 1959, p. 145.

2. K. Vepa Ram, *Small Industries in the Seventies,* Vikas Publications, 1971.

3. T.S. Papola and R.S. Mathur, *Intersectoral Linkages in Manufacture,* a paper published by Giri Institute of Development Studies, 1971, Lucknow.

4. *Ibid.*

5. A paper in "Small Scale Enterprises in Industrial Development" Edited by K.B. Suri, Sage Publications, 1988.

Appendix

Methodology

Sampling

Stratified random sampling has been adopted in the study. Six stratifications have been taken. The repair and maintenance group has been excluded. The product range is not wide and by eliminating the repair sector, strictly manufacturing activity has been retained in the study. Thus technological differences in the methods of production of different commodities have been reduced to a minimum.

Method

For finding out the relation between size and efficiency two methods have been adopted:

(1) The units have been divided into size groups and the appropriate ratios worked out for each size group: The ratios could have been worked out in two ways:

(a) Adding the relevant values of all the units in each size group and finding the average ratio as per the formula:

$$\frac{xi}{yi}$$

Where X and Y refer to the economic variables and i to the unit.

(b) Evaluating the ratios for each unit in a particular size group, adding all the ratios of the units in the size group and finding the average ratio as per the formula:

$$\frac{xi/yi}{n}$$

where x and y are the economic variables, i the unit and n refers to the number of units in size group. Most of the research work on similar lines has been done on the basis of formula (a). J.C. Sandesara* and Dhar and Lydall** have based their analysis on this method of calculation. But formula (b) eliminates the influence of any exceptionally big unit on the result and thus is statistical superior. Hence this formula has been used in the calculation of ratios instead of formula (a).

(2) The second method adopted is the Rank Correlation Coefficient as given by Mendall. This has been derived for all the ratios by ranking the units on the basis of the three criteria mentioned earlier, viz, capital investment, employment and capital intensity, separately.

The formula used for deriving the Rank Correlation Coefficient is:

$$r = 1 - \frac{di^2}{n\left(n^2 - 1\right)}$$

where 'di' stands for the difference between the ranks of corresponding 'x' and 'y' and 'n' for the size of the sample or population while 'r' is the coefficient of correlation, which reveals the degree of correlation that exists between the two variables. The variables in this study are size and the particular ratio being studied.

(3) The data was further subjected to step-wise Regression Analysis also, with certain equations, to find the influence certain variables exert in the determination of certain dependent variables.

---

* J. C. Sandesara, *Size and Capital Intensity in Indian Industry*, 1969, Bombay University.

** P.N. Dhar and H.F. Lydall, *op. cit.*

Section B

Status

5

Growth of SSI in Developed and Developing Countries

Last few decades have witnessed an interesting development in the field of small scale industry all over the world. The scenario has revealed significant importance being accorded to this segment in industrial policy and growth of economies. At the same time one also witnesses a phenomenal change in the structure of the industry, as revealed by a decline in their importance in areas of their prior dominance, and an increased coverage of new areas.

World Bank studies and those conducted by some other economists have revealed that the share of very small establishments (fewer than 10 workers) in manufacturing has been declining very fast with growth in manufacturing output. However, it remains very high in very poor countries. In Europe and North America SSEs in manufacturing sector are almost extinct. Undoubtedly the dominant cause, as explained by Corter, Berry & Ishaq.[1] is natural economic evolution induced by the growth of the market, scale economics, falling transport costs and changes in factor prices.

According to some surveys, in Taiwan employment in very small (non-factory) manufacturing establishments with fewer than 5 workers has been falling since 1915. In the postwar period, between 1954 and 1971, small manufacturing employment (4-49 workers), fell from 45 to 26 per cent of total, being attributable to extremely rapid labour intensive growth. Medium sized establishments (50-59 workers) held steady, while firms with 100-499 workers increased their share dramatically from 17 per cent in 1961 to 29 per cent in 1971. Firms with 100 or more workers accounted for 73 per cent of the total increase in manufacturing employment of nearly 800,000 workers. No information is available for the smallest size group in Korea before 1958, but the size group between 5-49 workers reduced its share of manufacturing employment between 1958 and 1975 from 54 to 17 per cent. Even in the size group 50-99, unlike in Taiwan, there was a decline in Korea, while the largest size group with more than 500 workers increased its share from 12 per cent to 44% of employment.

There is very little information available on size structure of enterprises other than manufacturing, even though there has been a striking growth of the service sector. There is some evidence to prove that in Taiwan service industries are the home of small enterprises.

Table 5.1 : Employment Growth in Some Non-manufacturing and Manufacturing Sectors in Taiwan 1961-71

Plant Size	Manufacturing		Non-manufacturing		Other	
	%	Workers	%	Workers	%	Workers
1-3	-12	-8	52	97	60	9
4-9	-	-	144	102	97	29
10-19	70	72	170	58	160	26
20-49	125	72	139	74	166	44
50-99	252	80	195	64	245	35
100-499	454	279	87	58	242	42
500 & more	230	302	82	78	131	77
Total	175	796	97	530	125	262
Per cent per Year	10.7		7.0		8.5	

Source: HO (1980, Tables 2, 3, D-34)

Though in Taiwan SSE accounted for a large amount of employment in the non-manufacturing and service sector, the share fell between 1961-71. The remarkable annual growth rate of manufacturing employment of 10.7% resulted in an absolute increase of 796,000 workers of whom 581,000 were in enterprises with 100 workers or more. Employment in smallest size group fell relatively. In the service industries fastest growth was in the range of 10 workers and above. Taking the total increase in non-manufacturing establishments, it is seen that the size group 1-10 still accounted for most new jobs in absolute terms.

In Philippines, while employment in household manufacturing has declined relatively, it has increased in absolute terms. So has employment in all other groups also. But there is no clear evidence of relative success by either large or small. And no information is available on non-manufacturing sector.

In Columbia, Cottage shop which includes household as well as workshops with less than 4 workers, declined considerably between 1939 and 1978 from 77% of all manufacturing to 44%, though growing absolutely. Within the factory sector, between 1953-1973, medium and large size segment of units grew faster than smaller size units, but after 1973, smaller size sector grew faster than medium and medium grew faster than large.[2]

In Malaysia, employment in informal manufacturing sector has not increased significantly since 1950s, but employment in formal sector has increased very fast[3]. Within the formal sector, the largest size group grew fastest.

For Singapore no information is available on household manufacturing sector. But while establishments with 10 or more workers increased their employment by about 13 per cent a year, the share of the size group 10-99 workers fell from 56 to 29 per cent.[4]

Inspite of limitation, of information, one can come to the conclusion that the share of the small scale household manufacturing sector and mini enterprises (1-3 workers) is falling in employment and more so in areas showing very high rates of growth of manufacturing employment. Similarly, where growth has been fast employment in larger enterprises has increased at a faster rate than in medium ones. On the other hand where growth in manufacturing has been more sluggish, relative employment in medium level enterprises has been more steady or even increased.

As a justification for support to SSE's, it is pointed out that these survive and flourish even in developed economies. However, it has also been observed that this is definitional jugglery, in the sense that what is small in developed economies is medium in UDCs and hence the rationale for the small size of the type in UDCs cannot be sustained on the basis of the existence of the relatively small size of enterprises in the developed economies. The change in the actual size group (the small defined as below 200 workers and medium as 200-499 workers) in the developed economies as compared to the underdeveloped ones, may be due to any of the factors associated with growth e.g. large size of the market.

According to a United States Small Business Administration report (March 1984), small firms excluding agriculture, with 1-100 employees accounted for about 36 per cent of total private employment in 1978 and firms with 1-20 employees accounted for about 19%.

In Japan, firms with fewer than 20 employees in manufacturing and fewer than 5 in commerce and services, employed 31% of workforce (excluding agriculture) in 1975.[5]

Generally, more information is available about manufacturing sector than about the other sectors. However, it has been noticed that with development, the share of service sector increases and small firms tend to dominate in service sector and construction rather in manufacturing, e.g. in USA, manufacturing, construction and retail trade firms with less than 500 workers accounted for 27, 81 and 62 per cent respectively of total employment in1982. Similarly in U.K., only 20 per cent of manufacturing employment was in firms with less than 200 employees while in construction, 33 per cent were in firms employing less than 25 workers.[6]

It has also been observed that the relative position of small firms and establishments has been declining specially since World War II and the decline has been greater, the smaller the size. In U.K. there was an absolute decline in the number of small manufacturing firms (less than 200 employees) also.

As against this, German manufacturing sector shows a relative tilt towards the small size plant. It seems to be a classic example to give for those who propagate that a large number of small size plants are compatible with high level development.

Japan also can be similarly cited. However, the relative low productivity and low wages in these, do not make them an ideal example.

Lately however, both in development countries of Europe and in UDCs, the decline of small manufacturing firms seems to have been arrested based on arguments other than efficiency rationale. The idea of 'small is beautiful', as propagated by Schumacher has gained popularity based more on socialist considerations rather than the economic rationale. The arguments against concentration of power through the growth of a crop of small enterprises, employment generation etc., have become a political slogan in the capitalist economies also.

The above review clearly shows that in manufacturing sector atleast the very small size has an unstable future with development, though as pointed out by IMD Little, John Page and Mazumdar,[7] there is no clear noticeable evidence of any relationship between GDP and size trends. But because with high level of development the relative share of manufacturing sector declines, and that of the service sector increases, a reversal in the trend of decline may be noticed in the more advanced economies. Decline in the status of SSI in developed and developing countries may also be arrested because of structural changes in the industrial sector with growth of the electronics industry and other fields dependent on high level of technical skill.

References

1. Cortes, Berry & Ishaq (1987) World Bank Studies.

   It is interesting to note here that almost all these studies have used labour employed as the basis for classifying units by size, inspite of the fact that capital has been recognised as a more meaningful criteria for such classification.The discussion in the previous section on the concept, has been on the significance of this indifference.

2. Cortes, Berry & Ishaq, 1983, Table 2.2.
3. Lim, Lee and Thye, 1981, Table 6-12;
4. Forg & Tom 1981, Table 4-9.
5. Kanede, 1980.
6. Bolton Committee, 1971.
7. I.M.D. Little, John Page and Mazumdar, "Small Manufacturing Enterprises: A Comparative Study of India and Other Countries."

6

Status of Small Scale Industry in India

Small Scale Industry has been in the limelight of discussion in India and has occupied an important place in the economy since before independence. However, its status has undergone a change with change in economic, social, political and technical environment.

Changed scenario has brought about a change in the nature structure and concept of small scale enterprises (SSEs), while retaining their importance. The objectives for which they were awarded importance have also undergone a change with the expansion of small scale enterprises in all areas—the traditional industries, modern manufacturing, electronics and service sectors. Growth of the SSEs in the latter two categories is indicative of coming of age of the economy, as also the emergence of a skilled and educated entrepreneurial class.

Another aspect which is of recent origin and associated with technological advancement, is the establishment of SSEs not as competitors with the large scale enterprises (LSEs) but as supplementary ancillary supporting units. Thus we see the emergence of a section of SSEs which have the patronage of LSEs and yet have a rationale for their independent existence.

Growth of the small scale sector is also associated with the emergence of the middle class as an important constituent influencing demand and of strong job consciousness among women. Both these factors have led to a mushroom growth of units producing consumer gadgets and processed food items, wayside fast food joints, beauty parlours, etc.

Thus, while on the one hand there has been a tremendous quantum jump of SSUs, a qualitative and characteristic change has also been witnessed.

In section I of this chapter, we will study the growth of the small scale industry in India in general, and section II will deal with structural analysis of the small scale units, their industry wise distribution, the urban rural divide and their organization etc.

Growth of SSI

There has been a phenomenal growth in small scale units, their number having increased from approximately 4= 1/2 lakh units in early 70s to about 8= 1/2 lakhs in 1990, and 20.8 lakhs in 1991. The provisional estimate for 1992 is 22.3 lakhs. Growth in the number of registered units has, however been much higher than in the number of unregistered units. While the number of registered units had increased from 1.6 lakhs in 1973 to 12.7 in 1989, it had increased only to 5= 1/2 lakhs for 2.5 in unregistered. This, in a way is indicative of qualitative change in the structure of the SSI.

Production of SSEs at current prices has almost doubled. However, at constant prices it has gone up almost 5= 1/2 times which means a fall in the value of their products over the period. This is surprising in view of change in the structure of this industry in favour of more sophisticated commodities. Investment on the other hand has gone up 7 times in the SSEs. The value of output in 1991 was Rs. 1,78,699 and the provisional figure for 1992 is Rs. 2,09,300 crores.

There has been a phenomenal growth in exports from this sector. They increased from Rs. 393 crores in 1973 to Rs. 7626 crores in 1989. A Qualitative change thus seems to have come about which raises the status of this sector from one justifiable only on sociological grounds, to one of significant contribution towards the growth of the economy.

As regards the traditional Khadi and Village industries, between 1960-1961 and 1989-1990, the quantity produced as well as value of Khadi has almost doubled. During 1992-93

Table 6.1: Estimates of No. of Units, Production of Small Scale Sector

At the end of year	No. of Units (Lakh Nos.) Cumulative		Total No. of Units (Lakh Nos.)	Production (Rs. Crore) at current prices	Production (Rs. Crore) at 1970-71 prices	Investment (Rs. in Crore)	Exports (Rs. in Crore) (Actual)
	*Regd.	Un-Regd.					
1973-74	1.64	2.52	4.16	7200	5161	2296	393
1974-75	2.22	2.76	4.98	9200	5450	2697	541
1975-76	2.46	3.00	5.46	11000	6425	3204	532
1976-77	2.68	3.24	5.92	12400	7078	3553	766
1977-78	2.96	3.74	6.70	14300	7980	3959	845
1978-79	3.34	4.00	7.34	15790	8797	4431	1059
1079-80	3.92	4.13	8.05	21635	10025	5540	1226
1980-81	4.48	4.26	8.74	28060	10906	5850	1643
1981-82	5.23	4.39	9.62	32600	11837	6280	2071
1982-83	6.07	4.52	10.59	35000	12800	6800	2097
1983-84	6.84	4.71	11.55	41620	14120	7360	2159
1984-85	7.55	4.85	12.40	50520	15810	8380	2553
1985-86	8.53	5.00	13.53	61228	17840	9585	2785
1986-87	9.48	5.14	14.62	72250	20187	10881	3648
1987-88	10.55@	5.28	15.83	87300	22742	12610	4535@
1988-89	11.70@	5.42	17.12	106400	25675	15229	5490
1989-90 (Prov.)	12.70	5.56	18.26	131553	28526	N.A.	7626

@ Revised.
* Registered with the State Directorates of Industries.
Source: Office of the D.C. (S.S.I.).

this sector produced goods worth Rs. 2670.4 crores and the estimated production during 1993-94 is Rs. 2898.5 crores. In 1992 it gave employment to 51 lakh persons which is expected to increase to 52.4 lakhs in 1993.

There has been a more than 5 fold increase in value of the product of village industries during the same period, showing clearly a faster growth of other traditional industries and a comparative handicap khadi faced in competition from mill made cloth. Its survival is clearly associated with governmental support and very little on independent growth.

Statewise Distribution of Units

Distribution of SSI between different states is given in the Table 6.3 and 6.4. The data refers to units registered with the Directorate of Industries as on 31.3.1988, and was compiled by the office of Development Commissioner, Small Scale Industries, Government of India.

The initial frame for the second census comprised 10.55 lakh units which were registered with the DIs of states/UTs. However, after closer scrutiny, some were found non-traceable, some did not respond, some did not come within the purview of SIDO, and yet some others were closed.

As can be seen from the Table, the largest concentration of the SSI is in Madhya Pradesh followed by Uttar Pradesh, West Bengal, Tamil Nadu, Punjab, Karnataka, Andhra Pradesh, Bihar, Gujarat, Maharashtra, Rajasthan, Kerala and Haryana.

Total employment in 1988 in the registered segment of SSI was 3665810. Largest share was that of Tamil Nadu (14.6%), followed by Maharashtra (9.7%) and Uttar Pradesh (9.5%). Lowest in the line are Daman & Diu, Sikkim, Andaman & Nicobar, Mizoram and Jammu & Kashmir. Surprisingly though the share of Madhya Pradesh in the total number of units is the highest (12.7%). Its share in total employment in such units is relatively low. Per unit employment is highest in Nagaland, followed by Sikkim, Dadra & Nagar Havaeli, Delhi, Tripura and Maharashtra. Total employment in the SSI segment rose to 129 lakhs in 1991 and is expected to have reached a figure of over 134 lakhs in 1993.

Table 6.2 : Production of Khadi and Village Industries Since 1960-61

(Quantity in Lakh square metres)

Year	(Value in Rs. Lakh)			Total Khadi & Village Industries Value
	Khadi Quantity	Value	Village Industries Value only	
1	2	3	4	5
1960-61	537.65	1423.29	3315.65	4739.14
1961-62	632.47	1690.98	3776.81	5467.79
1962-63	746.51	2121.56	4001.43	6122.99
1963-64	718.07	2209.43	4334.43	6548.86
1964-65	806.26	2098.38	4833.45	6931.83
1965-66	848.54	2630.86	5587.09	8267.95
1966-67	785.50	2784.34	5961.51	8745.85
1967-68	630.85	2429.07	7456.12	9885.19
1968-69	600.19	2337.72	7512.45	9850.17
1969-70	622.20	2563.54	7798.86	10362.40
1970-71	567.37	2584.61	8560.34	11144.95
1971-72	540.57	2778.46	9369.12	12139.95
1972-73	582.22	3158.24	10913.71	14071.95
1973-74	557.19	3272.40	12239.83	15512.23
1974-75	592.18	4327.58	13630.88	17958.46
1975-76	561.13	4673.27	14848.25	19521.52
1976-77	644.74	5603.31	17172.69	22776.00
1977-78	684.12	6488.93	19253.81	25742.70
1978-79	796.99	7654.00	24297.00	31951.04
1979-80	822.70	9203.00	34798.00	44001.00
1980-81	910.10	10685.00	45124.00	55809.00
1981-82	964.29	12340.00	54237.00	66577.00
1982-83	1079.10	14340.00	62060.00	76400.00
1983-84	1027.50	15348.00	72210.00	87564.00
1984-85	1039.80	15762.00	80706.00	96468.00
1985-86	1049.40	19501.00	92903.00	112404.00
1986-87	N.A.	21806.00	109866.00	131672.00
1987-88	1157.20	22751.70	126088.40	1488396.10
1988-89	1085.30	23535.00	144339.00	1677874.00
1989-90	1074.70	25787.65	170529.29	196317.24

N.A. — Not available.

Source : (i) KVIC Annual Report 1989-90.
(ii) Department of Industrial Development, Ministry of Industry.

Table 6.3: State/UT Wise Distribution of Units

Sl. No.	State/UT	No. of Units in the frame as on 31.3.1988	No. of Units found					No. of Units for which Data Tabulated	
			None-Traceable	None-Responding	None-SIDO and others	Working	Closed	Working	Closed
1	2	3	4	5	6	7	8	9	10
1.	Andhra Pradesh	54762	364	45	330	39210	14813	39210	14813
2.	Assam	8290	1588	100	440	4430	1732	4430	1732
3.	Bihar	53602	2026	394	824	35366	14992	34822	14812
4.	Gujarat	58328	2464	1440	265	35000	19159	34453	18977
5.	Haryana	48493	1338	892	1801	23481	20981	23356	20981
6.	Himachal Pradesh	10836	522	37	438	6983	2856	6983	2856
7.	Jammu & Kashmir	14631	669	540	311	9080	4031	9080	4031
8.	Karnataka	59469	2504	995	817	40525	14628	40525	14629
9.	Kerala	38030	67	25	458	25717	11763	25717	11763
10.	Madhya Pradesh	124553	8957	1099	2800	76218	35479	73892	35479
11.	Maharashtra	50589	2969	3665	3057	29973	10925	29856	10925
12.	Manipur	2641	192	168	34	2078	169	2078	169
13.	Meghalaya	748	17	6	1	588	136	587	136
14.	Nagaland	274		1	7	183	83	183	83
15.	Orissa	13892	1708	178	71	8328	3607	8287	3607
16.	Punjab	94544	16297	2756	327	51507	23657	45339	21701
17.	Rajasthan	50001	1493	527	564	29477	17940	29043	17528

1	2	3	4	5	6	7	8	9	10
18.	Tamil Nadu	33257	318	379	532	57213	24825	57213	24825
19.	Tripura	1443	-	-	31	809	603	809	603
20.	Uttar Pradesh	95285	3889	757	8	53370	37261	53282	37249
21.	West Bengal	94362	7101	1153	2003	46795	37310	45954	36607
22.	Sikkim	106	-	4	-	66	36	66	36
23.	Andaman & Nicobar	441	18	3	9	323	88	323	88
24.	Arunachal Pradesh	368	6	-	-	326	36	326	36
25.	Chandigarh	2014	-	58	6	1310	640	1310	640
26.	Dadra & Nagar Haveli	185	-	-	-	152	33	149	33
27.	Delhi	18293	2383	644	36	10188	5042	10038	5020
28.	Goa	3800	43	22	6	2772	957	2772	957
29.	Mizoram	1247	-	-	24	917	306	917	306
30.	Pondicherry	2159	108	83	9	1237	722	1221	722
31.	Daman & Diu	208	-	9	6	147	46	147	46
Total		986861	57041	15980	15215	593769	304856	582368	301390

Note : Union Territory of Lakshadweep had no registered unit as on 31.3.1988.
Source : Report on Second All India Survey of Small Scale Industry, Development Commissioner.

Table 6.4

Sl. No.	Name of State/UT	No. of Units	%age to total	Employment (Nos.)	% age of total	Per Unit Employment
1	2	3	4	5	6	7
1.	Andhra Pradesh	39210	6.73	276127	7.53	7.0
2.	Assam	4430	0.76	34475	0.94	7.8
3.	Bihar	34822	5.98	181781	4.96	5.2
4.	Gujarat	34453	5.92	276955	7.56	8.0
5.	Haryana	23356	4.01	105656	2.88	4.5
6.	Himachal Pradesh	6983	1.20	25536	0.70	3.7
7.	Jammu & Kashmir	9080	1.56	40655	1.11	4.5
8.	Karnataka	40525	6.96	244039	6.65	6.0
9.	Kerala	25717	4.42	169309	4.62	6.6
10.	Madhya Pradesh	73892	12.69	158808	4.33	2.1
11.	Maharashtra	29586	5.13	355900	9.71	11.9
12.	Manipur	2078	0.36	10216	0.28	4.9
13.	Meghalaya	587	0.10	3780	0.10	6.4
14.	Nagaland	183	0.03	3059	0.08	16.7
15.	Orissa	8287	1.42	69305	1.89	8.4
16.	Punjab	45339	7.79	206209	5.62	4.5
17.	Rajasthan	29043	4.99	122550	3.34	4.2
18.	Tamil Nadu	57213	9.82	536381	14.63	9.4
19.	Tripura	809	0.14	10069	0.27	12.4

1	2	3	4	5	6	7
20.	Uttar Pradesh	53282	9.15	348908	9.52	6.5
21.	West Bengal	45954	7.89	311838	8.51	6.8
22.	Sikkim	66	0.01	1033	0.03	15.7
23.	A & N Islands	323	0.06	1672	0.05	5.2
24.	Arunachal Pradesh	326	0.06	2771	0.07	8.5
25.	Chandigarh	1310	0.22	10579	0.29	8.1
26.	Dadra & Nagar Haveli	149	0.03	2115	0.06	14.2
27.	Delhi	10038	1.72	121972	3.33	12.2
28.	Goa	2772	0.48	19935	0.54	7.2
29.	Mizoram	917	0.16	4223	0.12	4.6
30.	Pondicherry	1221	0.21	8721	0.24	7.1
31.	Daman & Diu	147	0.03	1233	0.03	8.4
Total		582368	100.00	3665810	100.00	6.3

Soruce : Report on the Second All India Census of Small Scale Industrial Units Development Commissioner, Small Scale Industries.

With respect to investment in fixed assets Maharashtra had the largest share (13.5%), followed by Tamil Nadu (11.7%), Uttar Pradesh (10.6%), Gujarat (9.5%), all four states together accounting for nearly 45% of total investment in fixed assets. Karnataka, Andhra Pradesh and Punjab together accounted for 20%.

Per unit investment in fixed assets was lowest in Madhya Pradesh which had a preponderance of very small units. It was highest in Sikkim.

On the production front, Maharashtra again provided the lead with a share of 17.5% in the total, followed again by Tamil Nadu, Gujarat and Uttar Pradesh.

The distribution pattern of small scale units as presented in the above table does not necessarily reflect the extent of industrialization of a particular state, since, registration is voluntary, so that while in some state even the very small units have registered, in others, due to restrictions on setting up of units, even working units have not been registered,

Distribution of Units by Employment Slabs

The distribution shows concentration of 64.5% of the units in the employment slab 1-4 workers. These units accounted for 22% of total employment, 21% of fixed investment and 12% of total production. Units in the employment slab 100 and above were 0.4% of total SSUs and accounted for 13% of employment, 5% of fixed investment and 10% of production. It is also observed that per employee production was highest (1.6 lakhs) in the employment slabs 20-49 and 50-99 workers. Maximum employment was in the employment slabs 5-9 workers and maximum production in employment slab 20-49 workers. Per Unit production was highest in largest size group (100 and above). Similarly production per unit of investment and employment per unit of investment were highest in units employing 100 or more workers.

Thus according to this survey, when units are classified on the basis of employment, labour, productivity is maximum in the medium size group, while capital productivity was highest

Table 6.5: Distribution of Units by Employment Slabs

Employment Slabs	No. of Units	%age to Total	Employment (Nos)	%age to Total	Fixed Investment (Rs. lakhs	%age to Total	Production (Rs. Lakhs)	%age to Total
1-4	3,75,828	64.5	822579	22.4	199800	21.5	501235	11.7
5-9	1,35,577	23.3	880087	24.0	258073	27.7	992899	23.1
10-19	43 282	7.4	567530	15.5	180701	19.4	845844	19.7
20-49	20,832	23.5	617600	16.9	178978	29.3	1005496	23.4
50-99	4,733	0.8	311707	8.5	68581	7.4	502297	11.7
100 & above	2,116	0.4	466307	12.7	43470	4.7	449434	10.4
Total	5,82,368	100.0	3665810	100.0	929603	100.0	4297205	100.0

Source : Report on the Second All India Census of Small Scale Industrial Units. Development Commissioner, Small Scale Industries, 1988.

DISTRIBUTION OF UNITS, EMPLOYMENT, FIXED INVESTMENT & PRODUCTION AS PER EMPLOYMENT SLABS

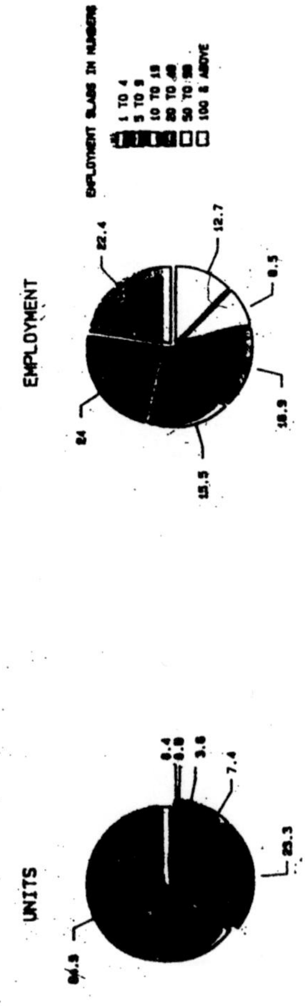

Table 6.6 : Distribution of Units by Investment in Plant and Machinery (Original Value) Slabs

Investment in P & M (Rs. lakhs)	No. of Units	%age to Total	Employment (Nos)	%age to Total	Fixed Investment (Rs. Lakhs)	%age to Total	Production (Rs. Lakhs)	%age to Total
0-1	4,82,452	82.3	1976227	53.9	308731	33.2	1207131	28.1
1-2	41,694	7.2	423244	11.6	101020	10.9	534417	12.4
2-5	34,362	5.9	511340	13.9	154487	16.6	770865	17.9
5-10	12,832	2.2	295365	8.1	112123	12.1	569843	13.3
10 & above	11,028	1.9	459634	12.5	253242	27.2	1214949	28.3

Source : Report on the Second All India Census of Small Scale Industrial Units Development Commissioner, Small Scale Industries.

DISTRIBUTION OF UNITS, EMPLOYMENT, FIXED INVESTMENT & PRODUCTION AS PER INVESTMENT IN PLANT & MACHINERY SLABS (ORIGINAL VALUE)

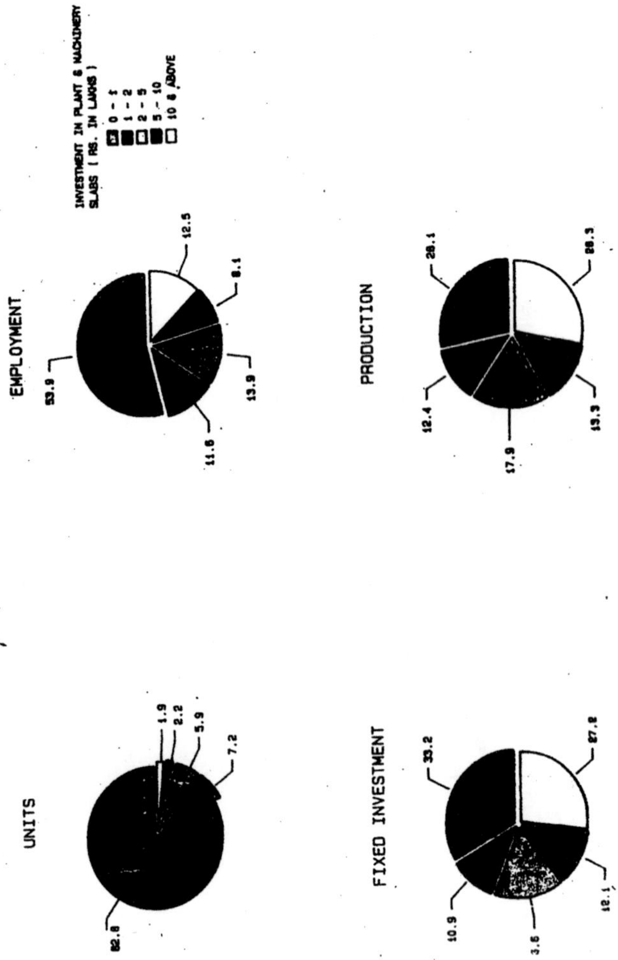

in the largest size group. Capital intensity was lowest in largest size group.

Distribution of Units by Investment in Plant & Machinery

The distribution of units as shown in Table 6.6 and chart 6.2 based on Second All India Survey of SSI reveals that 82.8% of the units covered in the census had investment in plant and machinery less than Rs. 1 lakh and accounted for 54% of employment, 33% of fixed investment and 28% of production. Per unit production was highest in investment slab Rs. 10 lakhs and above, and lowest in the slab less than Rs.1 lakh. Labour productivity was observed to be the highest also in the largest size group and lowest in the lowest size group. But capital productivity in terms of production per unit of fixed investment was highest in the second lowest size group (1-2 lakhs).

Organisational Structure

On the basis of the same survey 80% of the SSUs were proprietary units (Table 6.7 and Chart 6.3). They accounted for 51% of the employment, 42% of investment in fixed assets and 29% of production. Employment per unit and production per unit were highest among limited companies and lowest among proprietary units. Labour productivity was lowest among co-operatives followed by proprietorships.

Distribution to Units by Type of Activity

According to the survey, 50% of the units were engaged in manufacturing assembly (Table 6.8 Chart 6.4). Another 8% of the units had taken up manufacutre/assembly along with processing, job work and/or repairing/servicing activity. These 58% units accounted for 84% of total production. Per unit production was highest among the units undertaking manufacturing/assembly activity only, followed by units in processing activity. Lowest was among repairing/servicing units. Fixed investment also followed a similar pattern.

Regional Distribution

The distribution of small scale units as between, rural, urban and metropolitan towns according to All India Survey 1988 shows that these units have almost an equal pull in both sectors. 42% of the registered small scale units in the country are functioning in rural areas and 48% in urban areas. Ten per cent are in metropolitan towns, which, strictly speaking comes in the urban area category, so that the urban sectors share

Table 6.7: Classification of Units by Organisation

Type of Organisation	No. of Units	%age to Ttotal	Employ-ment (Nos)	%age to Total	Fixed Investment (Rs. Lakhs)	%age to Total	Production (Rs. Lakhs)	%age to Total
Proprietary	4,68,717	80.5	1854284	50.6	387174	41.6	1228326	28.6
Partnership	98,049	16.8	1288643	35.2	335563	36.1	2007683	46.7
Limited Company	12,283	2.1	439012	11.9	186242	20.1	953977	22.2
Cooperative	1,702	0.3	37449	1.0	5551	0.6	18326	0.4
Others	1,617	0.3	46422	1.3	15073	1.6	88893	2.1
Total	5,82,368	100.0	3665810	100.0	929603	100.0	4297205	100.0

Source : Report on the Second All India Census of Small Scale Industrial Units Devp. Commissioner, Small Scale Industries.

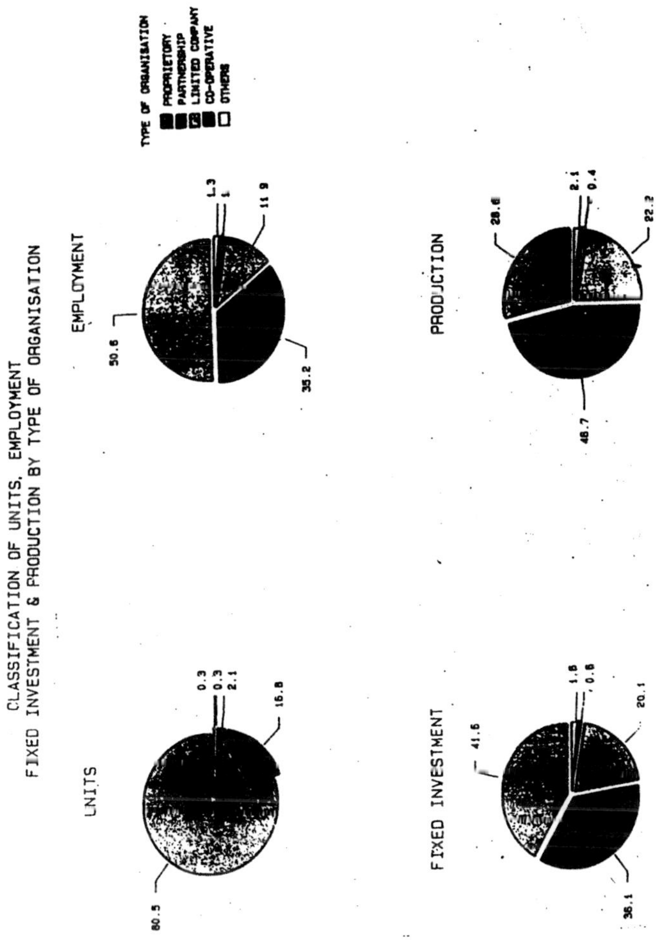
CLASSIFICATION OF UNITS, EMPLOYMENT
FIXED INVESTMENT & PRODUCTION BY TYPE OF ORGANISATION
UNITS
80.5
0.3
0.3
2.1
16.8
EMPLOYMENT
50.6
35.2
11.9
1.3
FIXED INVESTMENT
41.6
1.8
0.5
20.1
36.1
PRODUCTION
28.6
2.1
0.4
22.2
46.7
TYPE OF ORGANISATION
PROPRIETORY
PARTNERSHIP
LIMITED COMPANY
CO-OPERATIVE
OTHERS

would come to 58%. This information has important implications for policy formulations for the growth of SSI. It indicates that while support to the SSI is necessary for the development of the rural sector, it is equally significant for generating employment in the urban sector. Since information is not available on the non-registered category, which may itself form a large group, one cannot comment authentically on the whole SSI group. However, it may be safe to presume that the unregistered segment would mainly consist of the tiny sector, which would normally belong to the rural sector, thus bringing the share of rural sector closer to the urban.

Units in the rural sector accounted for 33% of employment, as compared to more than 70% in urban areas. Similarly, the share of rural units in total investment and in total production is also much less than their number. They accounted for 29% of total investment in fixed assets and 27% of production (Table 6.9).

Statewise distribution of SSI in rural and urban areas reveals that states and union territories like Dadra & Nagar Haveli, Arunachal Pradesh, Manipur, Mizoram, Himachal Pradesh and Kerala are dominated by industries located in rural areas. On the other hand, most of the bigger states have about 40% to 50% units located in rural areas, which conforms to all India average. Maharashtra and Gujarat are exceptions with about 80% units located in urabn and metropolitan areas (Table 6.10).

Distribution of Units by Categories

A study of SSUs from the point of view of the category of establishment reveals that out of a total of 5.82 lakh working units in the country in 1987-88, 560470 units, i.e. 96.2% were registered as small scale industries (SSI), 3029, i.e. 50% as Ancillary Industrial Undertakings and the remaining 18869 (3.2%) units, as Small Service Establishments (SSE).

Details of their share in employment, production, fixed investment, production and capacity are given in Table 6.11.

Their relative performance vis-a-vis SSI and SSE is also given in Table 6.11. It can be seen that judged by almost all efficiency ratios, the ancillaries have performed better than the other two categories. But their capital intensity is higher than the other two which is inherent in the very nature of ancillary relationship.

Table 6.8: Distribution of Units by Type of Activity

Type of Activity	No. of Units	%age Total	Fixed Invest-ment (Rs. Lakhs)	Investment in Plants & Machinery (Original Value)	%age to total	Production (Rs.Lakhs)	%age to Total
Manufacturing/ Assembling	2,92,301	50.2	626161	372822	67.4	3283879	76.4
Processing	88,711	15.2	100696	59994	10.8	557995	13.0
Job Work	70,399	12.1	68332	44093	7.4	90924	2.1
Repairing/Servicing	83,118	14.3	51307	21639	5.5	51929	1.2
All other (Combined)	47,839	8.2	83107	55710	8.9	312478	7.3
Total	5,82,368	100.0	929603	554258	100.0	4297205	100.0

Source : Report on Second All India Census of Small Scale Industrial Units, Development Commisioner, Small Scale Industries.

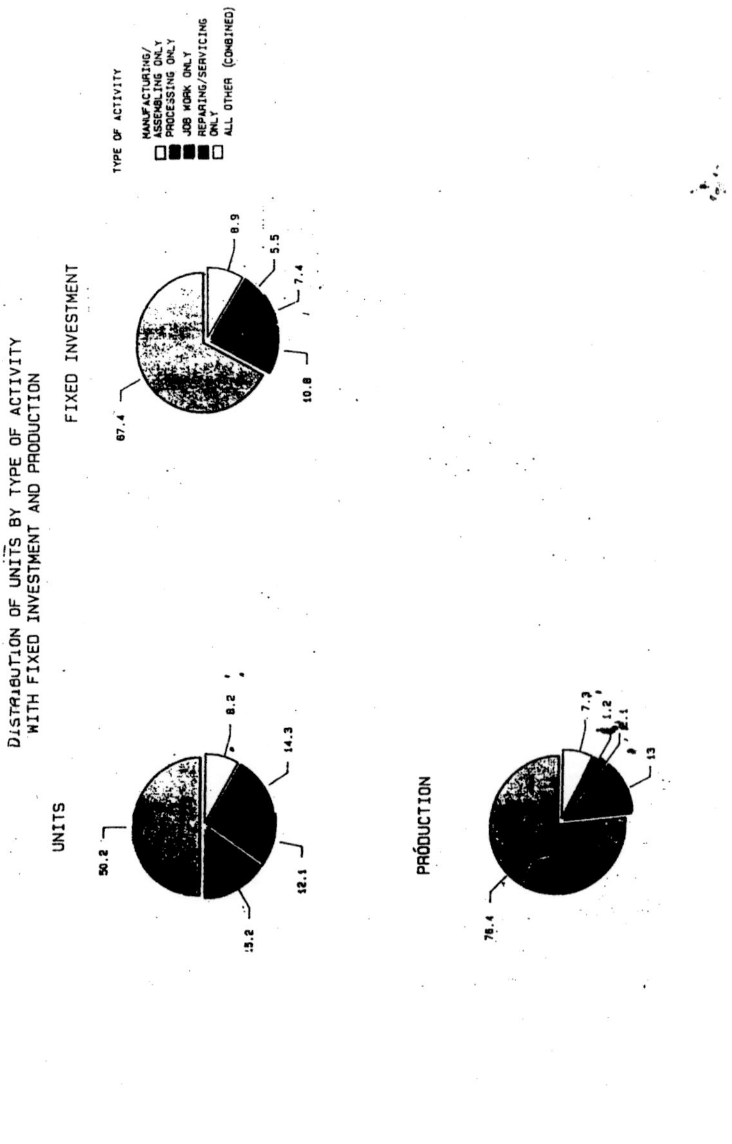
DISTRIBUTION OF UNITS BY TYPE OF ACTIVITY
WITH FIXED INVESTMENT AND PRODUCTION
UNITS
50.2
15.2
12.1
14.3
8.2
FIXED INVESTMENT
67.4
10.8
7.4
5.5
8.9
TYPE OF ACTIVITY
MANUFACTURING/
ASSEMBLING ONLY
PROCESSING ONLY
JOB WORK ONLY
REPAIRING/SERVICING
ONLY
ALL OTHER (COMBINED)
PRODUCTION
78.4
13
7.3

Table 6.9: Distribution of Units by Area of Location

Sl. No.	Area of Location	No. of Units	%age to Total	Employment (Nos)	%age to Total	Fixed Investment (Rs. Lakhs)	%age to Total	Production (Rs. Lakhs)	%age to Total
1	Rural	2,45,573	42.2	1221673	33.3	273008	29.4	1152234	26.8
2	Urban	2,79,359	48.0	1848616	50.4	482954	51.9	2187392	50.9
3	Metropolitan	57,436	9.8	595521	16.3	173641	18.7	957579	22.3
Total		5,82,368	100.0	3665810	100.0	929603	100.0	4297205	100.0

Source : Report on Second All India Census of Small Scale Industrial Units, Development Commissioner, Small Scale Industries.

Table 6.10: Location-wise Distribution of Units in Various States/UTs

S.No.	Name of State/UT	NUMBER OF UNITS					
		Rural	Urban	Metropolitan	Total	Backward	Non-Backward
1	2	3	4	5	6	7	8
1.	Andhra Pradesh	17608	18747	2855	39210	21809	17401
2.	Assam	1992	2438	0	4430	4430	0
3.	Bihar	14536	20286	0	34822	34822	0
4.	Gujarat	7248	20105	7100	34453	11588	22865
5.	Haryana	11140	12216	0	23356	11310	12046
6.	Himachal Pradesh	5259	1724	0	6983	6983	0
7.	Jammu & Kashmir	4400	4680	0	9080	9080	
8.	Karnataka	15467	20251	4807	40525	32145	8380
9.	Kerala	18093	7624	0	25717	12817	12900
10.	Madhya Pradesh	47555	26337	0	73892	62860	11032
11.	Maharashtra	6070	12308	11478	29856	13443	16413
12.	Manipur	1478	600	0	2078	2078	0
13.	Meghalaya	323	264	0	587	587	0
14.	Nagaland	54	129	0	183	183	0
15.	Orissa	4004	4283	0	8287	3303	4984
16.	Punjab	17126	28213	0	45339	24957	20382
17.	Rajasthan	14726	12681	1636	29043	16421	12622
18.	Tamil Nadu	16414	33086	7713	57213	28248	28965
19.	Tripura	365	444	0	809	809	0
20.	Uttar Pradesh	17191	32921	3170	53282	32106	21176

1	2	3	4	5	6	7	8
21.	West Bengal	20558	16519	8877	45954	26274	19680
22.	Sikkim	6	60	0	66	66	0
23.	A & N Islands	138	185	0	323	323	0
24.	Arunachal Pradesh	287	39	0	326	326	0
25.	Chandigarh	15	1295	0	1310	0	1310
26.	Dadra & Nagar Haveli	147	2	0	149	149	0
27.	Delhi	173	65	9800	10038	0	10038
28.	Goa	1705	1067	0	2772	2772	0
29.	Mizoram	790	127	0	917	917	0
30.	Pondicherry	622	599	0	1221	1221	0
31.	Daman & Diu	83	64	0	147	147	0
Total		245573	279359	57436	582368	362174	220194

Source : Report on Second All India Census of Small Scale Units, Development Commissioner, Small Scale Industries.

Table 6.11: Distribution of Units by Categories—Employment, Production Fixed Investment and Capacity

Sl. No.	Category of Units	No. of Units	Employment (Nos.)	Production (Rs. lakhs)	Fixed Investment (Rs. lakhs)	Capacity (Rs. lakhs)
1	Small Scale Industries (SSI)	560470	3591662	4230329	907794	8367462
	%age to Toal	(96.24)	(97.98)	(98.45)	(97.65)	(98.53)
2	Ancillary Indl. Undertakings (ANC)	3029	31290	40656	10314	67972
	%age to Total	(0.52)	(0.85)	(0.94)	(1.11)	(0.80)
3	Small Service Establishment (SSE)	18869	42858	26220	11495	56558
	%age to Total	(3.24)	(1.17)	(0.61)	(1.24)	(0.67)
	Total	582368	3665810	4297205	929603	8491992

Source : Report on Second All India Census of Small Scale Units, Development Commissioner, Small Scale Industries.

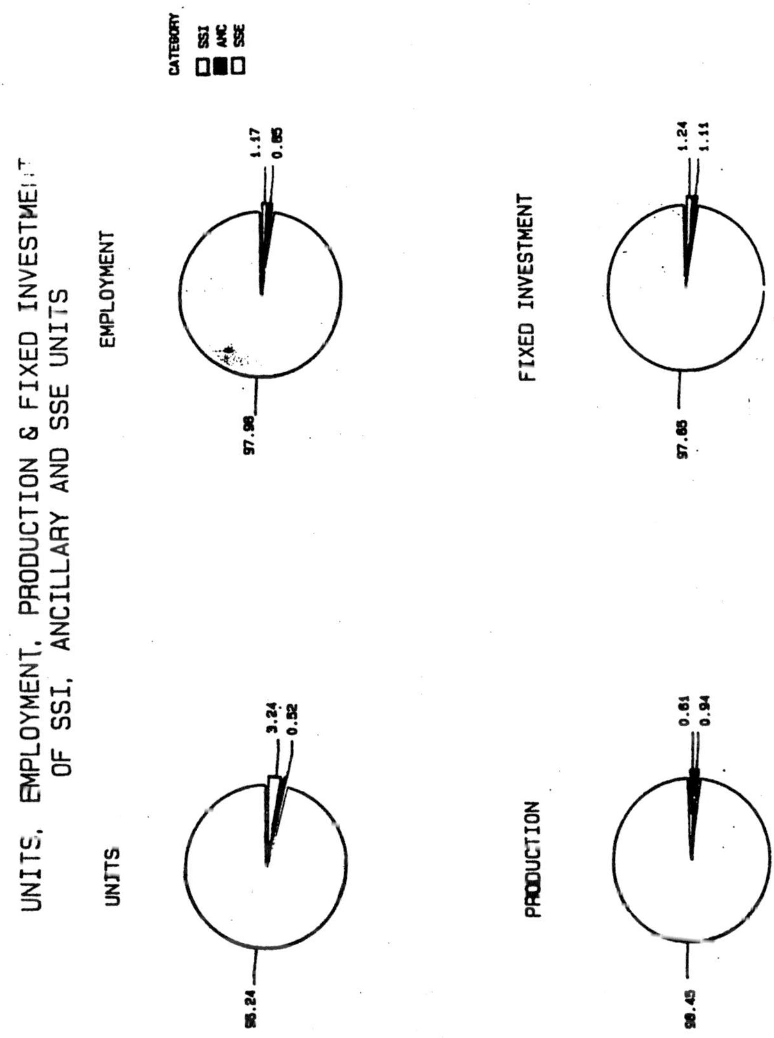
UNITS, EMPLOYMENT, PRODUCTION & FIXED INVESTMENT
OF SSI, ANCILLARY AND SSE UNITS
CATEGORY
SSI
ANC
SSE
UNITS
96.24
3.24
0.52
EMPLOYMENT
97.98
1.17
0.85
PRODUCTION
98.45
0.61
0.94
FIXED INVESTMENT
97.65
1.24
1.11

Table 6.12: Performance of Industries At 2-Digit NIC Level

Sl. No.	2-Digit NIC code	Industry Group	No. of Units	Fixed Investment (Rs. lakhs)	Investment In P&M (Book value)	Production (Rs. Lakhs)	Employment (Nos.)	Net value added (Rs. lakhs)	Exports (Rs.lakhs)	Capacity utilisation %age
1	2	3	4	5	6	7	8	9	10	11
1.	20 & 21	Food Products	96123	134072	48729	938561	481682	118740	53414	48
2.	22	Beverages, Tobacco & Tobcacco Products	3669	7153	1946	47247	73375	17742	1014	60
3.	23	Cotton Textiles	1451	4729	1939	30052	24725	4413	1319	68
4.	24	Wood, Silk & Synth. Fibre Text	1158	4011	1862	25795	12314	9269	344	74
5.	25	Jute, Hemp and Mesta Textiles	219	830	290	5649	2599	776	260	37
6.	26	Hosiery and Garments	39778	34976	9843	220756	198387	53453	72567	69
7.	27	Wood Products	54975	43428	11243	189803	229061	57651	3689	48
8.	28	Paper Products & Printing	33320	64241	27909	172260	199389	53013	2194	60
9.	29	Leather Products	24028	14648	3969	102581	81667	36624	45040	79
10.	30	Rubber & Parts Except Elect	25819	72340	34262	254170	188784	58228	3557	58
11.	31	Chemical & Chemical Products	25941	88117	33281	527273	313986	158348	19969	53
12.	32	Non-Metallic Mineral Products	31589	65363	24703	176804	446218	54680	4628	49
13.	33	Basic Metal Industries	14937	64046	29241	448517	202463	84994	8918	43

1	2	3	4	5	6	7	8	9	10	11
14.	34	Metal Products	65868	88590	31433	361578	372711	109528	12830	43
15.	35	Machniery & Parts Except Elect	40802	80825	33133	247428	279292	65762	6466	62
16.	36	Electrical Machinery & Parts	12283	45042	16317	259865	137260	58772	2678	42
17.	37	Transport Equipments & Parts	11325	28343	11594	108910	100360	24715	1822	60
18.	38	Miscellaneous Mfrg. Industries	8852	16055	5646	78953	65322	28501	5975	46
19.	97	Repair Services	80412	41416	9423	44165	192267	8935	1203	62
20.	99	Services not elsewhere Classified	613	2045	1100	2713	2720	581	0	63
21.	OT	Other Services and Products	9206	29333	12346	54145	61228	21380	2015	51
		Total	582368	929603	350209	4297205	3665810	1026127	249902	51

Note : For classifying the data (collected through the Census) industrywise, the National Industrial Classification (NIC) 1970 evolved by the CSO has been used. For broad analysis, the 2 digit level of this classification (i.e. major industry group level) has been adopted. A group 'OT' has been introduced in the Tables to accommodate industries and services which could not be covered by any of the 2 digit industry groups. For finer analysis, the 4 digit level (sub groups) of the classification has been adopted. The product classfication under each 4 digit codes runs into 9 digit codes.

Source : Report on Second All India Census on Small Scale Units, Development Commissioner, Small Scale Industries.

Table 6.13: Export by Performance Industries at 2-Digit NIC Level

Sl. No.	2-Digit Ind. Group	Description	No. of Units	No. of Exporting units	%age of Col. 5 to 4	Values of exports (Rs. lakhs)	Exports per exporting unit (Rs. lakhs)	%age to total exports	%age share of exports to production within idusry group
1	2	3	4	5	6	7	8	9	10
1	26	Hosiery and Garments	39778	948	2.38	72567	77	29.04	32.87
2	20 & 21	Food Products	96123	532	0.55	53414	100	21.38	5.69
3	29	Leather Products	24028	432	1.80	45040	104	18.02	43.91
4	31	Chemical & Chemical Products	25941	519	2.00	19969	38	7.99	3.79
5	34	Metal Products	65868	332	0.50	12830	39	5.13	3.55
6	33	Basic Metal Industries	14937	208	1.39	8918	43	3.57	1.99
7	35	Machinery & Parts Except elect	40802	355	0.87	6466	18	2.59	2.61
8	38	Miscellaneous Mfrg. Industries	8852	192	2.17	5975	31	2.39	7.57
9	32	Non-metallic Mineral Products	31589	155	0.49	4628	30	1.85	2.62
10	27	Wood Products	54975	159	0.29	3688	23	1.47	1.94
11	30	Rubber & Plastic Products	25819	153	0.59	3557	23	1.42	1.40
12	36	Electrical Machinery & Parts	12283	156	1.27	2678	17	1.07	1.03
13.	28	Paper Products & Printing	33320	92	0.28	2194	24	0.88	1.27
14	OT	Other Services and Products	9206	57	0.62	2015	35	0.81	3.72

1	2	3	4	5	6	7	8	9	10
15	37	Transport Equipments & Parts	11325	130	1.15	1822	14	0.73	1.67
16	23	Cotton Textiles	1451	18	1.24	1319	73	0.52	4.36
17	97	Repair Services	80412	78	0.10	1203	15	0.48	2.72
18	22	Beverages, Tobacco & Tobacco Products	3669	30	0.82	1014	34	0.41	2.15
19	24	Wool, Silk & Synth. Fibre Text	1158	6	0.52	344	57	0.14	1.33
20	25	Jute, Hemp and Mesta Textiles	219	2	0.91	260	130	0.10	4.60
21	99	Services not Elsewhere Classified	613	0	0.00	0	0	0.00	0.00
		Total	582368	4554	0.78	249902	55	100.00	5.82

Value of Exports Less than Rs. 50,000 has been shown as zero.

Source : Report on the Second All India Census of Small Scale Industrial Units, Development Commissioner.

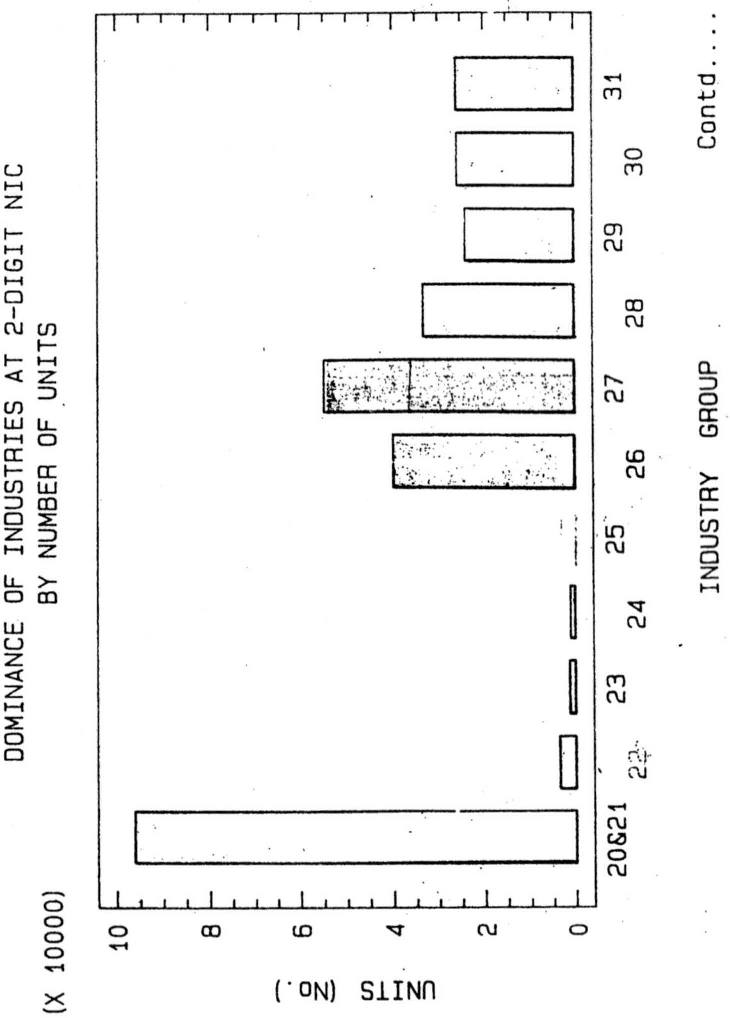
DOMINANCE OF INDUSTRIES AT 2-DIGIT NIC
BY NUMBER OF UNITS
(X 10000)
UNITS (NO.)
10
8
6
4
2
0
20&21
22
23
24
25
26
27
28
29
30
31
INDUSTRY GROUP

Contd....

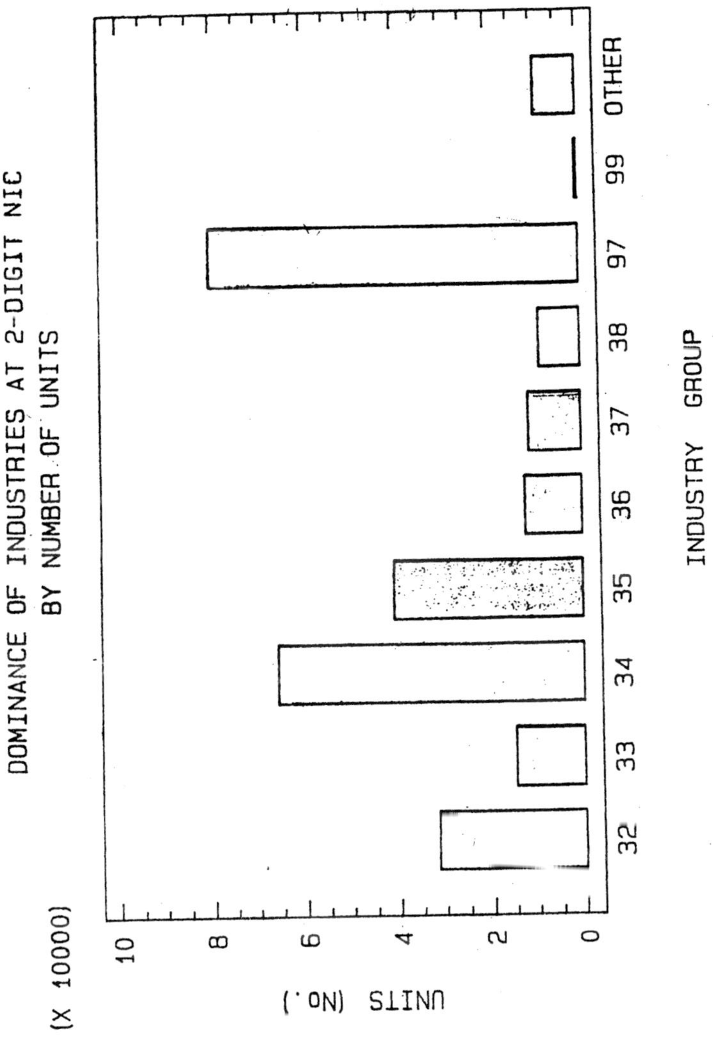
DOMINANCE OF INDUSTRIES AT 2-DIGIT NIC
BY NUMBER OF UNITS
(X 10000)
UNITS (NO.)
10
8
6
4
2
0
32
33
34
35
36
37
38
97
99
OTHER
INDUSTRY GROUP

It can be seen that while the share of SSI in employment and production is proportionate to the share in total number of units, the share of ancillaries in production, employment, investment and total capacity of all small scale units, is much larger than the share in the total number of units. On the other hand, in the case of SSEs the picture is opposite, which indicates that the average operational size of the ancillary units is larger than that of the SSI.

Dominance of Industries (At 2-Digit NIC level)

Range of industries covered by SSUs is very wide. But the dominance of industries as indicated by the number of units, level of production, employment, fixed investment, net value added and exports in each industry group differs considerably as indicated in the Table 6.12.

As can be seen, the largest concentration of units was in food products industry (96123 units), followed by Repair group (86412), Metal products (65868) and woodwork (54975).

The Engineering industry, (two digit classifications 30-38 in the table) accounted for one fourth of total number of small scale units in the industrial sector. In terms of production also, the food products industry dominated with a production of Rs. 9386 crores, accounting for nearly 22% of a total production of Rs. 42972 crores of all the small scale units. This was followed by chemical and chemical products accounting for 12.3% of total (Rs. 5273 crores), the two groups of the Engineering industry above accounting for nearly 34% of total production. Average production per small scale unit was Rs. 7.38 lakhs. The highest was in Basic metal industry (30.03 lakhs), and lowest in Repair/ Service sector (Rs. 0.55 lakhs).

Statewise spread of industries in terms of number of units and production are given in Table 6.15 and 6.16.

Out of total fixed investment of Rs. 9296 crores in all the 5.8 lakh units covered in the census, industry groups, Food products (14.4%), Metal products (9.5%) and chemicals and chemical products (9.5%) together accounted for 33% of the total fixed investment.

Per unit fixed investment was 1.6 lakhs on an average. The highest was in Basic metal industries (4.43 lakhs) and lowest (0.5 lakhs) was in Repair.

Total employment in SSUs was 36.6 lakh persons in 1987-

88, out of which food product accounted for 13.1%, Nonmetallic mineral products came next with a share of 12.2%, followed by Metal products, 10.2%. Per Unit employment was the highest in Beverages, Tobacco & Tobacco products (20%), and lowest in repair and services.

Exports

In terms of export performance, out of 5.8 lakh units surveyed, 4,554 units exported goods worth Rs. 2499 crores during 1987-88. The largest number of exporting units were from the hosiery and garments industry group (948), recording the largest value of exports. (worth Rs. 726 crores). Next came food products group with 532 units exporting Rs. 534 crores, worth of goods, followed by leather and leather products with exports worth Rs. 450 crores by 432 units. These 3 group of industries are export intensive industries in the SSI sector. Average per unit export was highest for Jute, Hemp and Mesta textiles with exports worth Rs. 130 lakhs. (Table 6.13).

Comparative Findings of the Two Surveys (1972 and 1987)

A comparative study of the 1972 and 1987 surveys brings out following points-

1. Units for which data was tabulated out of the total frame of registered units, had increased by 10%.
2. The distribution of units as between backward and non-backward areas shows a drastic change. While the percentage share of backward area rose from 35% to 62% in the Second Survey, for the non-backward region it fell from 65% to 38%. Thus the shares were reversed.
3. Fixed investment per small scale unit was marginally less in the second survey, but employment per unit of SSU was halved from 12 to 6 numbers. Employment per Rs. 1 lakh of fixed investment also declined considerably from 20.75 to 12.53, showing a general increase in capital intensity of SSUs, which could be attributed to change in the character of the product mix of the SSI.
4. By and large productivity of the SSUs seem to have increased. But while the output capital ratios show a marginal change, the ratios indicating labour productivity (Value added/employments, production/employment) show a marked increase, which seems to be related to increase in capital intensity.

Table 6.14 : Comparison of Main Findings of First and Second All India Census

Main findings of First and Second All India Census of small scale industrial units (SIDO) are given in Tabular form as under:

Item	First All India Census of SSI (1972)		Second All India Census of SSI (1987-88)	
A. Total Units as per Frame List	2,57,797 (as on 30-11-73)		9,86,861 (as on 31-3-88)	
Working Units	1,59,321		5,93,769	
B. Number of Units for which data was tabulated	1,39,577* (88%)		5,82,368 (98%)	
C. Distribution of units				
i. Backward Area	49,349 (35%)		3,62,174 (62%)	
ii. Non-backward Area	90,228 (65%)		2,20,194 (38%)	
Total	1,39,577 (1005)		5,82,368 (100%)	
	<u>Total</u>	<u>Per Unit</u>	<u>Total</u>	<u>Per Unit</u>
D. Investment in Fixed Assets (Rs.in lakhs) (Book Value)— constant prices (1972-73)	79,674	0.57	2,92,639	0.50
Investment in Plant & Machinery (Rs. in lakhs) (Original value)— constant prices	53,696	0.38	1,74,480	0.30
	<u>1972-73</u>		<u>1987-88</u>	
E. Production (Rs. in lakhs) at 1972-73 prices	260274	1.86	13,52,760	2.32
F. Employment (Nos.)	16,53,178	12	36,65,810	6
G. Net Value added at 1972-73 prices (Rs. in lakhs)	84,100	0.60	3,23,012	0.55
H. **Important Ratios**	<u>First Census</u>		<u>Second Census</u>	
(i) Production/Investment in Fixed Assets	3.27		4.62	
(ii) Net value added/Investment in Fixed Assets	1.06		1.10	
(iii) Gross value added/ Employment (Rs. 000)	6.20		9.49	
(iv) Net Value added/ Employment (Rs.000)	5.09		8.81	
(v) Production/Employment (Rs.000)	1.57		3.69	
(vi) Employment per Rupees one lakh of Investment in fixed assets	20.75		12.53	

Table 6.15 : Distribution of Units by States/UTs & Industry Groups (2 Digit NIC Level) and their Percentages

S.No.	State/UTs	Industry Groups (At 2 digit NIC Level)											
		20 & 21		22		23		24		25		26	
		No. of Units	% to Total	No. of Units	% to Total	No. of Units	% to Total	No. of Units	% to Total	No. of Units	% to Total	No. of Units	%to Total
1	2	3	4	5	6	7	8	9	10	11	12	13	14
1	Andhra Pradesh	10598	21.3	452	0.9	50	0.1	22	0.0	13	0.0	390	0.8
2	Assam	1376	23.7	3	0.1	4	0.1	0	0.0	0	0.0	200	3.4
3	Bihar	4365	11.1	145	0.4	23	0.1	19	0.0	14	0.0	2080	5.3
4	Gujarat	2414	6.5	174	0.5	50	0.1	35	0.1	17	0.0	1603	4.3
5	Haryana	2808	10.7	35	0.1	38	0.1	18	0.1	4	0.0	275	1.1
6	Himachal Pradesh	2083	23.0	23	0.3	15	0.2	292	3.2	4	0.0	723	8.0
7	Jammu & Kashmir	1447	13.7	20	0.2	26	0.2	11	0.1	1	0.0	994	9.4
8	Karnataka	10221	20.1	550	1.1	52	0.1	28	0.1	9	0.0	1750	3.4
9	Kerala	4791	15.7	443	1.5	8	0.0	3	0.0	3	0.0	1202	3.9
10	Madhya Pradesh	12608	14.6	60	0.1	65	0.1	35	0.0	21	0.0	14576	16.9
11	Maharashtra	2587	8.0	152	0.5	108	0.3	114	0.4	16	0.0	857	2.6
12	Manipur	391	15.8	1	0.0	1	0.0	0	0.0	0	0.0	398	16.1
13	Meghalaya	152	20.6	0	0.0	0	0.0	0	0.0	0	0.0	49	6.6
14	Nagaland	69	27.4	0	0.0	0	0.0	0	0.0	0	0.0	2	0.8
15	Orissa	2835	25.5	83	0.7	27	0.2	1	0.0	5	0.0	267	2.4
16	Punjab	4110	8.3	46	0.1	127	0.3	182	0.4	7	0.0	2105	4.3
17	Rajasthan	7812	21.2	71	0.2	58	0.2	38	0.1	13	0.0	1103	3.0
18	Tamil Nadu	3970	13.6	596	0.9	557	0.8	188	0.3	10	0.0	3450	5.2
19	Tripura	247	23.4	3	0.3	0	0.0	0	0.0	0	0.0	5	0.5
20	Uttar Pradesh	9618	15.3	307	0.5	143	0.2	74	0.1	26	0.0	2671	4.2

1	2	3	4	5	6	7	8	9	10	11	12	13	14
21	West Bengal	4779	9.4	270	0.5	55	0.1	57	0.1	48	0.1	3811	7.5
22	Sikkim	19	22.4	0	0.0	0	0.0	0	0.0	0	0.0	5	5.9
23	Andaman & Nicobar	84	20.6	5	1.2	0	0.0	0	0.0	0	0.0	1	0.2
24	Arunachal Pradesh	171	34.4	1	0.2	0	0.0	0	0.0	0	0.0	10	2.0
25	Chandigarh	42	3.1	2	0.1	0	0.0	3	0.2	1	0.1	16	1.2
26	Dadra & Nagar Haveli	20	11.8	0	0.0	0	0.0	0	0.0	0	0.0	0	0.0
27	Delhi	140	1.4	4	0.0	40	0.4	36	0.4	4	0.0	808	7.9
28	Goa	918	24.9	181	4.9	1	0.0	1	0.0	3	0.1	54	1.5
29	Mizoram	139	13.2	4	0.4	0	0.0	0	0.0	0	0.0	310	29.4
30	Pondicherry	263	17.7	33	2.2	3	0.2	1	0.1	0	0.0	60	4.0
31	Daman & Diu	46	23.8	5	2.6	0	0.0	0	0.0	0	0.0	3	1.6
	Total	96123	14.2	3669	0.5	1451	0.2	1158	0.2	219	0.0	39778	5.9

Table 6.15 Contd.......

S.No.	State/UTs	Industry Groups (At 2 digit NIC Level) 27 No. of Units	27 % to Total	28 No. of Units	28 % to Total	29 No. of Units	29 % to Total	30 No. of Units	30 % to Total	31 No. of Units	31 % to Total	32 No. of Units	32 %to Total
1	2	15	16	17	18	19	20	21	22	23	24	25	26
1	Andhra Pradesh	3598	7.2	2831	5.7	879	1.8	1551	3.1	1232	2.5	3193	6.4
2	Assam	569	9.8	88	1.5	16	0.3	291	5.0	175	3.0	290	5.0
3	Bihar	5714	14.6	1797	4.6	2128	5.4	1324	3.4	928	2.4	2133	5.4
4	Gujarat	2320	6.3	2003	5.4	169	0.5	1787	4.8	2868	7.8	2406	6.5
5	Haryana	2588	9.9	407	1.6	2835	10.8	663	2.5	611	2.3	632	2.4
6	Himachal Pradesh	1406	15.5	202	2.2	112	1.2	154	1.7	160	1.8	140	1.5
7.	Jammu & Kashmir	1622	15.4	218	2.1	420	4.0	154	1.5	157	1.5	281	2.7
8	Karnataka	3779	7.4	2623	5.2	1381	2.7	1570	3.1	1587	3.1	1422	2.8
9	Kerala	3812	12.5	2445	8.0	191	0.6	2679	8.8	1334	4.4	1837	6.0
10	Madhya Pradesh	8535	9.9	1613	1.9	4769	5.5	1272	1.5	941	1.1	4503	5.2
11	Maharashtra	1307	5.6	3205	9.9	267	0.3	2365	7.3	2796	8.6	1405	4.3
12	Manipur	702	28.4	37	1.5	11	0.4	98	4.0	13	0.5	57	2.3
13	Meghalaya	124	16.8	28	3.8	4	0.5	23	3.1	2	0.3	68	9.2
14	Nagaland	52	20.6	11	4.4	1	0.4	4	1.6	1	0.4	8	3.2
15	Orissa	711	6.4	556	5.0	56	0.5	400	3.6	293	2.6	685	6.2
16	Punjab	3270	6.6	980	2.0	5816	11.8	770	1.6	847	1.7	443	0.9
17	Rajasthan	3237	8.8	1036	2.8	601	1.6	648	1.8	932	2.5	3171	8.6
18	Tamil Nadu	2297	3.5	5253	7.9	1224	1.8	2812	4.2	5587	8.4	3283	5.0

1	2	15	16	17	18	19	20	21	22	23	24	25	26
19	Tripura	99	9.4	51	4.8	5	0.5	95	9.0	18	1.7	78	7.4
20	Uttar Pradesh	4429	7.0	3594	5.7	2013	3.2	2839	4.5	2674	4.3	3099	4.9
21	West Bengal	3383	6.7	2884	5.7	867	1.7	2789	5.5	1715	3.4	1992	3.9
22	Sikkim	3	3.5	15	17.6	2	2.4	3	3.5	4	4.7	2	2.4
23	Andaman & Nicobar	87	21.4	13	3.2	0	0.0	12	2.9	2	0.5	25	6.1
24	Arunachal Pradesh	102	20.5	1	0.2	0	0.0	6	1.2	1	0.2	4	0.8
25	Chandigarh	79	5.8	82	6.1	8	0.6	89	6.6	50	3.7	26	1.9
26	Dadra & Nagar Haveli	6	3.6	7	4.1	4	2.4	14	8.3	18	10.7	20	11.8
27	Delhi	143	1.4	996	9.8	222	2.2	1124	11.0	788	7.7	173	1.7
28	Goa	221	6.0	177	4.8	9	0.2	166	4.5	85	2.3	140	3.8
29	Mizoram	177	16.8	63	6.0	2	0.2	30	2.8	0	0.0	14	1.3
30	Pondicherry	93	6.3	98	6.6	16	1.1	69	4.6	110	7.4	52	3.5
31	Daman & Diu	10	5.2	6	3.1	0	0.0	18	9.3	12	6.2	7	3.6
	Total	54975	8.1	33320	4.9	24028	3.5	25819	3.8	25941	3.8	31589	4.7

Table 6.15 Contd.......

S.No.	State/UTs	Industry Group (At 2 digit NIC Level)											
		33		34		35		36		37		38	
		No. of Units	% to Total	No. of Units	% to Total	No. of Units	% to Total	No. of Units	% to Total	No. of Units	% to Total	No. of Units	%to Total
1	2	27	28	29	30	31	32	33	34	35	36	37	38
1	Andhra Pradesh	539	1.4	4257	10.9	2653	6.8	636	1.6	699	1.8	316	0.8
2	Assam	51	1.2	642	14.5	52	1.2	73	1.6	31	0.7	17	0.4
3	Bihar	536	1.5	4054	11.6	1134	3.3	371	1.1	505	1.5	422	1.2
4	Gujarat	2042	5.9	3805	11.0	5478	15.9	1168	3.4	658	1.9	887	2.6
5	Haryana	725	3.1	3051	13.1	1191	5.1	393	1.7	421	1.8	429	1.8
6	Himachal Pradesh	43	0.6	672	9.6	72	1.0	80	1.1	22	0.3	56	0.8
7	Jammu & Kashmir	109	1.2	1304	14.4	56	0.6	105	1.2	52	0.6	389	4.3
8	Karnataka	546	1.3	4173	10.3	2915	7.2	699	1.7	808	2.0	394	1.0
9	Kerala	250	1.0	2691	10.5	960	3.7	374	1.5	204	0.8	202	0.8
10	Madhya Pradesh	417	0.6	5938	8.0	1854	2.5	406	0.5	713	1.0	682	0.9
11	Maharashtra	1356	4.5	4218	14.1	3691	12.4	1585	5.3	983	3.3	749	2.5
12	Manipur	4	0.2	138	6.6	4	0.2	13	0.6	29	1.4	6	0.3
13	Meghalaya	1	0.2	46	7.8	0	0.0	4	0.7	1	0.2	4	0.7
14	Nagaland	0	0.0	17	9.3	0	0.0	1	0.5	1	0.5	2	1.1
15	Orissa	233	2.8	1026	12.4	178	2.1	116	1.4	117	1.4	64	0.8
16	Punjab	1735	3.8	4464	9.8	3687	8.1	625	1.4	1743	3.8	671	1.5
17	Rajasthan	431	1.5	3177	10.9	1144	3.9	258	0.9	398	1.4	230	0.8
18	Tamil Nadu	343	2.3	6074	10.6	6589	11.5	1250	2.2	880	1.5	999	1.7

1	2	27	28	29	30	31	32	33	34	35	36	37	38
19	Tripura	5	0.6	62	7.7	23	2.8	19	2.3	4	0.5	6	0.7
20	Uttar Pradesh	2157	4.0	5809	10.9	3806	7.1	1153	2.2	1097	2.1	1037	1.9
21	West Bengal	1398	3.0	8174	17.8	4090	8.9	1444	3.1	1043	2.3	751	1.6
22	Sikkim	0	0.0	1	1.5	0	0.0	4	6.1	0	0.0	3	4.5
23	Andaman & Nicobar	1	0.3	12	3.7	3	0.9	0	0.0	4	1.2	1	0.3
24	Arunachal Pradesh	0	0.0	13	4.0	0	0.0	0	0.0	2	0.6	0	0.0
25	Chandigarh	117	8.9	374	28.5	234	17.9	77	5.9	25	1.9	27	2.1
26	Dadra & Nagar Haveli	4	2.7	25	16.8	6	4.0	5	3.4	2	1.3	8	5.4
27	Delhi	812	8.1	1177	11.7	842	8.4	1289	12.8	787	7.8	443	4.4
28	Goa	25	0.9	323	11.7	51	1.8	91	3.3	47	1.7	22	0.8
29	Mizoram	1	0.1	38	4.1	1	0.1	3	0.3	4	0.4	6	0.7
30	Pondicherry	21	1.7	104	8.5	77	6.3	37	3.0	43	3.5	28	2.3
31	Daman & Diu	5	3.4	9	6.1	11	7.5	4	2.7	2	1.4	1	0.7
	Total	14937	2.6	65868	11.3	40802	7.0	12283	2.1	11325	1.9	8852	1.5

Table 6.15 contd........

S.No.	States/UTs	Industry Group (At 2 digit NIC Level) 97 No. of Units	97 % to Total	99 No. of Units	99 % to Total	Other Services No. of Units	Other Services % to Total	All Industries No. of Units	All Industries % to Total
1	2	39	40	41	42	43	44	45	46
1	Andhra Pradesh	4889	12.5	283	0.7	129	0.3	39210	100.0
2	Assam	519	11.7	32	0.7	1	0.0	4430	100.0
3	Bihar	6655	19.1	461	1.3	14	0.0	34822	100.0
4	Gujarat	3833	11.1	716	2.1	20	0.1	34453	100.0
5	Haryana	5861	25.1	365	1.6	6	0.0	23356	100.0
6	Himachal Pradesh	591	8.5	127	1.8	6	0.1	6983	100.0
7	Jammu & Kashmir	1467	16.2	238	2.6	9	0.1	9080	100.0
8	Karnataka	5041	12.4	890	2.2	87	0.2	40525	100.0
9	Kerala	2124	8.3	154	0.6	10	0.0	25717	100.0
10	Madhya Pradesh	13153	17.8	1663	2.3	38	0.1	73892	100.0
11	Maharashtra	950	3.2	611	2.0	34	0.1	29856	100.0
12	Manipur	132	6.4	41	2.0	2	0.1	2078	100.0
13	Meghalaya	77	13.1	3	0.5	1	0.2	587	100.0
14	Nagaland	12	6.6	2	1.1	0	0.0	183	100.0
15	Orissa	523	6.3	104	1.3	7	0.1	8287	100.0
16	Punjab	13202	29.1	475	1.0	34	0.1	45339	100.0
17	Rajasthan	4469	15.4	207	0.7	9	0.0	29043	100.0
18	Tamil Nadu	4117	7.2	1565	2.7	169	0.3	57213	100.0

1	2	39	40	41	42	43	44	45	46
19	Tripura	86	10.6	3	0.4	0	0.0	809	100.0
20	Uttar Pradesh	5954	11.2	769	1.4	13	0.0	53282	100.0
21	West Bengal	6150	13.4	249	0.5	5	0.0	45954	100.0
22	Sikkim	2	3.0	3	4.5	0	0.0	66	100.0
23	Andaman & Nicobar	71	22.0	1	0.3	1	0.3	323	100.0
24	Arunachal Pradesh	14	4.3	1	0.3	0	0.0	326	100.0
25	Chandigarh	48	3.7	8	0.6	2	0.2	1310	100.0
26	Dadra & Nagar Haveli	6	4.0	4	2.7	0	0.0	149	100.0
27	Delhi	116	1.2	86	0.9	8	0.1	10038	100.0
28	Goa	162	5.8	90	3.2	5	0.2	2772	100.0
29	Mizoram	106	11.6	18	2.0	1	0.1	917	100.0
30	Pondicherry	80	6.6	31	2.5	2	0.2	1221	100.0
31	Daman & Diu	2	1.4	6	4.1	0	0.0	147	100.0
	Total	80412	13.8	9206	1.6	613	0.1	582368	100.0

Source: Report on the Second All India Census of Small Scale Industrial Units, Development Commissioner.

Table 6.16: Distribution of Production by States/UTs & Industry Groups (2 Digit NIC Level) and their Percentages

S.No	State/UTs	Industry Groups (At 2 digit NIC Level)											
		20 & 21		22		23		24		25		26	
		Production	% to Total	Production	% to Total	Production	% to Total	Production	% to Total	Production	% to Total	Production	%to Total
1	2	3	4	5	6	7	8	9	10	11	12	13	14
1	Andhra Pradesh	169120	18.02	18462	39.08	1285	4.28	159	0.62	248	4.39	1454	0.66
2	Assam	10971	1.17	47	0.10	9	0.03	0	0.00	0	0.00	797	0.36
3	Bihar	12142	1.29	229	0.48	281	0.94	23	0.09	64	1.13	1456	0.66
4	Gujarat	35935	3.83	400	0.85	624	2.08	533	2.07	239	4.23	11940	5.41
5	Haryana	54082	5.76	777	1.64	823	2.74	133	0.52	69	1.22	4126	1.87
6	Himachal Pradesh	5370	0.57	32	0.07	26	0.09	256	0.99	76	1.35	584	0.26
7	Jammu & Kashmir	77[illegible]7	0.82	22	0.05	32	0.11	21	0.08	0	0.00	1186	0.54
8	Karnataka	71570	7.63	6094	12.90	640	2.13	101	0.39	28	0.50	5819	2.64
9	Kerala	44836	4.78	572	1.21	352	1.17	2	0.01	3	0.05	2384	1.08
10	Madhya Pradesh	64174	6.84	1245	2.64	177	0.59	133	0.52	194	3.43	4815	2.18
11	Maharashtra	90460	9.64	5187	10.98	3125	10.40	11875	46.04	400	7.08	35825	16.23
12	Manipur	490	0.05	2	0.00	0	0.00	0	0.00	0	0.00	239	0.11
13	Meghalaya	882	0.09	0	0.00	0	0.00	0	0.00	0	0.00	32	0.01
14	Nagaland	1450	0.15	0	0.00	0	0.00	0	0.00	0	0.00	21	0.01
15	Orissa	31217	3.33	680	1.44	159	0.53	0	0.00	77	1.36	592	0.27
16	Punjab	58322	6.21	42	0.09	5000	16.64	2489	9.65	125	2.21	17961	8.14
17	Rajasthan	48200	5.14	1106	2.34	506	1.68	847	3.28	140	2.48	2210	1.00
18	Tamil Nadu	102767	10.95	3855	8.16	14231	47.36	6452	25.01	577	10.22	58781	26.63

1	2	3	4	5	6	7	8	9	10	11	12	13	14
19	Tripura	1050	0.11	3	0.01	0	0.00	0	0.00	0	0.00	4	0.00
20	Uttar Pradesh	73546	7.84	4484	9.49	1587	5.28	723	2.80	659	11.67	9393	4.25
21	West Bengal	35126	3.74	1991	4.21	264	0.88	841	3.26	2500	44.26	18836	8.53
22	Sikkim	125	0.01	0	0.00	0	0.00	0	0.00	0	0.00	4	0.00
23	Andaman & Nicobar	198	0.02	10	0.02	0	0.00	0	0.00	0	0.00	1	0.00
24	Arunachal Pradesh	221	0.02	0	0.00	0	0.00	0	0.00	0	0.00	24	0.01
25	Chandigarh	945	0.10	2	0.00	0	0.00	20	0.08	2	0.04	35	0.02
26	Dadra & Nagar Haveli	159	0.02	0	0.00	0	0.00	0	0.00	0	0.00	0	0.00
27	Delhi	8777	0.94	461	0.98	806	2.68	1118	4.33	163	2.89	40842	18.50
28	Goa	3768	0.40	1037	2.19	73	0.24	31	0.12	84	1.49	997	0.45
29	Mizoram	199	0.02	3	0.01	0	0.00	0	0.00	0	0.00	250	0.11
30	Pondicerry	3649	0.39	354	0.75	51	0.17	37	0.14	0	0.00	88	0.04
31	Daman & Diu	1043	0.11	150	0.32	0	0.00	0	0.00	0	0.00	60	0.03

Table 6.15 contd........

S.No.	States/UTs	27 No. of Units	27 % to Total	28 No. of Units	28 % to Total	29 No. of Units	29 % to Total	30 No. of Units	30 % to Total	31 No. of Units	31 % to Total	32 No. of Units	32 %to Total
		Industry Groups (At 2 digit NIC Level)											
1	2	15	16	17	18	19	20	21	22	23	24	25	26
1	Andhra Pradesh	32757	17.26	8530	4.95	2306	2.25	23632	9.30	27741	5.26	13640	7.71
2	Assam	4725	2.49	225	0.13	22	0.02	2083	0.82	1287	0.24	1644	0.93
3	Bihar	6614	3.48	4028	2.34	1366	1.33	10483	4.12	4826	0.92	10892	6.16
4	Gujarat	11086	5.84	15803	9.17	340	0.33	27229	10.71	74719	14.17	14132	7.99
5	Haryana	5512	2.90	1341	0.78	1289	1.26	7462	2.94	32768	6.21	4492	2.54
6	Himachal Pradesh	2353	1.24	384	0.22	113	0.11	1255	0.49	1820	0.35	1395	0.79
7	Jammu & Kashmir	5907	3.11	978	0.57	412	0.40	831	0.33	1665	0.32	1145	0.65
8	Karnataka	12817	6.75	28960	16.81	3800	3.70	13819	5.44	18582	3.52	8083	4.57
9	Kerala	17577	9.26	5220	3.03	218	0.21	10360	4.08	8666	1.64	5616	3.18
10	Madhya Pradesh	16625	8.76	4643	2.70	1551	1.51	11793	4.64	12604	2.39	13286	7.51
11	Maharashtra	18844	9.93	33281	19.32	4853	4.73	51588	20.30	146571	27.80	33495	18.94
12	Manipur	933	0.49	73	0.04	14	0.01	181	0.07	67	0.01	310	0.18
13	Meghalaya	631	0.33	84	0.05	15	0.01	119	0.05	2	0.00	420	0.24
14	Nagaland	9232	4.86	32	0.02	3	0.00	19	0.01	4	0.00	44	0.02
15	Orissa	2902	1.53	1482	0.86	187	0.18	2855	1.12	3715	0.70	3300	1.87
16	Punjab	3708	1.95	3478	2.02	20931	20.40	8710	3.43	12437	2.36	2767	1.57
17	Rajasthan	2803	1.48	2566	1.49	345	0.34	4500	1.77	21867	4.15	20813	11.77
18	Tamil Nadu	6299	3.32	22147	12.86	34913	34.03	20903	8.22	47805	9.07	9774	5.53

1	2	15	16	17	18	19	20	21	22	23	24	25	26
19	Tripura	529	0.28	51	0.03	3	0.00	116	0.05	51	0.01	597	0.34
20	Uttar Pradesh	7889	4.16	13863	8.05	18743	18.27	16806	6.61	34101	6.47	20278	11.47
21	West Bengal	12973	6.83	9894	5.74	6757	6.59	13318	5.24	34359	6.52	6491	3.67
22	Sikkim	5	0.00	24	0.01	15	0.01	210	0.08	577	0.11	38	0.02
23	Andaman & Nicobar	423	0.22	32	0.02	0	0.00	23	0.01	0	0.00	52	0.03
24	Arunachal Pradesh	2172	1.14	0	0.00	0	0.00	14	0.01	4	0.00	64	0.04
25	Chandigarh	372	0.20	726	0.42	167	0.16	870	0.34	983	0.19	458	0.26
26	Dadra & Nagar Haveli	45	0.02	355	0.21	49	0.05	1065	0.42	2994	0.57	233	0.13
27	Delhi	2487	1.31	12091	7.02	4074	3.97	20637	8.12	24126	4.58	2053	1.16
28	Goa	1061	0.56	867	0.50	14	0.01	1610	0.63	3342	0.63	1033	0.58
29	Mizoram	265	0.14	124	0.07	1	0.00	81	0.03	0	0.00	90	0.05
30	Pondicherry	229	0.12	906	0.53	80	0.08	933	0.37	9162	1.74	147	0.08
31	Daman & Diu	28	0.01	71	0.04	0	0.00	665	0.26	423	0.08	22	0.01

S.No.	States/UTs	Industry Groups (At 2 digit NIC Level) 33		34		35		36		37		38	
		Production	% to Total	Production	% to Total	Production	% to Total	Production	% to Total	Production	% to Total	Production	%to Total
1	2	27	28	29	30	31	32	33	34	35	36	37	38
1	Andhra Pradesh	17040	3.80	15934	4.41	8433	3.41	13434	5.17	3746	3.44	1441	1.83
2	Assam	2352	0.52	3310	0.92	600	0.24	885	0.34	429	0.39	28	0.04
3	Bihar	8636	1.93	7818	2.16	2341	0.95	2844	1.09	2690	2.47	542	0.69
4	Gujarat	51379	11.46	23361	6.46	51141	20.67	19855	7.64	6911	6.35	7045	8.92
5	Haryana	22807	5.08	16521	4.57	8480	3.43	5669	2.18	4401	4.04	1924	2.44
6	Himachal Pradesh	4567	1.02	2098	0.58	397	0.16	2827	1.09	195	0.18	236	0.30
7	Jammu & Kashmir	617	0.14	5535	1.53	349	0.14	723	0.28	202	0.19	1081	1.37
8	Karnataka	14317	3.19	31299	8.66	12274	4.96	13247	5.10	4279	3.93	2043	2.59
9	Kerala	1887	0.42	7128	1.97	1945	0.79	2495	0.96	953	0.88	680	0.86
10	Madhya Pradesh	29082	6.48	14895	4.12	5303	2.14	8227	3.17	2120	1.95	726	0.92
11	Maharashtra	7236[illegible]	16.13	77452	21.42	56995	23.03	51393	19.78	21223	19.49	26106	33.07
12	Manipur	3	0.00	198	0.05	2	0.00	260	0.10	63	0.06	6	0.01
13	Megalaya	50	0.01	154	0.04	0	0.00	127	0.05	5	0.00	9	0.01
14	Nagaland	[illegible]	0.00	275	0.08	0	0.00	129	0.05	8	0.01	2	0.00
15	Orissa	9393	2.09	4125	1.14	1454	0.59	1953	0.75	374	0.34	108	0.14
16	Punjab	58554	13.06	22858	6.32	22136	8.95	4911	1.89	24208	22.23	4529	5.74
17	Rajasthan	14302	3.19	10310	2.85	3969	1.60	5461	2.10	1776	1.63	1437	1.82
18	Tamil Nadu	25477	5.68	29438	8.14	24513	9.91	24337	9.37	8211	7.54	4252	5.39
19	Tripura	143	0.03	236	0.07	14	0.01	51	0.02	11	0.01	5	0.01

1	2	27	28	29	30	31	32	33	34	35	36	37	38
20	Uttar Pradesh	37969	8.47	39914	11.04	18925	7.65	32341	12.45	824	7.55	14932	18.91
21	West Bengal	35138	7.83	26911	7.44	14154	5.72	15095	5.81	7797	7.16	3757	4.76
22	Sikkim	0	0.00	2	0.00	0	0.00	50	0.02	0	0.00	96	0.12
23	Andaman & Nicobar	0	0.00	67	0.02	7	0.00	0	0.00	26	0.02	0	0.00
24	Arunachal Pradesh	0	0.00	68	0.02	0	0.00	0	0.00	2	0.00	0	0.00
25	Chandigarh	2377	0.53	2545	0.70	1777	0.72	1302	0.50	300	0.28	137	0.17
26	Dadra & Nagar Haveli	110	0.02	324	0.09	81	0.03	406	0.16	3	0.00	206	0.26
27	Delhi	39161	8.73	17047	4.71	11633	4.70	49910	19.21	9617	8.83	6056	7.67
28	Goa	230	0.05	897	0.25	317	0.13	1184	0.46	546	0.50	1446	1.83
29	Mizoram	1	0.00	82	0.02	0	0.00	126	0.05	23	0.02	6	0.01
30	Pondicherry	371	0.08	612	0.17	167	0.07	442	0.17	566	0.52	94	0.12
31	Daman & Diu	187	0.04	164	0.05	21	0.01	181	0.07	0	0.00	23	0.03

Table 6.16 contd........

S.No.	States/UTs	97 Produc-tion	97 % to Total	99 Produc-tion	99 % to Total	Other Services Produc-tion	Other Services % to Total	All Industries Produc-tion	All Industries % to Total
		Industry Group (At 2 digit NIC Level)							
1	2	39	40	41	42	43	44	45	46
1	Andhra Pradesh	2369	5.36	90	3.32	7584	14.01	369405	8.60
2	Assam	706	1.60	9	0.33	106	0.20	30235	0.70
3	Bihar	2998	6.79	79	2.91	7429	13.72	87781	2.04
4	Gujarat	3187	7.22	130	4.79	2636	4.87	358625	8.35
5	Haryana	2445	5.54	3	0.11	268	2.34	176392	4.10
6	Himachal Pradesh	259	0.59	10	0.37	266	0.49	24519	0.57
7	Jammu & Kashmir	899	2.04	9	0.33	974	1.80	30305	0.71
8	Karnataka	2831	6.41	246	9.07	1838	3.39	252687	5.88
9	Kerala	1739	3.94	29	1.07	980	1.81	113692	2.65
10	Madhya Pradesh	2968	6.72	78	2.88	2096	3.87	197635	4.58
11	Maharashtra	4939	11.18	541	19.95	4666	8.62	751180	17.48
12	Manipur	93	0.21	8	0.29	44	0.08	2986	0.07
13	Meghalaya	148	0.34	1	0.04	24	0.04	2703	0.06
14	Nagaland	15	0.03	0	0.00	15	0.03	11249	0.26
15	Orissa	541	1.22	7	0.26	613	1.13	65734	1.53
16	Punjab	3354	7.59	25	0.92	1097	2.03	277642	6.46
17	Rajasthan	1988	4.50	32	1.18	398	1.66	146076	3.40
18	Tamil Nadu	2989	6.77	912	33.63	2367	4.93	451300	10.50
19	Tripura	81	0.18	0	0.00	9	0.02	2959	0.07

1	2	39	40	41	42	43	44	45	46
20	Uttar Pradesh	3621	8.20	33	1.22	14674	27.10	372705	8.67
21	West Bengal	4022	9.11	59	2.18	2722	5.03	253005	5.89
22	Sikkim	0	0.00	0	0.00	11	0.02	1157	0.03
23	Andaman & Nicobar	51	0.12	3	0.11	2	0.00	895	0.02
24	Arunachal Pradesh	53	0.12	0	0.00	0	0.00	2622	0.06
25	Chandigarh	53	0.12	24	0.88	43	0.08	13138	0.31
26	Dadra & Nagar Haveli	3	0.01	0	0.00	4	0.01	6037	0.14
27	Delhi	514	1.16	256	9.44	1235	2.28	253064	5.89
28	Goa	1043	2.36	122	4.50	174	0.32	19876	0.46
29	Mizoram	200	0.45	0	0.00	17	0.03	1468	0.03
30	Pondicherry	54	0.12	6	0.22	50	0.09	17998	0.42
31	Daman & Diu	1	0.00	0	0.00	2	0.00	3041	0.07

Source : Report on the Second All India Census of Small Scale Industrial Units, Development Commissioner.

Section C

Policy

7

Problems of Small Scale Units

As seen in the pregoing analysis, it has been accepted by economists and policy formulations all over the world that there is a rationale for the existence and encouragement of small scale units in the industrial set up of both developed, developing and under-developed economies, specially the ones which have surplus labour force.

However, it has also been realised, that the small scale entrepreneur faces problems in the process of setting up business and growth, which differ in nature as well as magnitude from those of large scale business.

Problems of Small Scale Enterprises in India

The problems generally faced by small scale entrepreneurs in India in the process of setting up and running their units, can be summed up under the following heads:

(1) Finance: Large units raise their finances by public subscription, equity and other securities, which are available for major capital investment without repayment liability and interest. Over and above this, an investment allowance, development rebate, depreciation etc. are also permitted, which help in developing a sound financial base by generating such reserves.

As against this, a small entrepreneur receives finance assistance for capital investment on which he immediately starts paying interest at substantially high rate. Sometimes, even the working capital is eroded during the course of a year, in the repayment of loan and interest. Such units need at least five to seven years to come out of this initial commitment and therefore find it difficult to develop or expand.

The financial problems of the small entrepreneurs can be summed up under the following heads:

(a) Inadequacy of fixed and working capital.

(b) Lack of collateral security/guarantor for raising loans.

(c) Unorganised finance sector offering loans at higher rates of interest.

(d) Inadequate loans financed by organised sector.

(e) Higher repayment instalments, or shorter repayment period for loans.

(f) Elaborate procedures and forms required to be filled by entrepreneurs for obtaining loans involving undue delay.

(2) Land/Buildings: Non-availability of land/buildings, particularly in industrial estates, is another problem faced by the small scale entrepreneurship. Even where these are available, the premises are often unsatisfactory and congested.

(3) Labour: The problems faced by the small scale units with regard to labour can be summed up under the following heads:

(a) Non-availability of skilled workers

(b) High real cost of labour

(c) Insecurity arising out of an exodus of labour to large firms.

(4) Marketing: While the number of small scale units and their production has gone up it has come to light that marketing of the products is creating a number of problems which can broadly be classified under the following heads:

(a) Inability to compete with large scale sector manufacturing similar products for a wider consumer market.

(b) Lack of appropriate product information and engineering support to manufacture products of the specified quality within reasonable time and cost.

(c) Lack of guidance to reach conventional market channels

and establish new channels for marketing.

(d) Lack of adequate support from larger organizations purchasing products of the small scale units, or through subcontracting by the large organizations.

(e) Inability of small scale units to reach export market on their own due to lack of adequate resources.

(f) Lack of adequate inputs of the required quality to manufacture product of the type in demand and according to the required specification.

(g) In case of a change in design of the product of a large scale unit which has ancillaries, the latter are left high and dry because of adequate technical and financial support to implement the required change in the components.

In all these areas, while government adopted certain measures to extend support to small scale units, the existing arrangement and coverage is inadequate having regard to the wide dispersal of engineering industry and the variety of products made by it. Though state level agencies like small Industries corporations are expected to play a role in market promotion, so far their activities seem to have been confined only to distribution of raw materials and, in some cases, procurement of goods required by government departments or agencies. It is, therefore, necessary that these corporations are fully developed with adequate professional and managerial talent to be able to afford extensive marketing support to the small scale units.

Another problem is that though government has reserved a number of items for exclusive purchase from small scale units, the purchasing agencies try to find some faults or the other to make purchases of specified items from such units. It has also come to light that certain state government departments are insisting on earnest money and security deposits even if such firms are registered with DGS&D and NSIC.

(5) Raw Materials: There is lack of adequate quantities and of good quality raw materials. The most important raw materials for engineering industry in the small scale sector are iron and steel and non-ferrous metals. With regard to supply of iron and steel, our inquiries reveal that the system of distribution is defective and the quantities earmarked are also inadequate for this sector. It has been reported that in a number of cases small scale units have hardly been given 10 tonnes of iron or steel in a period of six months. With this meagre tonnage these units cannot function economically.

In regard to non-ferrous metals, while the supply position of copper, zinc and lead appears to be quite satisfactory, it is not so in the case of aluminium.

Though the government has been importing to meet the gap between demand and supply, procedural delays hinder timely and adequate delivery. For commercial grade indigenous aluminium, there is no system for ensuring that the needs of the small scale units, particularly those producing articles of mass consumption like utensils etc. are met on a priority basis.

The government has adopted a policy of giving preference for small scale units in the matter of supply of raw materials required for execution of government orders. Small units are unable to take advantage of this scheme in the absence of matching support, as the present system does not ensure automatic supply of raw materials. Even those units that take orders, fail to meet the delivery commitments for no fault of theirs, resulting in penalties and loss of future business.

Besides, as prices of finished products are fixed as the basis of controlled prices of raw materials, the small scale units can never afford to buy inputs in the open market to meet delivery commitments, as they have no means of spreading the additional cost over a larger output, as in the case of larger units.

(6) Modernisation, Quality Control and Standardisation: Small scale industrial units in the engineering industry face problems of modernization, quality control and standardization. The engineering industry has immense potential to produce a variety of goods, but is unable to keep abreast with product design technological changes because of the above mentioned handicap.

Small units do not have trained engineers, R & D experts and quality control experts on their rolls due to lack of finances.

For consistency in the quality of the products, it is essential that there is strict control on the quality of the raw material as well as on the finished products. Non-availability of certificates for quality of inputs from government organizations is another problem.

There is no support for designs to small scale units e.g. machine tools and equipment building industry.

Though quality testing facilities have been provided by the government in certain industrial estates, small scale units are not able to avail of these facilities, due to lack of quality consciousness on their part.

The present coverage of products manufactured by small scale units under the 959 standards, is far from adequate.

(7) Power Failures: Frequent power failures and cuts are also affecting the efficiency of small scale units. Irregular power supply prevents full utilization of capacity and raises cost of production. Their individual power consumption is small. Therefore captive generation of power by installing their own generation sets is uneconomical.

Problems of Ancillary Development

While the Industrial Policy emphasizes economic federalism giving due emphasis to the growth of small scale units, in actual practice there is no mechanism by which products and services that can be efficiently made available by small units/ancillaries can be built into the production programmes of large scale industrial units.

A common problem faced by ancillaries is, that there is no continuing assurance of demand from large units so as to enable them to plan full utilization of their capacity. There is no legal compulsion on the large scale unit to continue to buy from the ancillary units, which can free itself from the arrangement any time it wants.

Another problem is lack of adequate support to existing ancillaries to modernize their product line to suit the changing need of the 'mother' unit. Capacities built-in the small scale units should not be rendered idle due to lack of modernization. Obligations of 'mother' unit in this regard should be spelt out and enforced.

Contractual obligations between 'mother' unit and ancillaries and generally between large scale and small scale units, should be subjected to certain norms of Fair Trade, specially with regard to timely payment of the dues of the small units, assistance in procurement of raw materials, and equitable arrangements for inspection of goods.

Problems Faced by Small Scale Units in Chandigarh

Some of the common problems faced by the small scale units in Chandigarh which came to light in the course of interviews conducted with some small scale entrepreneurs are given below:

(1) In Setting up Industry: The most common and critical problem faced in setting up an industry is of space availability. Development of plots/sheds in Industrial Areas is too slow. Besides, most of the sheds in Industrial Area I were allotted to persons who were not even remotely connected with industries. The sheds/plots which were allotted in Industrial Area II almost two years ago are still under development/construction. This space shortage has resulted in steep hike in rent of sheds.

(2) Finance: The following problems in borrowing from commercial banks were highlighted:

(a) Arranging 25 per cent margin money of the amount of loan sought, is the biggest problem.

(b) Arranging a guarantor for bank loan is also a problem, as the guarantor should have either a good business record with that Bank, or he should have immovable property/fixed deposit equivalent to the amount of the loan plus the required margin. A guarantor is required for even working capital loan.

(c) Time taken for sanctioning necessary loan is inordinate.

(d) Working capital loan is sanctioned for a period of one year and contract is renewed every year, depending upon the previous year's balance sheet. So if a small scale unit has not done well in the previous year due to some reasons, then getting working capital from banks is a big problem.

(3) Raw Material: Availability of general type of raw material is not a problem, but special category raw material, like special alloy steel, special sizes of angles, flats rounds etc. take six to eight weeks' time to get, as almost the entire supply is from Delhi only.

The quantity and quality of raw materials is not a problem. As raw material to Chandigarh is supplied from Delhi and other places, its cost goes up since it attracts Central Sales Tax.

(4) Power Supply: Though power supply position is satisfactory in so far as there are no erratic power cuts as in other surrounding areas (e.g. Panchkula), getting new power connection or increasing connected load is very difficult in Chandigarh. Waiting period for new connection/connected load increase is more than two years.

(5) Marketing and Demand: Most of the small scale units of Chandigarh are dependent upon the three large tractor manufacturers in the near vicinity, via Punjab Tractors Limited, Hindustan Machine Tools and Eicher Tractors. Any slump in demand for tractors or harvestor combines, immediately reflects on the working or affects the survival of these small scale units.

(6) Labour: There is a shortage of skilled labour which has raised their wage rate considerably. Unskilled and semi-skilled labour is available in plenty. But most of these labourers are migratory in character, coming from neighbouring states. These labourers cannot be depended upon for continuity of employment as they often go on long leave and sometimes do not return. The problem of this type of labour has specially become acute in recent times under a climate of political and social insecurity.

(7) Facility in Industrial Area: There is no labour colony near the Industrial Area, with the result that the workers have to come from far off places. This sometimes affects regularity of attendance.

(8) Government Agencies: The following problems were highlighted with regard to their dealings with government agencies:

(a) Government agencies give loans only for plant and machinery. No loan is available for working capital.

(b) Since government agencies are offering need money/capital subsidies only in notified backward areas, small scale units in Chandigarh are not benefited.

(c) Procedural formalities are very cumbersome. This includes disbursements of loans in instalments after government agencies' Inspecting Officers submit report of completion of a part of the project for which instalment was released.

Even though rate of interest of agency loan is lower than Bank loans, small industrialists perferred commercial banks to government agencies because of the reasons explained above.

In fact, all the units surveyed in the Industrial Area, Chandigarh, with regard to the role of the government had obtained loans only from commercial banks.

With regard to other facilities offered by government agencies, e.g. supply of raw meterial or toolroom facilites etc. one fact seemed to emerge that those entrepreneurs who had good educational background and social standing were fully satisfied with the facilities offered. However, those who were not well placed educationally and socially, faced some problems in availing of these facilities. One or two even pointed out that there was no toolroom facility available in Chandigarh, when actually there is such a facility available and is being availed of by the others. Another entrepreneur pointed out that there was irregularity in the supply of raw materials.

One thing that seemed to emerge in the course of the survey was the apathy on the part of the institutions towards maintenance of records and lack of co-ordination in the functions.

Suggestions

The units interviewed came forward with some suggestions to meet these problems:

(1) New industrial plots/sheds should be developed by the government and allotted to genuine entrepreneurs on the condition that they will start the unit within six months from the date of allotment of the plot/shed.

(2) New electrical connections and new load sanctions should be given within three months from the date of application.

Problems Faced by the Ancillary Units in Chandigarh with Regard to Their Linkage

Some of the ancillary units of Chandigarh were also interviewed and their problems with regard to their linkage with 'parent' unit ascertained. The problems highlighted by them are given below:

(1) The price of a component manufactured by an ancillary unit is fixed by the parent unit and it becomes binding for the year even if there is a steep rise in the prices of basic inputs like power, coal and steel. Because of this, ancillaries sometimes have to face a loss also.

(2) All the ancillaries are captive units, with their supply tied up to the parent unit only.

Suggestions

Some suggestions made to solve the problems faced by them were—

(1) Prices of components should be reviewed from time to time to mutual advantage.

(2) Inspection at the ancillary premises should be final and there should not be any rejection by the parent unit after that.

(3) 'Parent' unit should also give technical assistance for manufacturing jigs and fixtures etc. for the component.

(4) In the case of a new unit, 'Parent' unit should provide help in getting loans for setting up the unit.

(5) More than one ancillary unit should not be developed for the same component unless the first unit is unable to meet the increased demand of the 'parent' unit.

Closed Units

A considerable insight into the problems of the SSUs and their implications can be had from a study of the closed units.

According to the Second All India Census of SSUs, 3.05 lakh units were found to be closed during the census enumeration process. Over 50% of these had closed down before 1986. Approximately 79,000 units were reported closed during 1987-88. However, it is quite possible that these units may have been facing temporary closure with a good possibility of revival.

The highest percentage (13.9%) of the closed units belonged to the metal products industry. Next came food products (11.4%), repair service (9.6%) hosiery and garments (8.4%) and wood products (7.8%).

Urban areas accounted for 51.4% of closed units and rural areas 35.7%. 12.9% were in Metropolitan areas.

Amongst states, Uttar Pradesh accounted for 72.4% of closed units, West Bengal 12%, Tamil Nadu 8.2%, Punjab 7.2%, Haryana 7%, Gujarat 6.3% and Rajasthan 5.8%.

Of the total units closed as on 31.3.88, the last year for which the data is available, about 27.8% had closed down within 3 years of going into production. Another 21.6% had closed within 3-5 years. The remaining about 50% had a life span of about 5 years or more.

More than the number of closed units, the reasons for their closure are a reflection of the problems they face.

Financial problems were reported to be the reason for closure for a large percentage (35%) of units. This was more or less the case in every industry. This brings out the magnitude of the problem, and focuses on the need for special policy measures in the field.

In the case of 14.4% of the units, marketing problem was stated as the reason for closure, and here also the industry wise pattern was almost the same. Non availability of raw materials was stated as the reason for closure by 5.6% of units and 2.2% were stated to be closed due to labour problems. 19% reported more than one of the above reasons for closure, while 16% are reported to be closed for reasons other than the ones mentioned above.

Table 7.1: Distribution of Closed Units Yearwise At 2 Digit NIC Industry Group

NIC 2-Digit Code	Broad Industry Group with Description	Number of units closed in the area							
		Metropolitan		Urban		Rural		Total	%age to Total
		No.	% to total	No.	% to total	No.	% to total		
1	2	3	4	5	6	7	8	9	10
21 & 20	Food Products	1351	3.5	16592	10.7	16383	15.2	34326	11.39
22	Beverages, Tobacco & Tobacco	P85	0.2	993	0.6	989	0.9	2067	0.69
23	Cotton Textiles	131	0.3	542	0.4	232	0.2	905	0.30
24	Wool, Silk & Synth. Fibre Text	82	0.2	407	0.3	184	0.2	673	0.22
25	Jute, Hemp and Mesta Textiles	62	0.2	128	0.1	41	0.0	231	0.08
26	Hosiery and Garments	2943	7.6	10035	6.5	12218	11.3	25196	8.36
27	Wood Products	1283	3.3	10727	6.9	11568	10.7	23578	7.82
28	Paper Products & Printing	3837	9.9	7614	4.9	1829	1.7	13280	4.41
29	Leather Products	1435	3.7	4986	3.2	6894	6.4	13315	4.42
30	Rubber & Plastic Products	3880	10.0	11411	7.4	4821	4.5	20112	6.67
31	Chemical & Chemical Products	4110	10.6	12244	7.9	6715	6.2	23069	7.65
32	Non-metallic Mineral Products	1134	2.9	8492	5.5	10699	9.9	20325	6.74
33	Basic Metal Industries	1980	5.1	6223	4.0	1350	1.3	9553	3.17
34	Metal Products	5639	14.5	24592	15.9	11498	10.7	41729	13.85
35	Machinery & Parts Except Elect.	4285	11.0	12402	8.0	3313	3.1	20000	6.64
36	Electrical Machinery & Parts	2445	6.3	4141	2.7	991	0.9	7577	2.51
37	Transport Equipments & Parts	1073	2.8	3589	2.3	1211	1.1	5873	1.95
38	Miscellaneous Mfrg Industries	1145	2.9	3338	2.2	1281	1.2	5764	1.91
97	Repair Services	1238	3.2	13690	8.8	13938	12.9	28866	9.58
99	Services not elsewhere Classif.	44	0.1	137	0.1	33	0.0	214	0.07
OT	Other Services and Groups(CO)	762	2.0	2499	1.6	1476	1.4	4737	1.57
Total		38944	100.0	154782	100.0	107664	100.0	301390	100.0

DISTRIBUTION OF CLOSED UNITS
LOCATIONWISE

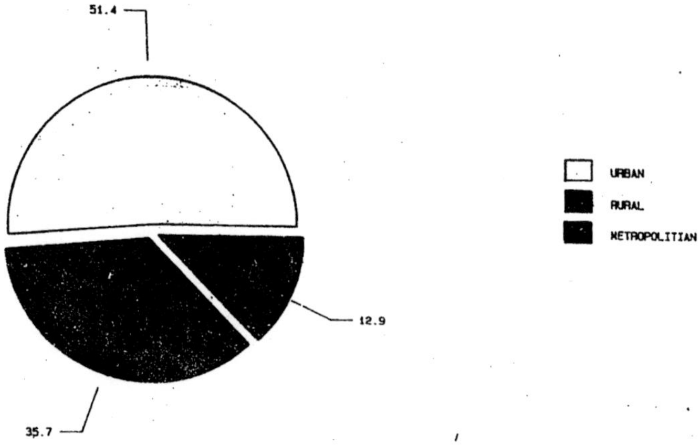

REASONS FOR CLOSURE OF UNITS

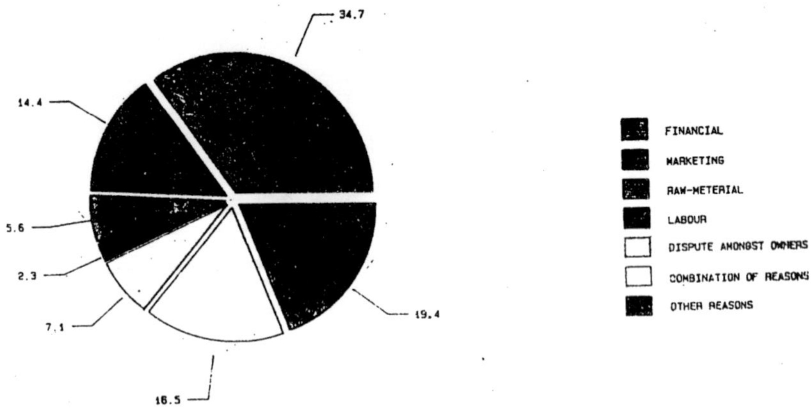

Table 7.2: Year-wise Closure of Units and Reasons for Closure

	Reasons for Closure	Number of Units Closed During									
		Upto 1980	1981	1982	1983	1984	1985	1986	1987	1988	Total
	-	2	3	4	5	6	7	8	9	10	11
1	Labour Problems	968	196	368	421	587	986	1333	1102	816	6777
2	Dispute Amongst Owners	1798	375	601	761	1260	1599	2110	1694	834	11023
3	Raw Material Problem	2516	541	1087	1116	1693	2499	3531	2804	1223	17010
4	Finance Problem	10901	3993	5594	6193	10443	16426	22247	19345	9526	104668
5	Marketing Problem	4237	1059	2189	2360	4340	6219	9814	8739	4494	43451
6	Natural Calamity	1477	363	625	523	1118	1435	2212	1719	783	10255
7	More than One Reasons (Combinations)	6768	1618	3389	2856	5873	7208	10682	7412	3932	49738
8	Others	8616	2269	3632	3847	6364	8788	10285	9414	5253	58468
	Total	37281	10414	17485	18077	31678	45160	62205	52229	26861	301390

8

Government Policy

An analysis of the handicaps and problems faced by the small entrepreneur at every stage of the business vis a vis a large entrepreneur, brings out the need for a positive policy by the government towards the small entrepreneur.

Due to unfair competition faced by the small entrepreneur in the absence of a supportive programme, a budding en trepreneur may experience failure even before he has been able to prove himself.

Moreover, certain inherent social benefits that are concom-mitant with the growth of SSUs, bring out the difference between social and private cost, a significant aspect in the formulation of government policy of intervention.

This intervention can take various forms depending on the social and economic goals towards which the intervention is directed. It can be both from supply side and demand side. The degree of intervention and the extent of discrimination between the small and the large will depend upon the nature of the market and the relative social advantage that the SSUs enjoy vis a vis the large scale units.

In recent years need for a positive policy towards the small scale sector has become stronger because of the magnitude of the problem of the educated unemployed. This has generated another rationale for protective intervention.

Government Programmes for Entrepreneurial Development in Small Scale Industry

It has been pointed out by Staley and Mores,[1] that in an underdeveloped country like India, while there is a comparative dearth of entrepreneurship, new entrants in the field face discouraging impediments on account of inadequate infrastructure.

It has now been generally accepted that entrepreneurship is not restricted to only those who are gifted with certain qualities. It can be developed. Towards this end programmes of entrepreneurial development have been taken up by most of the developing countries.

The major elements of entrepreneurial development are :

(a) Indentification

(b) Training

(c) Counselling

(d) Support—financial, fiscal and technical in setting and running a new enterprise.

A conceptual model worked out in SIET Institute, to categories the various activities of the organisations, has come out with three distinct categories:

(a) Stimulatory Activity

(b) Support Activity

(c) Sustaining Activity[2]

Stimulatory Activity refers to all such efforts that stimulate entrepreneurship in any society.

Support Activity refers to all such activities that help entrepreneurs in establishing and running their enterprises. This group of activities provides, nurtures and helps entrepreneurship to grow and survive after it has been stimulated.

Sustaining Activity: These activities are all those that help to ensure continued efficient and profitable functioning of an enterprise. After stimulation and establishment of a unit through adequate support, it may happen that a unit becomes sick, non-profitable, and non-viable due to many unforeseen and uncontrollable factors. Even well managed units may suffer closure for want of raw materials, non-availability of substitutes, lack of skilled hands, etc. Such casualties are comparative high in the small units than in the bigger ones. Accordingly, small entrepreneurs require a lot of sustaining activities by the promotional agencies.

Each activity discussed is important but it also supplements and interacts with the other two. The efforts to promote and develop entrepreneurship follow a cyclic form, i.e., it is imperative to have a certain amount of stimulatory activity, followed by an equal amount of support and sustaining activity.

In the absence of a balance, and when one is emphasised at the expense of another, e.g., if a promotional agency undertakes a programme for development of entrepreneurship and excessive emphasis is laid on stimulatory activity without creating a matching degree of support and sustaining activities, then the supply of entrepreneurs is no doubt accelerated, but soon they tend to get frustrated. This will discourage the succeeding group of entrepreneurs. Again the mortality rate of such units can rise. On the other hand, if excessive emphasis is laid on support activities, neglecting stimulatory and sustaining activities, the outcome will be of two types —

(a) Non-availability of entrepreneurship in a given region.

(b) An inflow of entrepreneurship into that region to avail of opportunities.

The first condition arises mainly because of lack of publicity of entrepreneurial opportunities and lack of local agencies to identify and train entrepreneurs.

A large number of units may be set up but the successful performance of these may be hampered because of lack of sustenance. Similarly, provision of sustaining activities, without matching degree of stimulatory and support activities, may result in lack of enough entrepreneurs to whom such services can be offered. Thus any planned efforts to develop entrepreneurship should balance these activities, to be fruitful.

These three activities can further be sub-divided as given in the chart below :

Various Sub-Activities Under Stimulatory, Support and Sustaining Activities

	Stimulatory	*Support*	*Sustaining*
1	Entrepreneurial education and planned publicity of entrepreneurial opportunity.	Registration of the unit	Modernisation
2.	Identification of potential entrepreneurship	Arrange finance for working and fixed capital for equipment	Diversification
3.	Motivational and inplant training to the entrepreneurs.	Provide land shed, power water, etc.	Expansion
4.	Help and guidance in selecting the product and preparing project reports	Help and guidance in obtaining and selecting machinery	Additional Financing for full capacity utilization
5.	Make available techno-economic information and feasible product profiles.	Supply scarce raw materials and/or import licences etc.	Defering repayments/ interest
6.	Evolve new products and processes suitable to local situation	Provide common facilities centres	Diagnostic industrial extension/ consultancy activities
7.	Train Officers to create local agencies for entrepreneurial counselling and promotion	Help in getting tax relief and other types of subsidy	Change/ modification in legislation/ policy for protecting recognition of enterprises

Cont.

	Stimulatory	*Support*	*Sustaining*
8.	Organise entrepreneurial forums	Other management consultancy including help in marketing the product.	Create new avenues for marketing.

It is generally seen that support and stimulatory activities are given greater emphasis than sustaining activities.

Indian Industrial Policies and Measures to Promote Small Enterprises

Traditional Small Scale and cottage industries had played an important role in the Indian economy before the industrial revolution. Manufactured goods such as Calicoes, muslin, metalware etc., had reached a high level of excellence and were in demand outside the Indian boundary also. The British rule, which exposed these industries to unfair competition from the budding mill sector of the west, saw their decline.

Interest in the handloom and other traditional industries again revived with the Swaraj movement and the patronage given to the 'Charkha' by Mahatma Gandhi.

The 2nd World War saw the growth of the mill sector in India, with the result the "Small" sector was exposed to competition from within the country also.

After independence, under government patronage, such industrial units again got a fillings. However, the policy towards the small scale sector has seen a dichotomy of opinion about the concept in the early stages of planning and even in early forties. In his introduction to the volume on rural and village industries, perpared by the National Planning Committee, T.K. Shah defined small scale industries as,

"Small Scale or Cottage industry may be defined to be an enterprise of a series of opreations carried on by a workman skilled in the craft on his own responsibility, the finished product of which he markets himself. He works in his own home with his own tools and materials.....these workers work mostly by hand labour and personal skill......He works, finally, for a market in the immediate neighbourhood, that is to say in response to known demand, with reference to quality as well as quantity. In contrast Pandit Jawaharlal Nehru, in a note to the NPC suggested in 1940, a three tier definition of Cottage, Small Scale and large industries, thus laying the foundation of the small scale industry as a distinct entity from the traditional cottage industry. The concept of the SSI was to include hired labour and/or mechanical power. He thus provided for capital intensity in the small scale industry."

This distinction between cottage and small scale sector was later to become the basis for differences in policy approaches towards the SSUs.

Soon after independence the small scale industries came to be divided into three categories (i) Those which are auxillary to large scale industries; (ii) those which are engaged in repair services; and (iii) those which are engaged in the production of finished goods. The small scale sector thus came to be visualised as a modern mechanical sector. Though this was in conflict with the concept of the small scale industry as envisioned by the Gandhians, in effect the post independence era saw recognition being accorded to both traditional and modern small scale industry.

The Industrial Policy resolution of 1948 saw the emergence of a dualist approach, viz emphasis on traditional as well as modern small scale sector. The same has continued to form the basis of industrial policy towards the Small Scale sector, to this day.

The 50's saw the development of another seeming contradiction in industrial policy. While emphasis on traditional small scale industry continued, there also emerged the Nehruvian view that capital intensive heavy industry was an essential concomitant to economic growth.

The two got reconciled in the theoretical model of Prof. Mahalanobis. In this model the small scale sector was accorded the function of maintaining an elastic supply of consumer goods to meet the expanding demand generated by the large scale capital goods sector.

The Industrial Policy Resolution of 1948 stated that these industries were particularly suited for better utilisation of local resources and for the achievement of self sufficiency in respect of certain types of consumer goods.

As a follow up to this approach in the Industrial Policy Resolution, an All India Cottage Industries Board was set up. Subsequently six other All India Boards were set up—The All India Handloom Board, the All India Handicrafts Board, the Coir Borad, the All India Handloom Board, the India Handicrafts Board, the Coir Board, the All India Khadis and Village Industries Board and the Central Silk Board for traditional industries, while the Small Scale Industries Board (SSIB) was set up for giving impetus to the urban small scale sector.

Government policy on industry was further elaborated in the Industries Development and Regulation Act (IDRA) of 1951. It provided for registration of units employing more than 50 workers employing power or more than 100 workers when not using power in industries listed in Schedule I of the Act. Besides, it also required a licence to be obtained for setting up any new unit or expansion in existing capacity of any unit above the minimum size, in the industries listed in the schedule. It thus automatically gave preferential treatment to the small scale sector by exempting them from the requirement of registration and licence.

The 7th Plan gave a boost to the small scale development programme by adopting a number of programmes.

(i)The number of items exclusively reserved for the SSI were increased progressively . (ii) Procedures for obtaining financial assistance from Banks and other institutions were liberalised (iii) Tiny units with investment limit of Rs. 2 lakhs and located in towns with population less than 50,000 were identified for special assistance and incentives. (iv) Raw material availability for SSUs was enhanced. (v) Value of import licences to small scale units was increased. (vi) Government's purchases from SSUs were increased and the policy of reservation of items for purchases from these units was strengthened. (vii) A comprehensive range of consultancy services and technical managerial, economic and marketing assistance was provided to the SSUs by the Small Industries Development Organisation (SIDO) through its network of service and branch institutes. (viii) A Council for Advancement of Rural Technology (CART) was set up to provide necessary technical assistance to the rural industries.

Several schemes of financial assistance specially to the smallest segment of SSI, were introduced. The Small Industries Development Fund (SIDF), the National Equity Fund (NEF) and the Single Window Scheme (SWS) were introduced. The SIDF provides refinance assistance for development, expansion, diversification and rehabilitation of new projects in tiny/small sector and also assistance for rehabilitation of viable sick units. SWS provides working capital loans along with term loans for fixed capital to new tiny and small scale units having project cost upto Rs. 5 lakhs and working capital requirement upto Rs. 2.5 lakhs. For meeting the long standing demand for the small scale industries for a separate Apex Bank providing assistance to them, the government set up the Small Industries Development Bank of India in 1989. In 1979, the District Industries Centres were set up in each district to arrange and provide a package of assistance and facilities for credit guidance, raw materials, training, marketing etc. including the necessary help to unemployed educated young entrepreneurs. The government also initiated the nucleus industry programme which involved development of a core unit around which a number of small units can grow in each area which was not industrially developed. The core units were to off load at least 50% of their manufacturing programmes to ancillaries.

To impart more vitality and growth impetus to this sector, the government announced a policy package for small, tiny and village industries in August 1991.

The policy statement recognised the fact that the SSI sector had emerged as a dynamic and vibrant sector of the economy during the 80's. In view of this fact the primary objective of the Small Scale Industrial Policy during the 90's would be to impart more vitality and growth impetus to the sector to enable it to contribute its full mite to the economy, particularly in terms of output, employment and exports. Efforts were to be made to deregulate and debureaucratise the sector with a view to remove all fetters on its growth potential, reposing greater faith in small and young entrepreneurs.

The investment limit for the 'Tiny' enterprises was raised from Rs. 2 lakhs to Rs. 5 lakhs, irrespective of location of the unit.

All Industry related services and business enterprises, irrespective of their location, were to be recognised as Small Scale Industries and their investment ceilings would correspond to those of 'Tiny' enterprises.

A separate package of incentives for the 'Tiny' sector has been introduced. While the small sector (other than 'Tiny' enterprises) would be mainly entitled to one time benefits, the Tiny enterpises would also be eligible for additional support on a continuing basis including easier access to institutional finance, priority purchase Programme and relaxation from certain provisions of labour laws.

It has also been decided to widen the scope of the National Equity Fund Scheme. The coverage of the single Window Loan Scheme has also been widened to facilitate access to a larger number of entrepreneurs.

In the field of finance, emphasis is to shift from subsidised cheap credit, except for specified target groups, and efforts would be made to ensure both adequate flow of credit on a normative basis and quality of delivery, for viable operations of this sector. A special monitoring agency was to be set up to oversee that the genuine credit needs of the Small Scale Sector are fully met.

Equity participation by other industrial undertakings in SSI to the extent of 24% of the total shareholdings, has been allowed. This is expected to boost ancillarisation and subcontracting, leading to expansion of employment opportunities. It is also expected to encourage modernisation and technological upgradation.

Regulatory provisions relating to the management of private limited companies are being liberalised. To enhance the supply of risk capital to the Small Scale Sector, limited partnership is to be allowed.

A begining has been made towards solving the problem of delayed payments to small industries by setting up of factoring services through Small Industries Development Bank of India (SIDBI).

To facilitate location of industries in rural/backward areas and to promote stronger linkages between agriculture and industry, a new scheme of integrated infrastructural Development for the SSI is being implemented.

A Technology Development Cell (TDC) was to be set up in the Small Industries Development Organisation (SIDO) which would provide inputs to improve productivity and competitiveness of the products of the small scale sector. The TDC is to co-ordinate the activities of all other technology aiding cells.

To expand the share of the SSI in the vast domestic market, market promotion would be undertaken through co-operative/ public sector institutions, other specialised/professional marketing agencies and consortia approach.

The Policy statement emphasised the need to widen and deepen complementarity in production programmes of large/ medium and small industrial sectors.

The statement also provided for the establishment of an Export Development Centre in SIDO to serve the small scale industries, through its network of field offices for the augmentation of exports of the SSI.

Modernisation and Technological upgradation was to be encouraged by creating greater awareness, supporting setting up of quality counselling and common testing facilities etc.

An orientation programme of modernisation and technological upgradation is to be pursued. Specific industries in large concentrations have to be identified for studies in conjunction with SIDBI and other banks, and support would be provided for modernisation of these industries on a priority basis.

To promote entrepreneurship, Entrepreneurship Development Programmes (EDP) would be significantly expanded. Industry Associations would also be encouraged to participate in this venture effectively.

EDP would be built into the curricular of vocational and other degree level courses. Women entrepreneurship could be specially encouraged and enterprises in which women entrepreneurs have a majority share holding and management control would be defined as "Women Enterprises".

Simplification of rules and procedures would be undertaken to reduce unnecessary interference and bureaucratic controls.

The Eighth Plan places greater emphasis on private initiative in industrial development. Since small scale and medium industries are more or less based on private initiative and entrepreneurship, they are likely to play an important role. Full employment being an important goal of this plan, and the problem of the educated employed assuming greater significance than before, the SSI will become a key instrument for the achievement of this objective.

Major areas of assistance for this sector that will receive attention are: (i) improving access of raw materials by encouraging industry associations to come forwards; (ii) timely and adequate availability of credit by strengthening SIDBI and NABARD; (iii) laying more emphasis on establishment of tool rooms and training facilities to upgrade technology; (iv) simplification of rules and procedures; (v) proper monitoring of projects by SFCs and commercial banks to prevent sickness at the incipient stage; (vi) improving marketability by inducting better technology; (vii) encouraging industry associations to form marketing organisations in a bid to improve the maketing infrastructure of small scale units.

In addition to the above, the Eight Plan aims to earmark a certain percentage of developed industrial area for small industries in the 70 growth centres envisaged to be set up during the plan period. Integrated infrastructure development centres (for tiny units in rural and backward areas) would be opened. Various procedural simplifications were introduced in 1993.

The Nayak Committee was set up to examine the problems of credit, sickness and other related issues in the SSI sector. The Committee submitted its Report in September 1992. The RBI announced a special package of measures to ensure adequate and timely credit to SSI sector. The salient feature of this package are :

(a) Bank should give preference to village industries, tiny industries and other small scale units in that order, while meeting the credit requirements of the small scale sector.

(b) They should step up the credit flow to meet the legitimate requirements of the SSI sector in full during the Eight Five Year Plan.

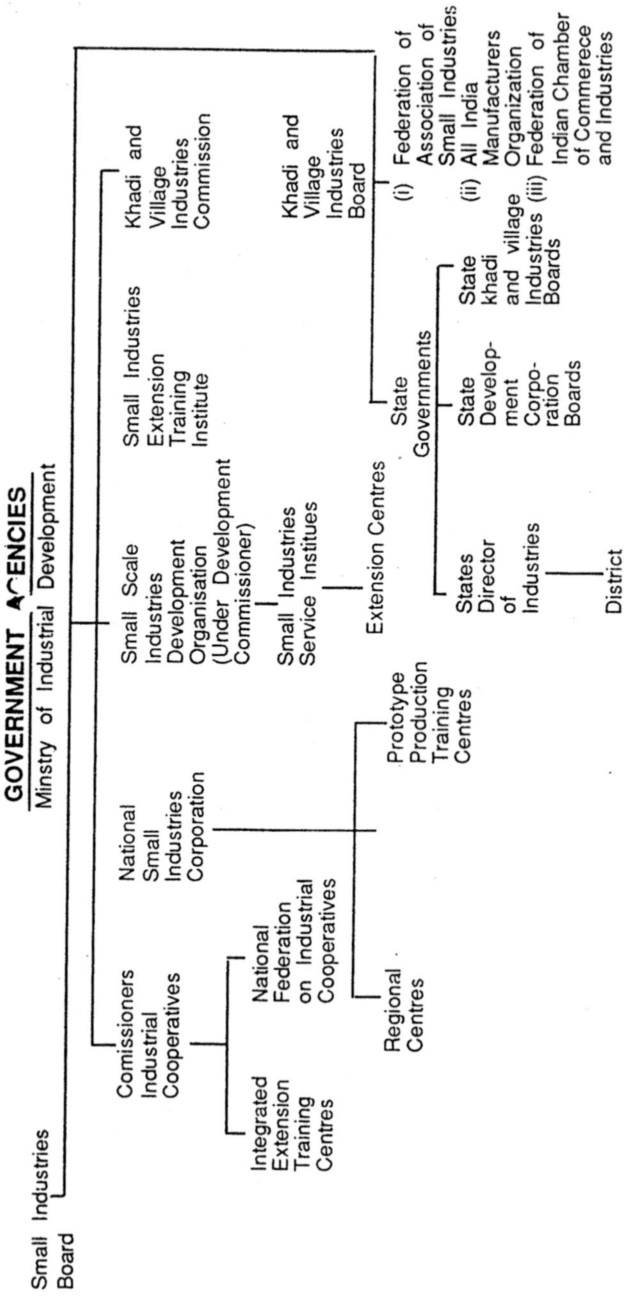

Note : Handloom, handicrafts and coir are dealt with Ministry of Foreign Trade through Special Boards.

(c) An effective grievance redressal machinery for the SSI in each bank.

(d) Banks should adopt the single window clearance scheme for SIDBI for meeting the credit requirements of small scale units.

Policy Measures to Promote Small Scale Enterprises

The policy instruments designed to encourage small scale units fall under the following broad categories:

(i) Fiscal incentives—Under this category come excise tax exemption and state tax exemptions, primarily sales taxes and turnover taxes on purchases of inputs. Other incentives include preferential pricing policies and various subsidies. Central government provides capital subsidy for new projects and rehabilitation and expansion projects in specified backward areas. State and local governments also provide subsidies consisting of interest rate and capital subsidies, water and electricity subsidies and subsidies for acquisition of land.

(ii) Quantitative restrictions on the output of large scale firms—Under this category comes the reservation of items for production by small scale firms. With the introduction of reservation in a product line, all expansion in the particular line is limited to small scale enterprises.

(iii) Infrastructure, Marketing and Industrial Extension services—These consist of the provision of infrastructure primarily in the form of industrial estates, marketing services, including export marketing and other industrial services, including technology development, extension and training.

The institutional set up for the provision of stimulatory, support and sustaining activities for the small scale entrepreneur is given in the chart.

References

1. E. Staley and R. Morse, *Modern Small Scale Industry for Developing Countries*, McGraw Hill Book Co., New York.

2. S.V.S. Sharma, *Small Entrepreneurial Development in Some Asian Countries— A Comparative Study*, Light and Life Publishers, 1979, New Delhi.

9

Critique of Government Policy

Any industrial policy towards the small scale sector has to be assessed in the context of the general and specific objectives for the achievement of which the policy is framed. And the extent to which a particular segment of the industry is expected to serve these objectives, has itself to be based on a clear perception of the 'area' that the particular segment is supposed to cover.

Ironically, as has been observed in the chapter on the definition of small scale industry, this very premise, i.e. the segment this concept represents, is not clear not only in India, but all over the world. Uniformity of opinion is only about the fact that the concept is related to size and not to product. Beyond that, there is no clarity. This lack of clarity as already observed, is on two fronts— the criteria to be chosen for measuring size and the limits to size to be set on the basis of that criteria. Since the two aspects in their global perspectives have already been taken up in the definition chapter, this section will be confined to the implications of this confusion in our policy towards the SSI.

Taking the criteria that was adopted, we have seen that over the years this has changed. In the beginning it was employment only. Later, to include developments in technology, the modern small scale sector, the criteria was changed to include the use of power and capital investment in plant and machinery. Subsequently labour was completely eliminated from the definition. It can be clearly seen how this would have changed the area covered by the small scale sector. Initially it was only the traditional sector. Later it came to incorporate the modern small scale sector also, which has subsequently gained more and more importance.

Apart from the area of coverage, what other implication can there be of this change in criteria i.e. from labour to capital? We have seen in the chapter on concepts, that the study conducted by the author brought out the fact that the results with respect to efficiency ratios and conclusions for policy may differ with respect to different criteria. The objectives for the achievement of which the small scale sector can be a means, depends upon the criteria adopted e.g., in the case of our plans, the socio-economic objectives of generating higher levels of employment, more equal distribution of income, regional balance in economic development, rural development etc. have been some of the important goals, for the achievement of which policy of support to the SSI has been adopted.

However, it is seen that the small scale sector does not necessarily have an edge over the large scale sector on all these fronts. Where it has an advantage, depends upon the criteria adopted. The basic premise on which the idea that "small is beautiful" was based, is the assumption that small scale units are labour intensive. However, our study proves that this may not be the case if the area demarcated for the SSI is on the basis of employment criteria. Some others who have used this criteria for their analysis have also come to a similar conclusion.

Thus we find that the formulators of the policy of support to the small scale sector for achieving their socio-economic goals, had based their policy on wrong premises when they defined it on the basis of employment criteria. It is another matter that the small scale sector at that time consisted basically of traditional household sector, and hence was inherently less capital intensive.

Revision in the definition, adopting capital as the criteria of size instead of employment, was also based on reasons other than the factors mentioned above. It was done to incorporate modern technology and industrial structure rather than due to the realisation of an inherent contradiction in the two criteria. So while the basic goals of policy remained the same, the criteria was changed— coincidentally for the better, for it has been seen that the capital investment criteria of size endorses the ideas on labour intensive character of the SSI, as also emerges as the most significant factor determining productivity. However, it is surprising that most economies still retain labour as the criteria of size for defining the SSI segment and so do the studies conducted by international institutions like the World Bank. Although retention of this criteria may be justified for the purpose of statistical uniformity, the fact that it can change the conclusions of the whole analysis, raises strong doubts about making simplifications in research.

Regarding the 'area' of the SSI, i.e. setting limits to size, we find that there have been continuous upward revisions in capital investment limits, to demarcate size in India. This makes it difficult to make intertemporal comparisons and to study the impact of policies.

However, such revisions could not have been avoided if the price escalation effects on size and changes in industrial structure had to be incorporated.

Apart from conceptual vagueness in the formulation of the policy for SSI, which is a weakness found in policy formulations almost everywhere, there have been certain probable misconceptions about the relative desirability of the small scale units vis-a-vis large scale units also.

The first and most important presumption as we have already observed, is that the small scale unit has a low capital labour or capital output ratio and high output labour ratio. As discussed in the earlier sections of this book, this generalisation about the labour intensive character of small scale units, does not always hold good, and may differ from industry to industry. Even within the same industry, there may be no uniformity. No observations about such a possibility have been made in the early policy formulations when a case was built for support to the small scale sector. One may however, again come to the defence of the Indian policy formulators on the ground that this is a lacuna prevailing in policy formulations of almost all countries. Besides, during the early industrial policy statements, the industrial structure was such that the existing small scale industry was inherently labour intensive, being generally traditional in nature.

A second misconception about the small scale units was that they can easily be regionally dispersed, so that growth of such units would automatically promote more balanced growth. This premise however, has already been disproved in practice. Studies conducted by many researchers have revealed that small scale units get attracted by availability of demand and infra-structure, and giving of financial incentives alone cannot attract them to backward areas. So there is no built in dispersal effect in the policy of promotion of the SSI. This mistake was later corrected to a certain extent by setting up "nucleus" centres with a large scale unit in areas where growth had to be promoted through the growth of small scale units. This also brought the concept of ancillary development into greater prominence. Ancillary growth however, has also not taken off in practice in the same manner in India as in some other countries like Japan, and a proper ancillary culture involving deeper and stronger linkages between the large and small units needs to be developed.

A third defective premise on which the policy is based is that the growth of the small scale units will promote a more equal distribution of income than the growth of large scale ones. This view itself is based on two presumptions (i) the SSUs can check the growth of monopolistic tendencies, and (ii) they look after labour better than the large units.

As regards the first presumption the SSUs by themselves cannot offer competition to the large scale ones. Often, their very survival in the face of existence of large scale units, is dependent upon demand and supply side interventions by the government. Hence, to expect that the SSUs can check the growth of monopolies by themselves is a very unrealistic presumption.

As regards the second presumption, studies have shown that wage per worker is higher in large scale units than in smaller units. This is partly due to labour regulations and trade union activity that the large scale units are subjected to, and partly due to the fact that these units can afford to pay higher salaries because labour productivity is generally higher in them.

From both these aspects the policy premise that the small scale units will promote more equal distribution of income, is wrong. However, to the extent that growth of SSI is associated with a rational growth of small scale entrepreneurial class, they have a positive effect on income distribution. In the long run however, in terms of higher incomes for the larger numbers, whether large or small units are more desirable, is debatable.

The new focus on the SSI as a means of providing self employment to the educated unemployed, is more in line with this rationale than the earlier more general approach to the problem of unemployment.

The programmes to improve the efficiency and viability of the small scale units, which the government has been pursuing, relate to supply of information, consultancy, entrepreneurship development, training, modernisation and technology support, industrial estates, raw materials, marketing, finance, reservation, ancillary development and so on.

Relative emphasis of these has been changing in conformity with the need of the changing industrial structure and nature of the sector. While emphasis was earlier on finance, raw material supply, information, marketing and reservation, it has now shifted to development of entrepreneurship, technology and modernisation, consultancy and ancillary development.

An assessment of the success of these measures requires a periodic review of the performance of these units. To quote from the government's policy statement of July 1980: "It is governments' considered view that all incentives given to industry must be performance oriented. It is therefore proposed that regular periodic assessment be made of the impact of these incentives, to the extent to which they have fulfilled their initial purpose. Unless it is apparent that the purpose is being served, government will review the system of incentives."

To what extent this exercise of periodic assessment can be indulged in fruitfully and accurately, can be gauged from the observations made by the Development Commissioner in the Report on the Second All India census of Small Scale Units, work on which was started in 1990 and took two years to complete.

"The magnitude of the task which has been completed can be appreciated in its right perspective, in the light of the fact that the data was collected for the survey by utilizing the services of 1448 number of enumerators. Decentralized processing of data was done at more than 30 different locations in the country and about 20 data entry agencies were engaged. Multi-location and multi-organisation involvement demanded innovations in project management."

This statement of the Development Commissioner of Small Scale Industry highlights the magnitude of the task to be undertaken for the collection of information in a country like India, as well as the necessity of giving extensive training to the staff involved in data collection exercises. Training has to include motivation to get correct information. Motivation depends on a clear understanding of the objectives of data collection. Lack of seriousness on this front has proved a serious hurdle in data collection, both at the government level and for the individual researcher.

Again, quoting the Development Commission in the 'Report on Second Annual Survey of the SSI':

"During the field operations in the first round (of the First Report) it was found that nearly 44% of the registered units were either closed or untraceable, indicating that closed units were not getting deleted from the registered records. Copies of the registration application form were not flowing into the office of the DC (SSI) from different states/UT Directorates of Industries as originally contemplated. Thus, data on total number of units, fixed investment in plant and machinery, employment etc. could not be updated meaningfully".

This statement clearly reveals that a flexible policy contemplated in the policy statements for the SSI based on regular periodic assessment of results of various packages for the SSI sector, can not be successfully implemented in the absence of an efficient data collection mechanism. This is partly responsible for the failure of the SSI policy on many fronts.

Inspite of this lacuna, we can draw certain conclusions about the success or failure of various programmes on the basis of various studies conducted by individual researchers and government agencies.

In the field of assistance for *long term finance*, it has been generally observed that the assisted units have not shown better overall performance than the non-assisted ones. J.C. Sandesara[1] on the basis of a study of 12 industries concluded, that while the assisted units had higher labour productivity, higher surplus per worker and higher average wage than non-assisted units in a majority of industries, the latter had higher profitability, higher capital productivity and higher surplus per unit of capital than the former in a majority of industries (Table 9.1).

Thus, while assisted units showed more efficient use of and reward to labourer, the non assisted ones showed a more efficient use of and reward to capital. Judged by the fact that capital, and not labour is the scarce factor, this does not speak very well towards the success of the financial support programmes. As far as better rewards to labour are concerned, this cannot be rationally explained and hence cannot form a good premise by which the programme can be assessed.

Judging by the growth rate of assisted vis-a-vis non-assisted units, Sandesaras' study shows lower growth rates for assisted units in 3 out of 5 industries for which a comparative analysis could be made.

The poor performance of assisted units may be due to excessive assistance given to the selected SSUs without proper assessment. This may lead to a waste of resources in the form of creation of excess capacity. It may also lead to adoption of capital intensive techniques which runs counter to the objective of creating more employment through the Small Scale industry. It increases the total cost of borrowing as well, inspite of lower cost of borrowing, because of easy and cheap availability.

It is also seen that easy entry causes excessive competition within the small scale sector. This may be increasing the 'death rate' in the small scale sector leading to more wastage.

'Waste' of assistance has been noticed in yet another form. Assistance may create what J.C. Sandesara calls ghosts. On the basis of ownership of a small shed and machinery, a unit may claim assistance meant for a small entrepreneur. But actually it may be run by a large manufacturer. Thus assistance meant for the 'small' and 'needy', may be actually claimed by an undeserving unit. Even to the extent that this assistance is

Table 9.1: Financial and Economic Ratios of Assisted and Non-Assisted Units

City/Year/Industry	Number of Units	Profits to Equity Capital (%)	Value Added to Total Assets	Value Added Per Worker	Surplus to Total Assets	Surplus Per Worker	Wages Per Worker	Total Assets Per Worker
1	2	3	4	5	6	7	8	9
I. Bombay (1976-77)	39							
1. *Metal Products*								
Assisted	8	14.25	0.21	9,198	0.11	4,793	4,073	44,470
Non-Assisted	5	6.46	0.22	6,454	0.04	1,258	4,603	28,891
2. *Machinery and Spare Parts*								
Assisted	9	21.39	0.40	14,090	0.09	3,194	10,582	35,450
Non-assisted	4	-114.59	0.06	1,088	-0.19	3,530	4,296	18,316
3. *Paper and Paper Products*								
Assisted	9	-3.19	0.13	5,244	0.04	1,601	3,506	40,433
Non-assisted	4	42.26	0.23	6,217	0.12	3,279	2,471	27,338
II. Hyderabad (1977-78)	59							
1. *Industrial Fasteners*								
Assisted	4	8.62	0.18	9,445	0.10	5,508	3,893	53,476
Non-assisted	3	20.44	0.31	6,798	0.14	2,969	3,414	21,582
2. *Printing Press*								
Assisted	2	-8.73	0.36	3,975	-0.03	-299	4,174	10,985
Non-assisted	6	6.36	0.21	6,147	0.07	2,131	3,784	29,223
3. *Chemical and Pharmaceuticals*								
Assisted	7	23.90	0.21	11,100	0.14	7,039	3,969	51,820

1	2	3	4	5	6	7	8	9	
	Non-assisted	7	24.12	0.32	11,465	0.11	3,905	7,426	35,554
4.	*Machinery and Spare Parts*								
	Assisted	14	25.93	0.36	9,348	0.12	3,241	6,044	26,357
	Non-assisted	16	48.31	0.35	9,684	0.13	3,718	5,731	28,006
III.	**Jaipur (1978-79)**	40							
1.	*Industrial Fasteners*								
	Assisted	4	-1.37	0.16	5,520	0.06	2,237	3,270	34,410
	Non-assisted	2	32.20	0.27	12,905	0.17	7,950	4,850	48,032
2.	*Metal Products*								
	Assisted	5	20.68	0.28	16,174	0.14	7,776	8,245	57,343
	Non-assisted	9	36.27	0.31	9,062	0.16	4,740	4,164	29,685
3.	*Electricals and Electronics*								
	Assisted	3	45.06	0.24	15.990	0.19	12,746	3,184	67,700
	Non-assisted	5	80.23	0.41	9,079	0.27	5,949	2,974	21,878
4.	*Plastic Products*								
	Assisted	2	45.48	0.28	27,738	0.24	23,252	4,411	97,989
	Non-assisted	3	5.19	0.19	4,109	0.05	1,192	2,909	22,155
5.	*Chemicals*								
	Assisted	4	-15.52	0.15	6,088	.0330	1,138	4,403	41,945
	Non-assisted	3	-12.87	0.10	5,561	.0336	1,812	3,688	54,004

The items included in the terms used here and the other tables are briefly described.

(a) Assets side: The term fixed assets used here includes land, building, plant and machinery, furniture and fixtures and other assets (such as office equipment and vehicles). They relate to net fixed assets, arrived at after deducting accumulated depriciation from their value at the time of installation or purchase. *Total Assets* relate to the net fixed assets, total current assets and other assets, such as deposits for water and electric connections.

(b) Liabilities : *Equity Capital* includes proprietary funds - paid up capital and reserves.

(c) Profits and Loss side : Output is arrived at by adding to net sales (gross sales less value of goods received, allowance, discount and excise) the differential values of closing and opening stocks of finished and semi-finished products, other income and work done for others. Value added is the net income produced by the units, and is arrived at by deducting the expenses of basic raw materials, power, other materials, miscellaneous expenses, depreciation and work done for others from the value of output. This is thus the sum of rent, wages, interests and profits. *Wages* include wages and salaries, benefits paid to employees as also management remuneration. Surplus is defined as value added less rent and less wages, and it thus includes interest and profits. Profits are the residual item arrived at by deducting interest from surplus, and are inclusive of taxes and provisions for taxes.

(d) Workers : Includes all workers, including owners and members of the family along with workers receiving wages and salaries in cash or kind.

Source : J.C. Sandesara "Small Industry Development Programmes in India", A Paper in "Small Scale Enterprises in Industrial Development" Edited by K.B Suri., 1988, Table 1.

Table 9.2: Growth Rates of Continuing Assisted and Non-Assisted Units (Per cent per annum, Compound)

City/Year/Industry	Number of Units	Total Assets	Fixed Assets	Equity Capital	Output	Value Added
1	2	3	4	5	6	7
I. Bombay (1972-73 to 1976-77)	23					
1. *Metal Products*						
Assisted	7	6.7	1.7	3.6	-1.41	-5.7
2. *Machinery and Spare Parts*						
Assisted	6	2.5	-0.7	10.2	8.9	4.9
3. *Paper and Paper Products*						
Assisted	7	16.3	14.0	11.3	9.4	11.2
Non-assisted	3	16.3	34.2	12.9	14.1	5.2
II. Hyderabad (1974-75 to 1977-78)	19					
1 *Chemicals and Pharmaceuticals*						
Assisted	2	14.9	1.9	15.6	125.8	*
Non-assisted	4	3.3	—	3.0	6.0	5.6
2. *Machinery and Spare Parts*						
Assisted		5.6	8.0	6.5	13.1	12.8
Non-assisted	5	32.3	16.9	6.7	37.3	33.8

*Here the rate of growth could not be worked out because of the data problem.

Source : J.V. Sandesara, "Small Industry Development Programmes in India", A Paper in "Small Scale Enterprises in Industrial Development" Edited by K.B. Suri, 1988, Table 2.

Table 9.3: Financial and Economic Ratios of 'Reserve' and Other Industries

City/Year/Industry	Number of Units	Profits to Equity Capital (%)	Value Added to Total Assets	Value Added Per Worker	Surplus to Total Assets	Surplus Per Worker	Wages Per Worker	Total Assets Per Worker
1	2	3	4	5	6	7	8	9
I. Bombay (1976-77)	39							
1. *Metal products*	*13*	*13.05*	*0.21*	*8,451*	*0.10*	*3,830*	*4,217*	*40,226*
2. Machinery & spare parts	13	14.08	0.37	12,377	0.07	2,308	9,753	33,192
3. Paper & paper products	13	-1.09	0.14	5,361	0.05	1,804	3,381	38,852
II. Hyderabad (1977-78)	59							
1. *Industrial fasteners*	*7*	*14.56*	*0.22*	*8,027*	*0.11*	*4,148*	*3,636*	*36,390*
2. Printing press	8	5.94	0.22	5,906	0.07	1,861	3,828	27,197
3. Chemicals & Pharmaceuticals	14	23.93	0.24	11,219	0.13	6,011	5,102	46,488
4. Machinery & spare parts	30	32.55	0.35	9,384	0.13	3,374	5,891	26,693
III. Jaipur (1978-79)	51							
1. *Industrial fasteners*	*6*	*11.71*	*0.20*	*7,449*	*0.10*	*3,729*	*3,683*	*37,969*
2. *Metal products*	*14*	*26.97*	*0.29*	*12,943*	*0.14*	*6,397*	*6,391*	*44,779*
3. *Agricultural equipment*	*5*	*-15.74*	*0.08*	*4,960*	*0.02*	*1,223*	*3,429*	*62,852*
4. Casting and rolling	6	30.88	0.38	8,765	0.14	3,212	5,542	23,300
5. Electricals & electronics	8	62.81	0.33	10,760	0.23	7,601	3,025	33,016
6. Plastic Products	5	26.38	0.24	9,925	0.16	6,622	3,279	40,822
7. Chemicals	7	-14.24	0.12	5,828	0.03	1,595	4,050	47,898

Note : Reserve industries are shown in italics.

Source : J.V. Sandesara, "Small Industry Development Programmes in India", A paper in "Small Scale Enterprises in Industrial Development" Edited by K.B. Suri, 1988, Table 3.

Table 9.4 : Growth Rates of Continuing Units of 'Reserve' and Other Industries (Per cent per Annum, Compound)

City/Year/Industry	Number of Units	Total Assets	Fixed Assets	Equity Capital	Output	Value Added
1	2	3	4	5	6	7
I. **Bombay (1972-73 to 1976-77)**	25					
1. Metal products	8	5.8	0.9	3.1	-1.4	-5.8
2. Machinery & spare parts	7	2.8	-0.6	9.8	8.2	0.6
3. Paper & paper products	10	16.3	21.9	11.4	10.1	7.9
II. **Jaipur (1974-75 to 1978-79)**	24					
1. Industrial fasteners	2	3.6	-2.4	-0.9	6.2	0.3
2. Metal products	7	4.9	-2.2	2.6	19.5	12.2
3. Agricultural implements	4	4.6	-4.5	8.3	-7.6	-32.4
4. Casting and rolling	3	12.6	5.1	10.9	23.7	-3.0
5. Electricals and electronics	3	16.3	13.8	1.8	18.9	-1.8
6. Chemicals	5	4.7	4.0	5.5	-2.8	-15.9

Reserve industries: In Bombay No. 1 and in Jaipur Nos. 1, 2 and 3.

Ranking: Bombay Industry No. 3,1,2 3,1,2 3,2,1 3,2,1 3,2,1
Jaipur Industry No. 5,4,2,6,3,1 5,4,6,2,1,3 5,4,6,2,1, 4,2,5,1,6,3 2,1,5,4,6,30

Source: J.C. Sandesara "Small Industry Development Programmes in India, "A paper in Small Scale Enterprises in Industrial Development" Edited by K.B. Suri, 1988, Table 4.

directed to a small entrepreneur via a 'ghost' entrepreneur, the cost of this assistance would have increased. The number of such 'ghosts' may not be insignificant as revealed by the number of units approached at their recorded addresses, found to be closed.

Better performance of the non-assisted units can be explained by the possibility of better entrepreneurial qualities emerging out of more difficult circumstances due to non-availability of assistance. It may ultimately lead to greater efficiency due to economy of scarce resources.

With regard to the programme of *'Reservation'* of a group of industries for the SSI sector, a judgement on the efficiency of this schemes can be passed again, by comparing the performance of units in the reserved category with those in the non-reserved category.

J. C. Sandesara, in the same study has made such a comparison. Of the 3 industries in Bombay which were taken up in his study, only metal products is in the reserve list. Of the six ratios studied, this industry was first only on surplus/total assets and surplus/worker. Besides, it had the highest capital intensity. With regard to growth indicators also, it ranked last on 3 out of 5. In Hyderabad and Jaipur, the picture was not very different.

Some idea of the performance of the SSUs in the small scale sector in the reserved category, can also be had from their capacity utilization. The Second All India Census of Small Scale Units reveals that capacity utilization on an average for the whole of India in the case of such units was 47.7%. Of the 15 'industry groups' reserved for the small scale sector, one third showed capacity utilization even less than the average. Of the 843 items falling in these 15 industry groups, 290 had capacity utilization less than 47%.

This phenomenon may be accounted for by the excessive entry of entrepreneurs in these categories, propelled by the advantage of reservation. However, this very factor may have led to the creation of excess capacity, waste of resources and may be lowering of profits. Thus, it comes out quite clearly that Reservation policy by itself cannot guarantee profits to the small entrepreneur. Competition from within the SSI sector itself in the absence of an equivalent growth in demand, can lower profitability. The same explanation can be given for Sandesara's results also.

Regarding the programmes of Industrial Estates, the presumption is that

(i) Provision of facilities for the setting up of small units like shed, water supply, electricity etc., would attract entrepreneurs to certain locations. So this programme could be used to achieve the objectives of balanced regional development.

(ii) Provision of these facilities and clustering of units, would lower their cost of production because of lower establishment costs, and create external economies of horizontal and vertical linkage.

As regards the first presumption, a number of studies have shown that mere provision of industrial estates facilities have not been a strong enough attraction for location of units. A number of sheds in various industrial estates remain unoccupied. The most compelling force propelling a unit towards a location is demand generated by the existence of large scale units in a particular area. To a certain extent, this point can be brought out by studying statewise distribution of the small scale units. The Second All India Survey of Small Scale Units shows that major concentration of units is in big industrialized states like Maharashtra, Uttar Pradesh, Tamil Nadu, West Bengal and Gujarat, indicating the influence that large units exert on the location of small scale units, and the insignificant influence of other incentives like setting up of industrial estates to disperse them in backward areas.

Regarding the premise that provision of infrastructure facilities and possibility of linkage would increase the efficiency of units located in industrial estates, studies have shown that there is no conclusive evidence to prove the same. In fact in most cases evidence is to the contrary.

In a study of small scale units of Udhna estate, R. L. Sanghvi, points out that the small units located in the industrial estate had a higher rate of return than those located in Surat. On the other hand, studies[2] of Somasekhera[3] conducted in Karnataka, show that all the industrial estates, except the Harihar Industrial Estate and Mysore Industrial Estate, were less viable economically than those located outside. The former had become more capital intensive, while the latter had reduced their capital output ratio.

Oomen in his study of Kerala units[4] observed "the objective of creating more output and employment has not been achieved satisfactorily in industrial estates of Kerala." The capital output ratio in these was even higher than that in the large scale sector.

The same observations have been made by Bandopadhyaya for units situated in Howra industrial estate and by Dhar and Lydall in their studies.

Somasekhara observes that the easy availability of finance in industrial estates led to over capitalisation, which led to higher inventories and fixed investment. They had a higher cushion against sales which meant higher interest cost.

Thus the majority of the findings corroborate the view that the programme of industrial estates has not been very beneficial to the small scale sector.

With regard to the other incentives, viz., land-shed, finance, machinery, raw material, marketing and technical assistances, it has been observed that there is a fundamental lapse in the dissemination of information about the availability of these incentives.

Besides, there was the problem of timely availability of assistance due to the complicated bureaucratic procedures associated with the processing of assistance.

Most units seem to have availed of the financial facilities offered but with respect to the other incentives, utilization does not seem to have been that good. The units seem to give more importance to timely availability of assistance, rather than to concessional terms. Studies show that many units, though wanting assistance, could not get it because they could not prepare their projects as per technical and other requirements, or could not satisfy the institutions on one or the other of several formalities. The aid giving agencies need to make more sincere efforts at counselling on these matters so that units do not miss out on aid availability because of these lapses. Impact of assistance programme can be increased if procedures are simplified and formalities reduced.

The findings that not many small scale units avail assistance related to raw materials, machinery on hire-purchase, technical assistance and preferential purchase scheme, underlines the need for a proper assessment of such programmes. Either the loopholes should be filled up or the schemes scrapped.

On the other hand the fact that many units avail the facilities related to land/shed and finance, points to the fact that these programmes need to be further strengthened.

Any discussion of the industrial policy of the government of India would be incomplete without a discussion of the implications and achievements of the policy with respect to the rural sector. Using growth of small scale sector for the development of the rural areas and solving the problem of underemployment has not been one of the strong planks of the policy. However, there has not been any substantial focussed effort to promote programmes of such dispersal. Even where such programmes were introduced, the success story has not been very good. Reason being, lack of proper research to assess the suitability of the region for the introduction of such programmes.

The result is that growth of small scale units has been mainly in urban towns. Industrially developed states accounted for nearly 70% of the registered small scale units. Even in these states the concentration is in the metropolitan or large cities and industrial complexes. The Second All India Survey of the SSI shows that the urban rural distribution of units is almost equal inspite of the existence of specific measures for Khadi and village industries. There is no authentic data available to assess growth of the household units. But it is believed that these have been declining in India, just as is the tendency in all developing and developed nations. Since the household units are mostly in the rural areas, it indicates the lessening importance of small units in rural areas over the years.

With respect to Khadi and village industries, the Sixth Plan document observed that :

> "Low levels of technology, resulting in poor productivity and inadequate returns, have continued to characterwise the traditional industries sector. Coupled with this, the problem of obtaining raw materials of desirable quality

at reasonable prices and lack of marketing arrangements, have deprived the artisans of a good part of the earning which should have accrued to them."

The Sixth Plan document also noted that the traditional sector continued to rely on non-institutional sources of finance, and most of the problems that bedeviled this sector at the time of independence continued to do so even now despite large sums spent on diverse specialised agencies like the KVIC and Coir Board and so on.

Quoting from L. C. Jain, who has strongly championed the cause of the decentralized sectors,

> "Financing arrangements for small scale industries and modern co-operative agro-processing industries have been developed fairly extensively. But institutional finance for cottage and village industries is practically non-existent. Even in Government purchases, the small sector has price preference and organisational back up, but not the cottage sector."

Generation of employment specially in the rural areas, and development of rural areas has been the focal point of the support programme for SSI and the traditional sector has been specially chosen for encouragement because of this objective. Considering this, lapses in policy implementation are a contradiction which cannot be explained. The result is that, even after a 'considerable amount of resources, bestowed through the Small Industries Development Organisation on the modern small scale sector, this effort has not been able to attack even the fringe of the problem of rural unemployment.

A more general criticism of the policy can be with respect to the obsession with the concept of size, that it exhibits. Assistance being totally related to size, it puts a premium on expansion and modernisation. Theory and practical observation have shown that there are economies to be gained from expansion; so that the small size in any industry is not the most efficient nor is the largest. In fact, the optimum size may be somewhere in the middle. Where exactly it lies, depends on the industry. Thus, support for a small size in general overlooks the efficiency aspect. The result is that, in many cases the units have deliberately avoided expansion, wanting to remain in a protective environment and virtually stagnating.

In yet other cases, they have decided to split their location (either horizontally or vertically) thus effectively increasing the scale of operations, but definitionally remaining small. In the Television industry and entertainment electronics like hi-fi music systems, tape recorders etc., on the other hand, units have availed of the liberal import policy for small scale units and reaped heavy profits by just assembling imported components in a market protected both from within and outside the country.

The question that arises is, whether putting premium on efficiency was the objective, or efficiency was the objective of promoting the SSI.

Assessment of Small Scale Industry Policy, 1991

Coming to a specific assessment of the latest policy statement (1991), by and large, the statement gives a new focus to the policy followed hitherto.

Looked at in a broader perspective of the objectives of overall industrial policy, and the Eighth Five Year Plan, emphasis is on efficiency through modernization, rural development and reduction of unemployment, specially among the educated.

Inclusion of the service sector in the small scale sector implies a recognition of the fact, that the economy has reached a level of maturity where the service sector is going to play a more and more important role. The removal of the location criteria from the definition of a "Tiny Unit", is a welcome step, specially in view of the fact that the service sector has been included in the SSI Category.

There is a recognition of the fact, that continuing support to a unit inhibits its growth and affects efficiency. In conformity with this, support on a continuing basis has been taken away from the SSI, and only one time benefits will be conferred, except in the case of 'Tiny' units. This is likely to remove the psychology of depending permanently on 'crutches', and encourage the small scale units to grow and modernise.

Emphasis on easy and timely availability rather than the cost aspect of financial assistance, if implemented properly, is likely to go a long way in removing one of the major hurdles in making financial assistance effective.

Allowing equity participation by the large scale and other

industrial units, will also go a long way in removing the financial hurdle in modernisation and growth, as also forge horizontal and vertical linkages.

The limited partnership clause will also help in removing financial constraints.

The policy statement recognises the lapses on the rural front and makes a special mention of the measures to be taken on this front, specially in the sphere of infrastructure development in rural areas. The statement is however silent on the traditional industry front, possibly because of the fact that this is a declining sector, which can exist only with continued support, and also because future growth of rural demand will be for products of the modern small scale industry rather than for traditional products. It thus lays emphasis on rural development and growth of rural employment on the basis of modern small scale industry.

The establishment of the Technology Development Cell also emphasizes the modernisation aspect.

Another unique aspect of the policy statement is a clear focus on the expansion of the Entrepreneurial Development Programme, in recognition of the fact that future growth of employment for the educated is to be fostered through self employment. It also recognises the fact that the problem of educated unemployed is going to be the most difficult problem in future.

The statement also recognises failures on the administrative front. It has emphasized the need for simplification of procedures and expansion of the Single Window Scheme.

On the whole, one can see that emphasis in this policy is on promoting efficient growth of SSI rather than on indiscriminate growth. This is a welcome change for it will improve the health of the small scale sector and reduce sickness. Besides, by improving the quality of product as well as service, it will improve the export potential of the sector.

There is however, no attempt to reduced emphasis on reservation of categories of industries for this sector, which has not been serving any useful purpose. Lastly, as has been experienced, good intentions are not enough. Lapses in implementation of policies have very often nullified the directions indicated.

References

1. J. C. Sandesara, 'Incentives and their Impact - Some Studies on Small Scale Industry", Economic and Political Weekly, Nov. 1982.
2. R. L. Sanghvi, Role of Industrial Estate in a Developing Economy, Bombay, 1979.
3. Somasekhara N, 'The Efficiency of Industrial Estate in India, Delhi, 1975.
4. M. A. Oomen, "Small Industry in Indian Economic Growth — A Case Study of Kerala, Delhi, 1972.

Bibliography

Anderson, D. and F. Khambata. 1981. "Small Enterprises and Development Policy in the Philippines: A Case Study", World Bank Staff Working Paper, No. 468.

Bagchi, A. K. and N. Banerjee (eds.). 1981. Change and Choice in Indian Industry, Calcutta, K. P. Bagchi & Co.

Balasubramanyam, V. N. 1984. The Economy of India, London, Weidenfeld and Nicholson.

Bandopadhyaya, Kalyani, *Industrialization through Industrial Estates,* Calcutta, Bookland Private Limited, 1963.

Berna, James J., *Industrial Entrepreneurship in Madras State* (Bombay, International Industrial Development Centre, Standard Research Institute, 1960).

Bhagwati, Jagdish N. and Chakraborty, Sakhmoy, *Contributions in Indian Economic Analysis : A Survey* (Bombay, 1971).

Bhavani, A. 1980. 'Relative Efficiency of the Modern Small Scale Industries.' M. Phil. Dissertation. University of Delhi : January.

Boon G. K. 1980. Technology and Employment in Footwear Manufacturing. Alphen a/d Rijn.

Rowden, R. J. and D. Mazumdar. 1982. 'Segmentation and Earnings Profiles in LDCs', Discussion Paper, No. 4, World Bank, Development Research Department, November.

Bredo, William, *Industrial Estates,* London, Collier Macmillan Limited, 1960.

Brown, A.J., *Industrialisation and Trade,* Oxford, Royal Institute of International Affairs, 1943.

Chakraborty, Sukamoy. "Time and Choice of Technique". The Economic Weekly, Sept. 15, 1956, pp. 1097-1098.

Cornelisse, P. A., F. Bishay, S. I. Cohen and P. Terhal, 1980.

Agricultural Processing Industries in the International Division of Labour, 'Discussion Paper, No. 49, Rotterdam, Centre for Development Planning, Erasmus University, January.

Datta, Amlan, *Economics of Industrialisation,* World Press Private Limited, 1952.

Datta, Amlan, *"Welfare Versus Economic Growth",* Indian Economic Journal, Oct, 1956.

Dhar, P. N. and Lydall, H. F., The Role of *Small Enterprises in Indian Economic*

Development, Delhi, Asia Publishing House, 1961.

Dhar, P. N., *Small Industries in Delhi*, Bombay, Asia Publishing House, 1958.

Florence, P. S. *Investment, Location and Size of Plants*, London, Cambridge University Press, 1948.

Fong, pang Eng., and Augustine Tan. 1981. *'Employment and Export-Led Industrialization: The Experiences of Singapore'*, in Rashid Amjad (ed.), The Development of Labour Intensive Industry in ASEAN Countries, ILO, ARTEP.

Goldar, B. 1982. 'Unit Size and Economic Efficiency in Small Scale Washing Soap Industry in India', *Artha Vijnana*, March.

Government of India, Planning Commission, *Draft Second Five Year Plan*, New Delhi.

Government of India, Planning Commission, *Draft Five Year Plan* New Delhi.

Government of India, Planning Commission, *Sixth Five Year Plan*, New Delhi.

governmentof India, Planning Commission, Sixth Five Year Plan, New Delhi.

Government of India, *Annual Report of SIDO*, Development Commissioner, Small Scale Industries, New Delhi, 1983-84,

Government of India, *Annual Survey of Industries Annual Report*, Central Statistical Organisation, New Delhi, 1982-83.

Government of India, Ministry of Industry, *Development of Small Scale Industries in India: Prospects, Problems and Policies. Report of the International Perspective Planning Team*, New Delhi, 1963.

Hajra, S., "Firm Size and Efficiency in Manufacturing", *The Economic Weekly*, August 1965.

Handbook of Statistics, Association of Engineering Industry, New Delhi, 1979-80.

Heemst, J. J. P. van. 1982. 'Scale, Organisation and Efficiency in Footwear Production: An Analysis of some Ghanaian Data', Occasional Papers, No. 95, Institute of Social Studies, March.

Ho, S. 1980. 'Small Scale Enterprises in Korea and Taiwan', World Bank Staff Working Paper, No. 384.

Hicks, J. R., "World Recovery after war — A Theoretical Analysis", *Economic Journal*, June 1947, p. 160.

Jalan, Bimal N. 1978. 'Production in Tiny, Small and Large Scale Sectors: A Note, *Economic and Political Weekly*, Bombay, 20 May.

Kaneda, Hiromitsu. 1980. 'Development of Small and Medium Enterprises and policy Response in Japan: An Analytical Survey', Studies in Employment and Rural Development, No. 32, World Bank mimeo, October.

Kashyap, S. P., "Government Sponsored Industrial Growth: The Jaipur Estates", *The Economic Weekly*, June 1964, 16, pp. 1021-1027.

Khan, R. R. 1979. Management of Small Scale Industries, New Delhi, S. Chand & Co.

Kurien, C. T. 1978. 'Small Sector in New Industrial Policy', *Economic and Political*

Weekly, 4 March.

Kuyvenhoven, Aries, 1980. 'Technology, Employment and Basic Needs in Leather Industries in Developing Countries', Discussion Paper No. 51, Rotterdam, C. D. P., E. U. R.

Lakdawala, D. T. and Mehta, B. V., "Small Scale Units in Engineering Industry", *The Times of India Supplement*, 28 February, 1958.

Lakdawala, D. T. and Sandesara, J. C., *Small Industry in a Big City* : A Survey in Bombay (University of Bombay, 1960).

Lakshman, T. K., *Cottage and Small Scale Industries in Mysore* (Mysore, 1966).

Little, I. M. D. 1982. 'Indian Industrialisation 1857-1947', in M. Gerowitz et al., The Theory and Experience of Economic Development: Essays in Honour of Sir Arthur Lewis, London, Allen and Unwin.

Little, I. M. D. 1987. 'Small Manufacturing Enterprises in Developing Countries', The World Bank Economic Review, Vol. 1. No. 2.

Mahalanobis, P. C., "The Approach of Operational Research to Planning in India", *Sankhva*, Dec. 1955-56, pp. 3-130.

Mazumdar, D. 1983. 'The Role of Small Scale Enterprises in the Indian Economy', World Bank mimeo, June.

Mc Crorry, T. T., *Small Industry in a North Indian Town* (Delhi, 1956).

Mehta, B. V., "Size and Capital Intensity in Indian Industry", Bulletin of Oxford University, Institute of Economic Statistics, 1969, 31, 189-204.

Nanjnudan, S., Robinson, H. S. and Staley E., *Economic Research for Small Industry Development* (Bombay, 1962).

Naqvi, K. A., "The Economic of Ambar Charka", *The Economic Weekly*, July 1958, 8, pp. 833-34.

Nurkse, Ragnar, "Reflections on India's Development Plan"; *Quarterly Journal of Economics*, 1957, 71, pp. 188-204.

Ohkawa, K., and M. Tajima, 1978. 'Small-Medium Scale Manufacturing Industry: A Comparative Study of Japan and Developing Nations,' International Development Centre of Japan, March.

Ojha, P. D. 1982, 'Finance for Small-Scale Enterprises in India,' Reserve Bank of India Bulletin, November.

Page, John and Steel, William, "Small Enterprise Development—Economic Issues from African Experience", *World Bank* Technical Paper, No. 26, 1984.

Papola, T. S. and Mathur, R. S., Inter-sectoral Linkage in Manufacturing A Case Study of Metal Engineering Industry in Kashmir, Giri Institute of Development Studies, Lucknow, 1978.

Papola, T. S., and V. N. Misra. 1980. 'Some Aspects of Rural Industrialization, *Economic and Political Weekly*, October.

Pillai, P. P. 1978. 'Scale and Efficiency of Small Scale Industries in India, *Asian Economic Review*, 8 April.

Prakash, Prem, "The Relationship between size and Productivity in selected Indian Industries", *Asian Economic Review*, May 1961, pp. 237-248.

Raj, K. N., "Small Scale Industries — Problems of Technological Change: Parts I & II", *The Economic Weekly*, April 1956, 8, pp. 435-438.

Rangarajan, C. 1980. 'Innovations in Banking: The Indian Experience, Impact Deposits and Credit,' Domestic Finance Studies, No. 63, World Bank, June.

Robinson, Joan, "Choice of Technique", *The Economic Weekly*, June 1956.

Roden, Rosenstein, "How to Industrialise an Underdeveloped Area", in W. Isard (Ed.), *Regional Economic Planning Technique*, Paris, 1961.

Rosen, George, *Industrial Change in India, Industrial Growth, Capital Requirements and Technological Change*, Centre for International Studies, HIT, Greece, 1958.

Saito, K. A., and D. R. Villaneuva, 1980. 'Transaction Cost of Credit to the Small-Scale Sector in Philippines,' Domestic Finance Studies, No. 53, World Bank, Public and Private Finance Division, December.

Sandesara, J. C. 1981a. 'The Small Industry Questions: Issues, Evidence and Suggestions,' in A. K. Bagchi & N. Banerjee (eds.)

Sanderara, J. C., *Size and Capital Intensity in Indian Industry* (University of Bombay, 1969)

Sandesara, J. C., *"Scale and Technology in Indian Industry"*, Bulletin of the Oxford University, Institute of Economics and Statistics, 1956, 28, pp. 181-188

Sanghvi, R. L. *Role of Industrial Estates in a Developing Economy*. Multi-Bombay Technical Publishing Co., 1960.

Sen. A. K., "Labour Cost and Economic Growth", *The Economic Weekly*, Sept., 1956, 8, pp. 1159-1169.

Sen, A. K. *Choice of Techniques: An Aspect of Theory of Planned Development* Oxford, Blackwell Publishers, 1962.

Sen, A. K., "On Choosing Techniques", *The Economic Weekly*, July 1956, 8, 857-858.

Sharma S. V. S., *Entrepreneurial Development in Some Asian Countries — A Comparative Study*, New Delhi, Light and Life Publishers, 1979.

Shetty, M. C. *Small Scale and Household Industries in a Developing Economy* (Bombay, 1963)

Singh, Baljit, *The Economics of Small Industries — A Case Study of Small Scale Industrial Establishments of Moradabad* (Delhi, 1961).

Spengler, J. J., *"Cottage Industries: A Comment", Economic Development and Cultural Change*, 1956-57, 5, pp.371-373.

Staley, E. and Mores, Richard, *Modern Small Industry for Modern Countries* New York, McGraw Hill Co., 1969.

Suri, K. B. 1983. 'Quality and Marketing of Laundry Soap,' Development Economics Department, World Bank mimeo, June.

Tambunlerchai, Somsak, and Chesada Loohawenchit. 1981. 'Labour Intensive and Small-Scale Manufacturing in Thailand,' in Rashid Amjad (ed.), The Development of Labour Intensive Industry in ASEAN Countries, ILO, ARTEP.

Thirlwall, A. P., *Growth and Development*, London, Macmillan Publishers, Limited, 1972.

Tinbergen, T., "Mill Versus Cottage Industries," *The Economic Weekly*, Jan. 1957, 9, pp. 81-83.

Tyabji, N. 1980, 'Capitalism in India and the Small Industries Policy,' *Economic and Political Weekly*, October.

United Nations, Department of Economics and Social Affairs, *Industrial Estates in Asia and the Far East*, New York, 1962.

Uppal, J. S. (ed.) 1978, India's Economic Problems, An Analytical Approach (2nd, ed.), New Delhi, Tata McGraw-Hill.

Vakil, C. N. and Brahmananda, P. R., *Planning for an Expanding Economy* (Bombay, 1956).

Varma, R. 1980. 'Employment and Production in Small Scale Industries: Some Findings of the Reserve Bank of India Survey,' Reserve Bank of India Occasional Papers, Bombay.

Virmani, Arvind, 1982. 'The Nature of Credit Markets in Developing Countries: A Framework for Policy Analysis, 'World Bank Staff Working Paper, No. 524.

Watanabe and Susumme, "Reflections on current Policies for Promoting Small Enterprises and Subcontracting," *International Labour Review*, 1974, Vol. 110, No. 5.

White, L. J. 1978. 'Appropriate Factor Proportions for Manufacturing in Less Developed Countries. A Survey of the Evidence, '*Economic Development and Cultural Change*, Vol. 27, No. 1.

Index

Our Outstanding Books

1. **Recent Trends in Public Administration/** *P. R. Dubhashi*

The collection of papers under the title "Recent Trends in Public Administration" deals with a whole range of issues relating to Public Administration which has a crucial role to play in modern India. These papers are classified into six parts viz. general, policy making, bureaucracy, training, politics, administration and public interest and administration of public enterprises. In these papers Dr. Dubhasi brings to bear his experience, knowledge and deep reflection relating to public administration which has been the characteristic feature of his writings over the last several years.

The collection will be found useful to the students of public administration, practitioners of public administration and citizens for whom public administration exists.

1995, xii+ 292p., ind., 23 cm.
ISBN 81-7479-003-9 **Rs. 430**

2. **The New Political Elite - the inconsequential MP? Volume 2/***Gautam Vohra*

The Inconsequential MP? is the second volume of a three-part study on 'The New Political Elite' which was undertook by the author some years ago to get an idea of the nature and style of functioning of political masters. This volume is based on extensive interviews with the MPs belonging to different political parties in Maharashtra. It is in this context that the author has posed the question in the title of the book, asking whether the new MP, the MP of the nineties, is of any consequence.

1994, viii+229p., bib., ind., 23 cm.
ISBN 81-7479-001-2 **Rs. 340**